A Guide to Effective
MUSIC
SUPERVISION

Title III project "Widening Cultural Horizons" Merced County, California

*Music supervision exists for one purpose only —
that the joy of music reaches in fullest measure
to each of these children.*

A Guide to Effective
MUSIC
SUPERVISION

Second Edition

Rudolph H. Weyland

Supervisor-Coordinator
of Music Education
Tulare County
Visalia, California

WM. C. BROWN COMPANY PUBLISHERS
DUBUQUE, IOWA

Dedicated
to
La June

Preface

Eighty-five per cent of all children in elementary schools in the United States receive from their classroom teachers basic instruction in the several aspects of general music. Despite the wishful thinking and impassioned pleas of music teachers, this fact is not about to change appreciably in the immediately foreseeable future. This has nothing to do with philosophical arguments on either side, for instance, the classroom teacher's role or the general music specialist's role. To the contrary, it's a fact of life, with its numerous but relatively low ratio of exceptions, that (1) there are not enough specialists to do the job, (2) there is not enough money to pay them if they were in abundance.

Music supervision must be geared to provide such dynamic leadership that these eighty-five per cent are also musically affected in a positive way. It must open doors so musical growth can take place in spite of the many possible inhibiting factors.

Musical growth is natural. It will move along on its own unless there are too many impediments. The music supervisor's job involves clearing the musical path of any impediments and at times of changing the course so the flow is smoother and more consistent.

Happily, music supervision has come more of age during the past few years than during several decades prior. Music supervisors are more *task oriented* and *mission minded* than before. They have accepted the *task* of unlocking the gateways to music and clearing the roads of impediments. They have accepted as their *mission* that music must be brought by the best possible means to all children of all ages, of all races and of all economic and social strata.

No matter how one wishes to assess it, music supervision is a process of continuous evaluation. It places a value judgment on the total music situation in a district or area, or on a specific aspect of it, at the beginning of the term. From time to time thereafter it looks at what is happening in the light of the *mission*, resets its course and moves forward again. There is not a single act that the *task-oriented* music supervisor does that is not concerned with evaluation.

Today the involvements of the music supervisor are more than the weekly classroom visitation. They include every facet of the school and all affective facets of the community. They also include all of the forces that affect the cultural growth of the child. The present day supervisor is aware of the multiplicity of forces that affect and shape education, and he places himself in a position so he can influence such forces.

The intent of this revised edition of *Guide to Effective Music Supervision* is to give the future supervisor the necessary backing so he can cope with the many forces that are useful in bringing music to the many. This edition also hopes to provide systematic and concrete guidance for the new supervisor and reinforcement for the experienced supervisor.

Acknowledgments

This revised edition may be the author's way of saying "thank you" to the many colleagues, both in music supervision and those teaching future music supervisors, for their generous comments. Most treasured were the several poignant criticisms; they helped steer the production into its present and hopefully more usable form. The Music Educator's National Conference's permission to use and cite from its many publications is gratefully acknowledged as is the kind permission from the several music series publishers (American Book Company, Holt, Rinehart & Winston, Inc., and Follett Publishers) to adapt materials from their scope and sequence charts; ideas from A.S.C.D. and Phi Delta Kappa publications for their usefulness in keeping music supervision in line with current educational thinking; also, the 'coming of age' of music supervision per se witnessed during the past several years gave courage and incentive to the present revision. Not to be minimized is the valiant work of Fred Westphal, the music editor for the Wm. C. Brown Company Publishers, who recognized the worth of the ideas the author tried to convey and who steered these ideas into a more acceptable and communicable form.

Contents

The Job
of Music Supervision

...the needs
...the bases
...the process
...the problems

MUSIC
LEARNINGS
1-14

CREATIVE
ARTS CAMPS

ARTS
FESTIVALS

FINE ARTS
YOUTH
CORPS

DIMENSIONS
IN
MUSIC SUPERVISION

* * * *

FINE ARTS: PROGRAMS
AND SERVICES

YOUNG
PEOPLES
CONCERTS

ARTIST
CULTURE
POOL

OPERA,
BALLET AND
LITTLE THEATRE

SMALL
ENSEMBLE
CONCERTS

MUSEUM AND
ART GALLERY
TOURS

YOUTH
SYMPHONY
ORCHESTRA

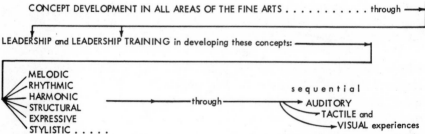

CONCEPT DEVELOPMENT IN ALL AREAS OF THE FINE ARTS . . . . through ⟶

LEADERSHIP and LEADERSHIP TRAINING in developing these concepts: ⟶

MELODIC
RHYTHMIC
HARMONIC
STRUCTURAL
EXPRESSIVE
STYLISTIC . . . . .

sequential

through ⟶ AUDITORY
⟶ TACTILE and
⟶ VISUAL experiences

Chapter 1

The Need
for Music Supervision

Historically, one of the most distressing things that could happen to an elementary classroom teacher was the periodic visit by the music supervisor. Remember the day the music supervisor visited you? Of course, you had the advantage of a rich musical background. But the teacher next door "couldn't sing for sour apples"; neither could he read a note. How did the music supervisor affect him? You may have been a music supervisor for years but still experience that unwanted feeling upon stepping into the grade teacher's room.

There will always be a need for music supervision despite strong feelings about it. This need exists because music is a rightful heritage of every child, and we have promised to give each child his share. Since all cannot teach music equally well, the trained supervisor-helper is needed to assure minimum music instruction.

Most schools today have to depend increasingly on the classroom teacher to teach music because (1) there are not enough school music teachers to go around, (2) there are far too many children for the few public school music teachers to serve effectively, and (3) there are not enough being trained to even begin to fill the need.

This dilemma (teaching music without adequate preparation) with which classroom teachers are faced has been compounded by the added responsibilities of the *self-contained classroom*. The good that could come from this concept has been overshadowed by (1) a lack of music teaching in the grades, (2) the absence of a consistent music education program in the schools, or (3) sporadic instruction in music.

Today's public school music teacher has to be regarded as a leader in music education in order to get the job done. His responsibility

3

is to provide leadership toward a coordinated program of music education. Instead of replacing the classroom teacher, he is expected to strengthen and supplement what the teacher does. It has been difficult for him to assume this role of leadership since frequently he has had no specific leadership training.

This role of the school music teacher has focused attention on a larger proportion of people from whom leadership is expected. It is for these that this book has been prepared.

A program of music supervision based upon sound leadership principles will stand. It is either made or broken by the deeds of the people placed in charge, namely the supervisors. Programs fail usually, not because of the absence of musical ability or a deficiency in teaching ability, but because of the misapplication or ignorance of supervisory techniques.

The Public School Music Teacher Becomes Consultant

The school music teacher needs guidance in the techniques of supervision. Even before he has had a chance to mature in his ability to teach music he is confronted with the challenge of being both teacher and consultant. His personal choice, training, or experience has very little to do with his new assignment. The fault is with the school that is faced with a need because (1) there are too many classrooms for the music consultant to meet regularly, and (2) most teachers are providing less than a reasonable minimum of musical experiences for their children.

In such cases, the young, inexperienced music teacher is tossed into a veritable arena of raging problems which he bravely tries to resolve. If things go well he receives plaudits from the amphitheater, boos and brickbats when he fails! His preservice training did not prepare him for this.

He searches for help and advice in professional journals and in the few available music education textbooks, also for a positive working framework which can be adapted to his particular circumstances. If nature endowed him with the necessary knack for handling difficult situations, he would tend to survive; or if he was one of the very few fortunates whose administrators joined him in the arena to give him professional aid, he could succeed.

Music Supervision Is a Job To Be Done

There is a strong need for clarification of the role of the music supervisor, or of just what his job is. The clues offered here suggest to the reader that he can see failures of music supervisors as tactical mistakes in dealing with the people who come within the scope of their influence; and successes, because important amenities in social relationships were observed.

Merely having taken a course called Music Supervision is no assurance that applications to local situations will be made. Not until the experiences of many supervisors are reconciled with educational aims and with an accepted philosophy of music education can the leader offer valid advice to the beginner. There is a need to clarify the *job to be done* in keeping with educational principles.

Some teacher-training institutions list courses in Music Supervision. Only when these courses are taught by people who are experienced music supervisors, schooled in current educational aims and in theories of supervision, can they be of benefit to the novice. An acquaintance recently took a course in music supervision. His comment was, "We learned about many new ways to teach music, especially in the grades, but nothing was said about supervision."

It would have been better had this person taken a course in general supervision. At least, he would have been exposed to modern leadership theories as they relate to educational philosophy and aims. Most music teachers believe that music is different, is approached differently, and has aims that go beyond those of many other subject areas. Therefore, this area of educational endeavor needs to be treated separately and with due regard for music's idiosyncrasy, thus placing music in proper perspective as an educative influence differing from the materialistic disciplines.

The New Music Consultant

The new music consultant needs supervisory techniques to assure reasonable success in the difficult job confronting him. Supervision techniques have changed over the past years. The emphasis of yesterday is not the concern of today. There was a time when the supervisor was expected to inspect the school and all that pertained to it. This type of supervision gradually gave way to a system of school visitation. This was after districts had greater assurance that they had reasonably qualified teachers. Still later the emphasis was on teacher improvement. Inherent in this approach is the theory that people have the power to change and improve other people.

Since teachers really don't change because someone wills it so, this mode of supervision gradually gave way to other attempts to improve instruction. Good teaching ideas went through a process from fads to methodologies. Finally, it became fashionable to apply a method to a teaching situation with vigor. According to this theory children are equally educable, and educators subscribed to the idea that if one taught a certain way *long enough and hard enough* most children would eventually learn. Discrepancies in this type of arrangement were not so pronounced years ago, when only the children of the select few were exposed to anything beyond a minimum educational program. However, when the children of all of the people were welcomed into school, new ways to provide better learning had to be devised.

A later stage of supervisory concentration was the attempt at improving the teaching climate. It seemed feasible that by rearranging a classroom situation or one in which learning takes place, many educational ills would be solved. But that did not do the job. Teaching still remained a complex matter and learning remained as complex as ever.

Another attempt by supervisors at solving educational problems was focussing attention on the learner himself. This approach took into account the findings of newer schools of thought produced by the still infant field of educational psychology. It looked at the learner both in and out of context of the classroom. It looked at him as an individual, his development, his peculiar tendencies and potentials, and as an individual controlled by certain natural or inherent factors and environmentally produced proclivities. This focus on the learner contributed toward a broader understanding about learning.

Recently supervision has concentrated intently on the total educational scene, referred to as the *teacher-learner situation.* Here the pupil, the teacher, and the body of materials to be learned, all were to be placed in an atmosphere guaranteed to insure optimum transfer of learning. The teacher, in this instance, is not so much the instructor as the arranger of a learning situation and the catalyst in various arrangements designed to promote learning.

Today educators are more willing to subscribe to the hypothesis set forth by Jerome Bruner,[1] "that any subject can be taught effectively in some intellectually honest form to any child at any stage of development." Also, what is taught in school should have such importance and such pertinence that it can serve us in the future. This implies a greater concern for quality of content. It also implies a mandate for the educator to choose either teaching for facts or for concepts and principles. To the music supervisor it means seeing basic overriding concerns and basic principles of operation that have relevance at most times and in most situations.

For Whom This Is Written

This book has been written specifically for people from whom leadership in music education is expected:

1. The public school music teacher
2. The full-time music teacher or director of school music activities or organizations
3. The musically talented classroom teacher
4. The combination special music teacher-consultant
5. The school administrator
6. The college teacher of supervision and music supervision
7. The prospective classroom music specialist and potential music consultant
8. The music supervisor

The public school music teacher's problems are inherent in the changing role from classroom music teacher to a professional music consultant. It is hoped that this book will be a practical guide in helping him assume leadership and in giving him program direction based on workable educational principles.

The full-time music teacher with too little time for working with teachers is expected to provide music leadership for his school community over and above his regular teaching assignment. His is a job of supervision over and above music teaching, since he is held responsible for the promotion of the total music program.

His daily schedule is complex. He may be responsible for two periods of band each day, two choral groups, and a period for sectional instrumental instruction. During the remainder of the day he may hop around to the various grade rooms, teaching fifteen minutes in each or either helping some teacher or giving suggestions to small groups of teachers. After school his time is pretty well taken up in participating in community music activities.

The musically talented classroom teacher is the musical leader in the schools that do not employ a regular music teacher. He may have some musical training and considerable talent. The entire music program revolves about whatever leadership he is able to give. The program may succeed or fail, depending on how he handles the various situations that confront him. Such music leadership is often expected of kindergarten teachers, because they ordinarily have more musical training than other teachers. Much is expected of them. The morning schedule may be taken up with teaching the kindergartners. The afternoon may be assigned to instructing upper grade glee club and teaching music in some of the other grades. Frequently, the teacher may be expected to plan and execute the annual Christmas program and the graduation exercises. In the absence of more qualified music personnel they automatically become the unifying influence for music not only on the school staff but also in the community. In essence they are the supervisor, the director, and the music administrator; therefore, they need to know much about music supervision so they can give effective direction to the music program.

The combination music teacher and consultant is found frequently in small cities. The school in a town of this size has enough work for a full-time consultant or supervisor, but probably assigns a person to teaching music one-half day and supervising the remainder of the day. This dual responsibility exists for a number of reasons, among which are (1) the cost of employing a full-time person, (2) the inability to find a fully trained person, or (3) the lack of administrative understanding of the need for a full-time supervisor. It results usually in considerably less than excellent effectiveness in either of the responsibilities. This often is the public school music major's first job. For this reason alone can his problems be most complex and extremely varied.

The full-time music consultant ordinarily has no scheduled teaching assignment. He is either in charge of elementary classroom music supervision, or he may be assigned to a combination of elementary and secondary supervision. Or, he may be either a special vocal or instrumental music supervisor. His title is any of these: consultant, director, supervisor, or coordinator.

This position exists at the several levels of school organization, state, county (intermediate unit or parish), and city or large district level. No matter where it exists, the job expectations range all the way from administrative duties to supervisory duties. Wherever this position is found there is always the connotation and expectation of educational leadership. The problems, ideas, and issues dealt with herein are directly applicable to good modern music supervision; and those who aspire to such positions need direction because (1) the role of leadership in music education is still quite misunderstood in many areas; (2) the problems are many and common to most music supervisors; and (3) there are definite and constructive guidelines that are applicable in any kind of music supervision or leadership situation. Actual practice needs to be modified in light of the real goals in music education.

The school administrator needs to be aware of principles of music supervision in order to reflect the best in music education thinking and to be able to reconcile what he knows about supervision to the urgencies of music education. He also needs to be in a position where he can guide and orient music supervision personnel. As the *key person* responsible for the total educational program he needs to use these ideas in all types of school situations. As the official educational leader in his school community, the administrator is in the position to promote, initiate, and carry out a good music program. He is also in the position to encourage good music education leadership on his music staff.

The teacher of music supervision can profitably use the materials and ideas herein, since they are factual, practical, anecdotal, and in keeping with modern theories of supervision; also, because they agree with the best we know about music education. Current courses in music supervision too often are merely advanced courses in teaching methods. Indeed most college music education instructors are well trained in the many important aspects of music education, but are not experienced in the complexity of present-day school systems to fully appreciate the interrelationships involved in modern supervision. They must understand that music supervision is as much dependent on people working together for the improvement of a situation as it is on the musical acuity of the supervisor.

The student of music education also needs to know and appreciate the many problems involved in a role of leadership. He will learn that music supervision requires not only skilled musicians and music teachers but that it also requires people possessing good leadership qualities and skills. He may some day become the supervisor. Even if this doesn't happen he needs to understand the supervisor's relationship to him as an educator.

This book provides many vicarious experiences which can be a guide through the perplexities he is bound to face someday when he becomes the leader.

What You Will Find in This Book

The student of music supervision is keenly interested in the *what, why, when,* and *how* of the responsibilities he assumes when he accepts the position of music consultant for a district. He seeks justification of his role, for clarification of it in relation to the total educational program. He wants to know about the problems he is likely to encounter. He needs to know his responsibilities toward others, simple directions for successful operations, basic principles from which to operate, useful materials, and his responsibility to himself and to his profession.

No one text can presume to provide answers to all of the perplexities concerning music supervision. However, this volume represents an attempt to apply principles of good supervision to typically recurring situations in music education. In their order, these are the considerations:

A. *The Job of Music Supervision* (Need, Bases, Process, Problems)
B. *The Music Supervisor and His Job* (Activities, Interrelationships)
C. *The Music Supervisor's Responsibilities* (Program Administration, Curriculum Implementation, Learning Facilitation, Materials Facilitation)
D. *The Music Supervisor as a Leader* (Pacesetter in Decision Making, Research, Professional Growth, Creative Thinking, and Evaluation)

Even with these considerations the writer does not presume to present the ultimate in coverage about good music supervision. This work will have served most adequately if it draws attention to the complexity of music supervision. It will have served well also if it draws attention to the fact that music supervision implies a *job to be done* in the area of educational leadership according to well-defined concepts.

The music supervisor's title is not necessarily a *sine qua non* for carrying out the responsibilities of music supervision. No matter what the title, there is a *job to be done* with peculiar challenges of its own. Please understand, the lone music person, or the musically inclined person in the isolated small school community, is as much a music *supervisor* as is his big-city counterpart. The only difference is in the terrain and the complexity of relationships each encounters.

A brief résumé of some of the sole existing authoritative sources for music supervision will be presented. They are the *Research Bulletin Number 18*, published by the Music Educator's National Conference,[2] and Chapters II and III of MENC Source Book Number 2, *Music in American Education*.[3]

The process involved in music supervision as described in Chapter 3 involves any or all of the following considerations:

1. Continual program and process evaluation of what transpires locally in music education.
2. Continual and highly technical service of a musical and a leadership nature.
3. Leadership, both musical and educational, possessing a high degree of competency attested by training and experience.
4. Democratic leadership of such caliber that it draws out the finest music teaching ability of teachers and brings it to fruition in an all-inclusive music program that fosters human and aesthetic values.

5. Skill in human relations so that confidence and harmonious relationships are established. Musical ideals and values flow readily when understandings have been established.
6. Skills that help people work together for the accomplishment of mutual musical goals. It takes skill to get the job done, and this is accomplished by centering attention on the job itself, and not on the individual.
7. Personnel administration with particular emphasis on utilizing the right talents for the right situation.
8. Taking a look at oneself as music supervisor to see and determine, as nearly as possible, the causative factors that spell success or failure of the program.

Constantly recurring problems in music supervision are presented in Chapter 4 and are, for the most part, anecdotal accounts of typical problems encountered by music supervisors in various situations. This chapter points out that problems arise from circumstances or situations, even from certain arrangements of interrelationships. The idea is fostered that many problems encountered by music supervisors often arise because of improper communication circuits or connections. These connections cannot be remedied by the supervisor alone. Others in and near the affected relationship must also share in the responsibility of correcting the situation.

The six areas productive of certain kinds of recurring problems are these:

1. Working with *other than* music supervisory personnel
2. Working with individual teachers
3. Working with administrators
4. Working with music specialists
5. Working with beginning music consultants
6. Working through proper channels of communication

To avoid problems in these areas the music supervisor must have been well schooled in many aspects of human relations.

The routine life of the music supervisor is treated anecdotally in Chapter 5. The events must be understood in terms of short and long-range goals; and the daily minutiae that engage the music supervisor can be a part of a long-range pattern of action reflecting a definite philosophy. The various accounts include (1) activities of a full-time music teacher also carrying out a program of music supervision; (2) a page out of the diary of a busy rural music supervisor; (3) a weekly report of the music supervisor; (4) a first semester report of field activities of the music supervisor; (5) the annual report of the music supervisor in terms of general goals; and (6) a brief summary of major accomplishments during the five-year tenure of a music supervisor.

Chapter 6 discusses how the music supervisor promotes proper inter-relationships with those who come within the range of his influence. To set up such working relationships it is necessary that all affected individuals be considered and approached differently. The problems of working with each of these is accentuated by the fact that there are various kinds of people and each of these has to be approached with due regard for his idiosyncracies.

That the music supervisor also administers the music program is pointed out in Chapters 7 and 8. One cannot separate administrative from supervisory responsibilities. Each of these areas overlaps other areas in its everyday workings. When supervisory responsibilities are delegated to the specialists, they have to be accompanied by obligations and prerogatives of an administrative nature so that the assigned function can be carried out.

The emphasis is on *the job that needs to be done.* This can be done best when a coordinated system of music supervision is developed and carried out. Such a coordinated program must be administered wisely in order to do the greatest good.

Chapter 9 describes the more prominent devices or in-service aids as preferred by hosts of teachers, such as the following:[4]

1. Supervision by technical assistance
2. Demonstration lessons
3. Grade-level meetings
4. Supervisor arranging teacher visits to other schools
5. Teachers helping formulate school policy with reference to the music program
6. Constructive criticism
7. Supervisor recommending new methods and techniques
8. Area meetings in music
9. Utilizing the outside expert
10. Providing growth opportunities for potential leaders
11. Working with teacher training institutions
12. Workshop type in-service programs in music education
    a. Consecutive workshops
13. Action research

Rationale for printed materials and audiovisual materials as a rein-forcement and a stimulant to teaching is presented in Chapter 10. Certain films, equipment, autoharps, songbells, and recordings are among the many items that can be used effectively, also regular series of music books, printed materials, charts, and pamphlets whereby the teacher can be helped to grow in her music teaching ability.

Chapters 11 and 12 indicate that decisions must be based on accepted principles. The music supervisor must be aware of the principles that have affected programs and progress of the field of music education in the past. Among these are the *aims of music education*. These could readily become philosophical guideposts for thinking about various aspects of music education:

1. Are the currently accepted aims in music education good?
2. If they are really good can the supervisor make wise decisions because of them?
3. How does knowledge of *child growth and development* influence planning a program of music education?
4. How do you feel about such issues as music reading, rhythms, use of preorchestral instruments, competition festivals, marching bands, integration with other learning areas, methods of teaching rote songs, dealing with the poor singer, and many other problems that by their nature involve certain educational principles?

According to Chapter 13 research findings are needed in order to improve any aspect of the music program. Research arises as a need after the existing music programs have been evaluated and found wanting in some respect. Such research will follow either of the several directions:

1. The supervisor availing himself of the research done by others
2. The research carried on by the music supervisor himself
3. The research that the supervisor causes others to do through action research right on the job, also called *innovations* (trying new ways)[5]

In order to avoid a proliferation of obsolete programs that have determined the course of music education in the past, there is a need for new ways of performing research basic to music education and disseminating it. Music education, as well as other aspects of education, surfeits in cliches that stop short of the intended practical application, at the classroom door. An answer to this may be a *closer relationship between research and practice.* Equally important ought to be the courage to discard the *insignificant* and *ineffective,* and to replace these with something more *effective* in transmitting true musical values.

Chapter 14 discusses many aspects of the professional growth of the music supervisor. Present-day leadership requires that its implementors deliberately keep informed of the newest trends and findings available.

For this reason there have developed various types of supervisory and music education organizations. Each of these has official publications and research findings of its own that can keep the music supervisor abreast of current ideas.

The various leadership roles which are expected of the music supervisor are also devices whereby he can grow professionally. These may include officerships in local, regional, state, or national organizations that promote either music education or the supervision of music.

The final chapter attempts to identify a direction in which music supervision ought to move in order to be more effective. It refers to the music supervisor's greatest challenge as an indefinable substance closely akin to professional integrity and search for truth through objective evaluation. This idea needs to be reemphasized again. It is the writer's hope, however, that it will stimulate thinking outside of the realm of acceptable and respected frameworks in order to come up with realistic and more feasible ways of transmitting musical values.

We may have built up systems and rituals around movements and gadgets in our search for finding more acceptable ways of getting music taught. We justify these as being educational because we reason that they agree with certain basic principles of education. The job can be done more effectively, and with more real musical values evolving. The final chapter deals with this kind of critical evaluation.

Again, here the *basic concepts in music education,* as developed in the National Society for the Study of Education 1958 Yearbook will be identified as challenges to the forward thinking music supervisor.[6]

This book is addressed to the many who are charged with leadership in music education, such as administrators, music teachers, college music teachers, students of supervision and of music supervision, and to music supervisors themselves. Its content is designed to meet the needs in many kinds of music supervisory situations. Its anecdotes may lend authenticity because they are factual and have been drawn from the experiences of many supervisors from several states. It is no panacea, but it hopes to offer direction.

QUESTIONS FOR DISCUSSION, THOUGHT AND STUDY

1. According to the outlines presented in this opening chapter, what is really the scope of music supervision?
2. Who are the music personnel in your school community? Which of these acts in the capacity of supervisor? Is this person really the supervisor in name, or does he carry out the responsibilities of this leadership role?

3. Try to obtain an administrative organization chart from various-sized school systems. On these look for the position of the music supervisor. To whom is this person responsible? What are the duties that are outlined?
4. Does the music supervisor that you know really affect the music education program? Or does it really not make any difference if there is anyone on the job?

NOTES

[1]Jerome S. Bruner, *The Process of Education,* (New York: Vintage Press, 1963), p. 33.

[2]Music Education Research Council, *Music Supervision and Administration,* Bulletin No. 18, (Washington, D.C.: MENC, 1945), pp. 4-30.

[3]Music Educators National Conference, Source Book No. 2, *Music in American Education,* (Washington, D.C.: MENC, 1955), Chapters II and III.

[4]Henry Antell, "Teachers Appraise Supervision," *Journal of Educational Research,* XXXVIII: (April 1945), pp. 606-611.

[5]Berlie Fallon, *Educational Innovations in the United States,* Phi Delta Kappa, (Bloomington, Ind., 1966), pp. 95 and 162.

[6]Madison Thurber and others, *Basic Concepts in Music Education,* 57th Yearbook, National Society for the Study of Education (Chicago: University of Chicago Press, 1958), pp. 3ff.

COMMUNITY INVOLVEMENTS
Regional Arts Council—Schools—Legislators
Civic and Service Groups—Individuals

A necessary feedback system
for supervision to assist
in directional goals

Chapter 2

Bases for Music Supervision

An Observer's Point of View of Music Supervision

No matter what his title is, most school districts employ a music supervisor. You may call him a specialist, a music consultant, a special music teacher, a helping teacher in music, a public school music teacher, or even a director of music education, or a coordinator of music education. Again, no matter what you call this person, the function of the music supervisor is well defined, accepted and respected by all in the community: by the children, their teachers, the administrator, and other school employees, also by the board of education and the school patrons.

This person, whom we call the music supervisor, may be the band teacher, the chorus teacher, the orchestra leader, or the one who goes into each elementary classroom either to teach music to all the children or to help the classroom teacher in his music teaching responsibilities. His function is well defined and accepted by all. And he is not without respect and high regard by all who come within range of his influence. Those who have the opportunity to observe the music supervisor and who react and place a value on his actions are the children, the teachers, the administration, the board, and the community.

There are many more people who look at the music supervisor, categorize him, help him, promote him, criticize him, or even castigate him. The five groups listed are the ones in most immediate relationship to the learning situation.

The Children Look at the Supervisor

Students, whether or not they have learned to like music, are sure in their feelings about the school music leader. They may not be able to verbalize them as effectively as adults, but they recognize that, were it not for this person, music might have been accorded a lesser place in the school program. They also know to whom they can direct their inquiries about music.

The Classroom Teacher Looks at the Supervisor

The classroom teacher knows his potential source of help. Whether he chooses to work closely with the school music leader or avoids him, this is certain, he knows what the supervisor stands for.

Different teachers may recognize the supervisor's function in different ways; nevertheless they are quite sure and aware of his sphere of influence. They may resent his intrusion into their domain, even though they wish they could do what he is trying to do for them. Many classroom teachers have had the bitter experience of the periodic and dreaded visit by the music supervisor. These dreaded visits still happen today in some places. However, currently more teachers are anticipating with pleasure the experience of being enriched musically by today's music supervisor when he appears on the scene. The teachers know that his function is to arrange situations so that more music values are transmitted to more children.

The Administrator Looks at the Supervisor

The administrative department knows the function of the music specialist as something that goes beyond teaching music or supervising teachers. The specialist was hired as a person with special competencies in music. So the administrator looks to him as a musical leader for his school and for his community. He wanted more than a baton-wielding leader or conductor. The administrator recognizes the need for one who could lead the children and his community to desire and cherish music. He also needs a musical adviser, someone to outline for him what it takes to make children musical; what it takes to make the school musical; and what it takes to make a community sensitive to music's power. The administrator may not be musical, but he knows enough about its values to appreciate its presence.

He recognizes music for its cultural and public relations values, but also he is aware of what it does for the individual child in his school, especially the child who cannot be reached through other means. He also is aware of the added cost to his school. It is costly! The music specialist, therefore, has to justify many musical purchases to him personally. Frequently, he has to sell the administrator on the advisability of purchasing certain items so that children can have a richer music instructional program. Through these various kinds of contacts the administrator becomes quite acquainted with the school music leader.

The Board of Education Looks at the Music Supervisor

When the local board hires a music teacher, it wants more than a teacher of music. It wants someone who can give musical leadership which will reflect itself in the school music program and have its power felt in the community. It wants a music adviser to suggest necessary and costly musical purchases and someone to advise of the material needs to be considered in setting into motion a balanced and inclusive musical program. It wants someone to tell about trends in music education so that wiser and more intelligent decisions can be made. Furthermore, it wants someone to stimulate promotion of cultural activities. The board wants to be known for wanting and promoting the ennobling things in life. To them the academic subjects are the self-evidents of education and they regard music as a specialty needing more than *self-evident* treatment.

The Community Looks at the Music Supervisor

The community sees the music supervisor, regardless of a contractual agreement that exists, as the music leader. In fact, music is in our schools today because the parents in the community wanted it for their children. This fact has been dramatically demonstrated throughout the ages. The community wants music in its concert halls, its recreational centers, and in its churches. It also desires its people to learn to love music for the enriching effect it has on humanity. The community looks up to its music teachers for leadership in developing its greatest musical potential.

The school music specialist is accorded prestige on a par with that of the community's best or greatest citizen. Since the community members are preoccupied with more mundane problems, music teachers are entrusted with the task of providing leadership in music for the community. This role is not always simple or easy. They have to reconcile their own personal inclinations and desires with the cultural status of the immediate situation lest they lose effectiveness in the community. They become known for musical astuteness and ability to convince people of the desirability of having music instruction in schools and music activities in the community.

The music teacher's job expectations go far beyond that of the regular academic teacher. These responsibilities he cannot avoid! He and the coach are the ones from whom so much is expected and who are respected by so many. This acceptance helps to accentuate the universality of music's appeal. It points out that man yearns for and strives for the things that ennoble the spirit and enhance living beyond life's barest sordities.

The responsible music person does many things that are usually self-understood:

1. Assuring music a place in the curriculum
2. Helping determine the degree of status music enjoys in the school
3. Speaking for music in educational circles
4. Seeing to it that the school has proper and adequate facilities to teach music effectively
5. Introducing music to adults and children through a program of education
6. Being a good musician
7. Being a good diplomat
8. Constantly promoting music for all
9. Constantly working toward defending and improving the status of music in the school
10. Working closely with leaders in other learning areas to insure equitable representation of music in the curriculum

In essence, he is a musical ambassador. As such, he must accept these job expectations as challenges over and above being an able musician. He must be able to speak convincingly for music in education. He must possess an aptness to project ideas to others. He must possess a personality that is able to meet other people and make friends with them easily. The success of a school music program is dependent upon the musicality and the personality of the person charged with the responsibility of promulgating it.

The music leader can do much to counteract the factors that contribute toward the failure of a school's music instructional program. Some of these are (1) apparent administrative indifference to the music program, evidenced by preoccupation with problems other than music; (2) unsympathetic attitude of classroom teachers for the music program, and lack of inclination on their part to accept any responsibility for carrying out part of the teaching of music; (3) a local board of education's refusal to purchase the necessary materials and equipment needed to develop a good program of music education; and

(4) what people often refer to as *the low cultural level of the community*.

It goes without saying that his responsibilities include finding and raising the cultural level of the community, enlisting sympathetic teacher support and participation in the program, getting administrative attention and agreement to a program of music education, and demonstrating to a governing board and to the community the wisdom of a coordinated program of music education. The specialist must accept the challenge of being the ambassador of music, the guardian of music's rightful place in the educational scheme, and the untiring champion and promoter of music as a great and ennobling art.

It was only a century and a quarter ago when Lowell Mason demonstrated to the Boston Board of Education that music, as a subject for instruction in the schools, was feasible. Through his influence the board has on record this classic statement: "Through vocal music you set in motion a mighty power which, silently, but surely, in the end, will humanize, refine, and elevate a whole community."[1] It was at this time when Mason introduced music reading and the art of singing to children in the public schools. True, children have always sung, and they have presumably sung in schools also, but never before has this been a curricular consideration in American schools.

It doesn't matter now that Lowell Mason was a self-taught musician, a bank clerk, and one who was an enthusiastic supporter of the educational ideas of Pestalozzi. What really matters is that his leadership ability prompted him to introduce singing and a system of music reading into the schools. His deeds interested many educators in the efficacy of teaching music in the schools. His *teacher institutes* held in various cities imbued an entire generation of teachers with enthusiastic interest for teaching music in the schools. His sense of educational dedication and his dynamic leadership was a springboard from which started the phenomenal growth in music education so evident today in almost every rural community, village, and city throughout the United States.

Mason not only was a fine self-taught musician, and a teacher keenly interested in the best educational trends of his day; he was, in essence, the first music supervisor. Whether he actually was called a supervisor is not important. This is important, though: His leadership ability extended far beyond the bounds of the classroom and the immediate school environs and affected music education for generations. This is the mark of a music supervisor. He was a leader of teachers and a man of superior vision whose educational influence is still appreciated today as a milestone in music education.

The following guidelines drawn from the life and activities of Lowell Mason lend a feasible pattern for music supervision today: He was a master teacher, an expert musician, a compelling personality, a possessor of missionary zeal, a research worker, an experimentalist, an indefatigable worker for community music, a leader in music education thinking, an organizer of in-service programs for teachers.

Essentially, this is the job expected of music supervisors everywhere. Today there are hundreds of Lowell Masons. There may be thousands who aspire to such a leadership role. Many supervisors have not as yet begun to realize their potential in terms of influence for the good of music education. Some of these lack training or experience, and some of these lack adequate personalities for the role of music leadership.

The clergyman, the grocer, and the lawyer each has services peculiar to his calling or trade which he offers to those who need or want them. The services of these are offered even in the remotest corners of a sparsely populated state. The importance of their profession or trade is not lessened by locale. Needs and desires of people for their goods and services are the same no matter where they are found. Accessibility, geography, climate, and even social complexity does not lessen the need of the potential leadership expertise.

The school music leader in a rural area deals with the same musical phenomena, music learning problems, and musical ideals as does the director of music of a large city school system. He seeks the same values for his constituents. His concerns differ not so much in kind as in relationship to the amount of the people served. He may have an excellent choral group, but a smaller one than his *big city* counterpart. The people and music are the same. Locale may be different; and there may be a difference in the degree of social complexity. The challenges and obligations confronting the music supervisor differ but slightly. The music supervisor in the small community enjoys a high esteem, as does the general medical practitioner in the same community. The small town musical specialist very frequently is supervisor, specialist, and teacher, while in the larger urban center these same obligations are carried out by an organization of personnel delegated to do specialized jobs. The needs, the children, the music, and the desired values are the same wherever one goes.

Most classroom teachers are adequately trained in general curriculum areas. It can be expected that they teach effectively in those areas. Because of deemphasis on the fine arts in preservice training many of these teachers are deficient in the skills needed to promote artistic values. Specialists need to be employed to rectify this.

Even with the employment of only one music specialist on a school staff, there is an implication of supervision, because he is expected to exert musical influence throughout the school community. Besides filling in the musical deficiencies caused by the inability of others to teach music, he also provides leadership in the school and in the community. The position of music supervisor developed from such a base.

In large communities a superior or senior music teacher is designated to be *in charge,* or responsible for the flow of the program at the different educational levels. Relieved of direct teaching duties he assumes the job of coordinating the efforts of other music teachers.

As music education advanced, it was felt that children at all levels should have a greater share of regular instruction in music. And, with emphasis on the *self-contained classroom,* teachers found themselves often willing, but unable to carry on a music program without specialized help. Classroom music teaching specialists appeared, however, in insufficient numbers to be of real help. A solution to the dilemma lay in the direction of someone coordinating the talents and efforts of many to produce a good classroom music instructional program designed to affect all children. The music supervisor gradually assumed these coordinating functions.

This can be called systematic *program administration.* It may mean merely taking care of details such as arranging for music and equipment for a teacher, or getting permission from a principal to hold an in-service meeting. The music supervisor administers the total school music program.

Music supervision is a *job to be done* . . . and whoever happens to be handy or employed with music responsibilities had better do the job.

A Documentary View of Music Supervision

Most of the authoritative information about music supervision has been written within the past twenty years. In 1948 the Music Educators National Conference published Research Bulletin No. 18, entitled *Music Supervision and Administration in the Schools.*[2] This bulletin and the extended review of it in the *Conference's Source Book Number II, Music in American Education,*[3] Chapters II and III, are the only official documents available as a guide to supervisors. Because of this, their content will be noted here. The writers attempted to reconcile music education ideals with concepts about general supervision and administration thus:

The Music Educators National Conference, from its organization in 1907, has sought to improve the practice of the teaching of music by improving standards and constantly reinterpreting the principles of music education both to music teachers and to educators at large. The Conference feels that the time has come for a restatement of the whole question of supervision and administration in relation to music education. Some excellent formulations concerning supervision in its more general aspects have already been made, but a similar statement in relation to the peculiar problems of music instruction still needs formulation.[4]

Prefaced with this statement it briefly developed the history of music supervision from 1853, when, in Cleveland, classroom teachers were given guidance in the teaching of music by specialists.

Part I discusses the origin and trends of music supervision. It differentiates between administration and supervision, referring to it as an evolutionary process starting with teaching and proceeding through supervision to administration.

Supervision arises from teaching pressures and *administration* arises from administrative pressures.

Part II outlines supervision at various levels where it is or ought to be found. The *outline of music supervisory functions* is included because of its clarity.

Supervision

1. combines supervisory with administrative functions, and
2. operates without administrative responsibility and is concerned with the conditions which surround learning.

State Supervision is to provide musical opportunities for all children, and see to it that

1. teachers employed to teach in the rural and smaller elementary schools are adequately prepared to teach music
2. practical suggestions are furnished to these schools for the carrying out of a minimum program of music instruction.

A state music specialist is available to larger schools for help or advice (currently in 34 states)

1. developing course of study
2. working out satisfactory schedule arrangements for music teaching
3. building suitable music rooms
4. supervising teachers and seeing that the first emphasis in school music is placed upon fine classroom teaching.

In each case the particular needs of the school determine the statewide program of music supervision. (See ideas listed on pages 133-135.)

COUNTY MUSIC SUPERVISION
  I. Administration of the Program
    A. Promotional Activities

      1. Contacting community agencies to enlist interest in the school music program
      2. Organizing inter-school music activities
      3. Organizing music programs that feature several schools
      4. Contacting newspapers, radio stations, and active organized groups
    B. Activities Concerning Personnel
      1. Selecting and recommending competent teachers and supervisors
      2. Organizing music staff to assure smooth functioning
      3. Establishing and maintaining a good attitude toward music by others in education
    C. Activities Concerning the Music Curriculum
      1. Guiding development of a balanced vocal and instrumental music curriculum
      2. Guiding information of music education philosophy and aims
      3. Promoting relationships between music and other curricular offerings
    D. Activities Concerned with Scheduling
    E. Activities Concerned with Finance
    F. Activities Concerned with Equipment
    G. Activities Concerned with the Physical Conditions Under Which Music Teaching Is Carried On
    H. Activities Concerned with Records (Personnel, Monies, Inventory)

  II. Supervision
    A. Teacher Training and Guidance
    B. Inspection
    C. Research
      1. Setting up testing devices
      2. Evaluating books, materials and equipment
      3. Checking professional literature for aids
      4. Assisting in assembling of curriculum materials
      5. Preparing courses of study

  III. Miscellaneous Supervisory Procedures (Bulletins, Communications, A-V)

SUPERVISION IN CITIES AND TOWNS
  I. Types of Organization
    A. Supervisor is chief music teacher
    B. Principal is responsible for quality of the instructional program in his building (line and staff)

C. Cooperative plan—principal and supervisor work together accepting joint responsibility for the program.

II. Functions of the Supervisor
(1) learning (2) training (in-service) (3) guidance program (4) community relationships (5) research

III. Characteristics of Competent Supervision
(Taken from Seventh Yearbook of Department of Supervisors and Directors of Instruction)
(1) Philosophic (2) Cooperative (3) Creative (4) Scientific (5) Effective

IV. Personality and Training of the Supervisor
Sound emotional balance; liberal education; specialized training; practical experience in field of service; broad professional outlook; adherence to democratic principles; philosophy based on an understanding of social needs and purposes; appreciation of the need for balance in the social, emotional, spiritual, physical, and mental growth of children

(Values of supervisory program dependent upon the qualities of personality and leadership displayed by the supervisor)

V. Techniques of Supervision
Visitation (scheduled, unannounced, on call, by appointment); individual conference, teachers' meeting, demonstration lesson, the supervisory visit, the course of study, the supervisory bulletin, tests and measurements

VI. Illustrative Types of Supervisory Programs
A. *The unorganized program* in which the supervisor attends to so many unnecessary details that those needing help are not reached
B. *The empirical program* in which the supervisor finds and determines the concentration of effort for the year and sets up in-service programs to reinforce the goals
C. *The survey or fact-finding program* in which the supervisor finds out from teachers what is needed and builds in-service programs around these expressed needs

An objective of a supervision program is the development of teacher initiative; and such initiative is developed only if there is a sincere recognition that teachers differ, not only in skill or in level of training, but also in the matter of interest. In modern supervision the teacher, the administrator, and the supervisor work together to develop an entire program that affects most children.

Part III outlines the responsibilities and activities of the music administrator.

A. Determining and implementing a school policy regarding music
B. Formulating, revising and applying the music curriculum
C. Providing opportunities for the personnel in the program to become unified and vitalized
D. Directing needed studies and investigations; devising and gathering records, evaluations and reports
E. Assisting in formulating the music budget and assuming the main responsibility for carrying it out
F. Establishing and maintaining desirable public relations

A music administrator must be a musician among musicians and an educator among educators. In the discussions of Research Bulletin No. 18 there is a strong indication that supervision and administration overlap in many of their functions. It is never all supervision and no administration or vice versa.

Music in American Education[5] describes two leadership positions in music education. In each case the title refers to the job to be done.

Administration of a Music Education Program emphasizes the job, and not the position, of the person. It is a job to be done because of certain situations. The *first situation* is found in cities with less than one hundred thousand population. These are some of the areas of concern:

1. Duties within department: in-service for teachers, materials, course of study, special teachers, schedules, personnel, testing records
2. Financial: budgeting and all pertinent problems
3. Extra-departmental duties: community efforts, civic music groups, adult classes, liaison between school and community
4. Promotional: publicity, public relations, news, radio, T-V
5. General Education: working with administration to interpret music program to those in charge of total educational program

The *second situation* is found in cities of more than 100,000 population (an arbitrary dividing line). These are some of the general considerations:

A. Personnel
   1. Selection of staff by music administrator
   2. Assignment of teaching load determined according to needs in the department
   3. Staff development through workshops, teachers' meetings, classroom demonstrations and discussions, techniques and methods classes, bulletins, teacher-supervisor-administrator planning.
B. Organization through various levels of instruction
C. Continuity between administrative levels

D. Materials and supplies services
E. Research and records
F. Curriculum development
G. Budget making
H. Promotional activities and public relations
I. Interadministrational relationships

Both administrative and supervisory responsibilities overlap in one position as they do in most other types of music supervision positions. Accordingly, music supervision today is a dual type of responsibility. The technical aspects of one are necessary for the other. Where there is only one person, he or she must assume both the administrative aspects of the music supervision program and the strictly supervisional aspects. To be an effective supervisor and music administrator one must be an educational leader.

Music in American Education discusses music supervision as it is found in various size communities. The current philosophy of supervision is also discussed. The terms consultant, counselor, teaching supervisor, supervising teacher, helping teacher, chairman, and the like are used. They indicate an acceptance of the gradual change in supervisional emphasis from ancient *inspection* through the *line and staff* operation to that more currently espoused in educational circles: *working together* and co-relationships.

The section entitled *Qualifications of a Music Supervisor* contains the ingredients that can spell success on the job. These are some of the considerations:

1. *Demonstrated success as a teacher.* The ability to see things as the teacher sees them, but with the essence of recognized success as a teacher of music.
2. *Some degree of maturity.* A young person can also be mature, especially if he is known for his teaching success and his emotional maturity.
3. *Personal qualities including good human relations.* (See Chapter 3 of this book).
4. *Recognized skill as a musician.* The supervisor ought never to have been the unsuccessful band director, choral director, or the Johnny come lately in music. He should typify musical stature as a fine articulate musician.
5. *Professional training above that of the average teacher.* So that the scope and depth of musical and education training will be of such magnitude that it will command the respect of others in the system, especially the special music teachers.

6. *Broad educational understanding.* This is necessary if music is to survive as a curricular consideration. Being able to see the school's view and the administrator's view, also being conversant in educational issues, seeing the relationship of music to the curriculum, all of these are indispensible understandings. He must be a master of music, but also a student of many areas of education.

Much emphasis is placed on music supervision as a service to schools and to education. These are some of the services:

1. To the teachers in the classroom
    a. Teacher-pupil-consultant planning
    b. Actual participation with the class
    c. Assistance with resource person
    d. Evaluation of group activity
    e. Helping the individual child
2. Services for the teacher
    a. Individual conferences
    b. Group conferences
3. Services to teachers in the use of audio-visual materials
    a. Assistance in the use of the phonograph
    b. Assistance in the use of the tape recorder
    c. Evaluation of commercial phonograph and tape recordings
    d. Assistance in planning live radio programs
    e. Assistance in selecting recorded programs for broadcasting to schools
    f. Assistance with resource materials to be used in preparation for listening to radio or television programs
4. Services for the teacher in in-service professional growth
    a. Participating in group consultant planning
    b. Group leadership
    c. Demonstrations or actual teaching when requested by the group
    d. Assistance to teachers who prepare classes for observation by others
    e. Presentation and evaluation of new materials and equipment
    f. Assistance as resource person to any group
    g. Assistance in orientation programs for new teachers
5. Services for school-community relations
    a. Liaison agent between school and community
    b. Generator of public relations
    c. A member of the community
6. Services for the school principal
    a. Conferences with groups of principals
    b. Conferences with individual principals

7. Services for the music staff
   a. Cooperation with the music director
   b. Cooperation with other musicians

Summary

This chapter tried to present supervision as it appears to many people and what it actually is today. It leaves much room for amplification, agreement or disagreement. The following chapter will deal more with the person doing the job. The program is important, also the kinds of qualities that are needed by the individual person responsible for the program.

Music supervision is available at various levels including the state, the county (called intermediate unit or parish in some areas), the very large city, the medium sized city, the small city and the rural community. In each of these a person is vested with the responsibility of carrying out the challenges and mandates of the position.

The qualifications of the persons holding these positions are similar. They may increase somewhat in kind with the magnitude of the situation. The responsibilities at each level are quite similar. These responsibilities do not change in quality or kind, only in amount. Leadership is the same wherever it is found.

The difference is in the degree or amount of face-to-face relationships encountered. The smaller the supervisory jurisdiction, the less these responsibilities are delegated. Even in a complex large city system there is a reasonable amount of face-to-face contact with the teacher-pupil situation. For instance, in a large metropolitan area like Los Angeles, one person is designated as Supervisor-In-Charge. Besides him there is a corps of instrumental and vocal music supervisors, each assigned to various districts in the city. They work through the various music directors and individual school principals. Many individual schools in such a city have their own full-time music specialists.

In a large city one often finds a multi-leveled situation with each level working closely with the one on either side. A face-to-face relationship similar to that in a much smaller school system is possible. It is, however, more complex.

The music director in a small community teaches, supervises and administers the music program himself. He does many of the same things that the big city music administrator does, except that he has less time in which to do them, and much less help to carry out these responsibilities. He is in the same relationship to the big city music administrator as the teaching principal is to the city school administrator. The problems are no less intense for the music teaching supervisor-administrator as are the problems of the big city music director.

QUESTIONS FOR DISCUSSION, THOUGHT AND STUDY

1. Select a small town where there is no official music supervisor but which employs a single music teacher. Describe how this person also acts as music supervisor.
2. What is the technical difference between each of these: supervisor, co-ordinator, consultant, helping teacher, demonstration teacher, director, music administrator?
3. Show how each of the positions listed above could overlap in function, expectation and responsibility.
4. Justify the contention that music supervision is a *job to be done* no matter where the school is.
5. Find out more about the history of music supervision in America. List a music education leader for each generation since the middle of the last century. What were some of their individual contributions?
6. List twelve nationally known leaders in music education today. For what is each known?
7. What trends can you note from the accounts in *Music in American Education* and in *Research Bulletin* Number 18?
8. How would you reconcile music supervision with the job of educational leadership?
9. Select a town of 6000 population. Assume you are teaching music a half of each day and are expected to carry out a program of music supervision the remaining time. Outline what you would consider an adequate program. List the many factors involved. List also your own personal attributes that you propose to bring to the job.

NOTES

[1]Russel Squire, *Introduction to Music Education*, (New York: The Ronald Press Company, 1952), p. 6.
[2]Music Education Research Council, *Music Supervision and Administration*, Bulletin No. 18, (Washington, D.C.: MENC, 1945), p. 12.
[3]Music Educators National Conference, Source Book No. 2, *Music in American Education*, (Washington, D.C.: MENC, 1955), p. 12.
[4]*Music Supervision and Administration.*
[5]*Music in American Education.*

M. Hohner, Inc., Hicksville, L.I.

Chapter 3

Music Supervision
as a Process

Many attributes of music supervision are closely related to general educational supervision, and to accepted principles of personnel management. Some of the attributes of successful music supervision discussed herein are these:

1. Program and process evaluation
2. Technical aid of a musical and leadership nature
3. Democratic dealing with situations and people
4. Musically and educationally competent leadership
   (developing leadership in others; two-way loyalty; building, promoting, and maintaining morale)
5. Skill in human relations (harmony promotes effectiveness)
6. Skill in group process
   a. Power over vs. releasing power in others
   b. Changing people
7. Skill in personnel administration
8. Skill in self-evaluation

These attributes will be discussed briefly here, and will be treated anecdotally later.

Program and Process Evaluation

Music supervision is a process that goes beyond the individual charged with the implementation of it. It is something that occurs in the wake of music educational leadership. This process has something to do with function, aspects, purposes, goals, and outcomes. For this reason the chief function of music supervision today ought to be the evaluation and improvement of the many factors affecting music learn-ing.[1] This recognizes several subsidiary functions:

a. evaluation of a program of music education and evaluation of the process of teaching music in terms of a cooperatively agreed upon philosophy and statement of aims. This evaluation is continuous. It is part of preplanning, process, and conclusion of all valid learning.
b. development of processes to carry out aims in music education that are not only concerned with the end results, but also with the effects of music while one is experiencing it, or while one is being taught.
c. setting up of personnel and working relationships in order to imple-ment aims and at the same time protect and stimulate the individ-uality and creativity of persons involved in the process of teaching music.

Music supervision involves looking at what we have and determin-ing where we are going in music education. It implies a methodology of instruction; it involves working closely with others, and it makes allowances for the myriads of problems involved in the implementing of goals.

Technical Service of Music and Leadership Nature

Music supervision is technical service aimed at improving the factors which affect the child's musical growth and development. This takes into account many factors. Evaluation has already been mentioned as one. By evaluating, one looks for ways to improve the teaching of music, both in the self-contained classroom and in the specialized choral and instrumental programs.

To evaluate means answering these questions:

1. For whom do we really want music?
2. What kinds and how much music is to be taught?
3. Who should teach the music?
4. In what ways does the present music curriculum foster the desired aims?
5. Do the methods used impart musical values?
6. Do the teacher's attitudes and actions reflect the aims of music education?
7. Are environment, equipment, and materials in keeping with aims and philosophy?
8. Is the school policy on important issues conducive to good music teaching and learning?
9. Is the community attitude conducive to carrying out an inclusive philosophy of music education?

10. How does the learner (pupil) affect carrying out aims? How do his own interests, background, his social, emotional, and moral traits affect carrying out goals?

These items go into looking at music education as it is perceived in terms of goals. If we believe certain things about music education, we will implement music education in certain ways. If *we really want all children to learn and partake of more and better music,* we will function to that end, not losing sight that music learning and music itself are processes.

Supervision Is Not Easy

The old saying, "If you can't teach, supervise," is an unrealistic assessment. The intricacies of modern education have certainly vitiated the notion that it was possible to hide behind supervision. One cannot merely wish to be a music supervisor because of such advantages as an easier work load, or greater influence and prestige. Music supervision is not easy and not always pleasant. Supervisors have never been rated high in effectiveness even among sincere and fair-minded teachers. These are some of the criticisms leveled at supervision over the years:[2]

1. It costs too much.
2. It is undemocratic. It destroys teacher individuality and initiative and inhibits the teacher emotionally.
3. It lacks objective, valid and reliable principles and criteria for self-evaluation.
4. Its personnel lack adequate training and personality.
5. It lacks a planned program.

These criticisms are frequently true. A single ill-worded even though justifiable criticism can negate the good that many praiseworthy deeds accomplish and can do a long-term disservice to the concept of good music supervision. We all know this happens. Teachers have told us. Instances may be rare, but they do wield an undue proportion of adverse influence.

Good music supervision facilitates the learning process. It takes away wasted motion in music learning. Merely by promoting the wise use of costly equipment and materials a good music supervisor helps the school to be more economical and efficient toward the accomplishment of goals. The program is costly if materials, equipment, personnel, and time are not used to fulfill the aims of music education.

Democratic Music Supervision

Good music supervision is democratic. It respects the integrity of the individual, whether he is a student, a teacher, part of the administration, the board of education, or the community. When aims of music education are identified in terms of goals (end goals) and process, then music supervision must necessarily be democratic. The democratic process reconciles the concept of continual growth in learning musical concepts. Undemocratic supervision implies concern only with the end result of music instruction.

Good music supervision is built upon objective, valid, and reliable principles and employs pertinent criteria for evaluation. These criteria also are concerned with means to the goals.

Musically and Educationally Competent Leadership

The person who is entrusted with the responsibility of setting up, promoting and carrying out a program of music education in the school needs to be highly skilled in several areas: (1) He is a trained musician who has a feeling for, and a good understanding of the many types of music and the many media by which music reaches people. (2) He can also perform on some musical instrument with sufficient skill that he can convey a musical message with ease. This skill is very important, since music must be performed and the supervisor often finds himself in a position where he must demonstrate a musical point. He should be able to demonstrate the whole of music—rhythm, harmony, melody, texture, form, and structure—all in one sitting. The quintessential for a music supervisor is musicianship—that attribute that sets him apart from a mere translator of music symbolism. Without it his pronouncements are meaningless. Musicianship is not readily measured. No totally satisfactory recipe exists for it.

It can be recognized when it presents itself. State departments of education and other educational certifying agencies have attempted to set up formulas that identify good music teachers and music supervisors. Even these agencies vary in ideas about what constitutes a sufficiently musical person for this job of educating children. Teachers colleges, universities, and state departments spell out varying ways by which one can become recognized as having the necessary musical acuity to teach. True, unmusical practitioners of music can meet these standards, while some truly musical people may encounter difficulty in becoming certified.

Musicianship is readily recognized even by the nonmusical layman. Children, teachers, administrators, boards of education, and communities can detect musicianship in their music teachers. They merely look at what is happening to their children musically, and the manner in which this is happening. They can tell whether musical values are being transmitted.

In 1921 the Music Educators National Conference (MENC) endorsed a program for becoming a music teacher. Basically, very little has been changed in this format over a period of forty-five years. This plan required that one-half of the units toward a degree were to be in music; of these, one-half in theoretical subjects and the other half in applied music. On the master's degree program out of a total of thirty semester units, twelve were recommended for music, half of these on theoretical subjects and half in applied music. Even these programs did not assure musicianship. Without it musical values just won't move. Musicianship must be present to cause music to flow from its source to the recipient.

In 1953, the MENC Commission on Accreditation and Certification in Music Education, in cooperation with the National Association of Schools of Music and the American Association of Colleges for Teacher Education, prepared a guide for the preservice training of the special music teacher.[3] It does not vary significantly from the 1921 statement. It carefully spells out the road to musicianship, culture, and teaching acuity, and thereby suggests a reasonable guarantee for quality.

The introductory statement sets the tone, philosophy, and purpose of the document. This is followed by an outline of suggested minimum course content, however, with a section of suggested precollege music training for the prospective teacher. The specific areas touched upon are as follows:

1. The precollege music training
2. Music education subject content: general culture, basic music course, musical performance opportunities and requirements, professional education

As music becomes an increasingly powerful force in American life and education, it becomes increasingly necessary that the training programs of school music teachers be subject to periodic examination. The following schedules serve as a guide for such examinations and assist schools in giving attention to both the broad and the specific needs of the training program for the student who is preparing to be school music teacher.

Schedules for the evaluation of teacher education in some other fields might be limited in scope to include either the elementary or the secondary level. These schedules include *both*. In most areas of this country a school music teacher must have had training at both levels if he is to be prepared to meet the requirements of the teaching positions most commonly found.

These schedules make possible for *every* student some training in both the vocal and the instrumental areas, but to develop one major performance field. This broadens the general musical understanding of every student; also many school music teachers find it necessary to teach both vocal and instrumental music.

The percentages suggested in these schedules are a *minimum* requirement.

Precollege Music Training

The prospective music education student shall have had previous musical training. It is recommended that high school music teachers guide students who anticipate making music education their major field into the most valuable music study sequences possible. It is desirable that the student's high school provide opportunity to acquire some knowledge and develop proficiency in the following areas:

A. Musical performance, including piano, minor instrument, major instrument, and a variety of instrumental and vocal ensemble experiences
B. Basic music (fundamental theory)
C. Music history and literature

Outstanding musical preparation of a student ought to be recognized by entrance proficiency auditions at the college level enabling the student to substitute other areas of study at the college level for those in which he is already prepared.

Subject Content Areas in the Music Education Curriculum

I. General Culture

MINIMUM requirement suggested: 33% of the total (120 semester hours) required for an undergraduate degree.

The purpose of this area of the curriculum is well stated in the National Association of Schools of Music By-Laws and Regulations, 1949, p. 20.

> This area of preparation should assist the individual (prospective teacher) to take his place in a democratic society and a world order; to gain a cognizance of the scientific contributions to mankind; to recognize and accept the responsibility of living in a social relationship; and to evaluate the cultural heritage. He should be able to use, adequately, the English language and should acquire the ability to recognize and solve problems independently.

The courses in this area include the following, some of which may be specific institutional or state requirements:

A. Non-music subjects, to include a non-music minor if required
B. Any psychology course other than Educational Psychology
C. Music literature, history, and/or appreciation
D. The basic survey type of course, where required: 1. Humanities; 2. Social Sciences; 3. Natural Sciences. (In some cases subjects listed under A, B and C above are, or may be, included in certain surveys.)

BASIC MUSIC

MINIMUM requirement suggested:

14% of the total (120 semester hours) required for an undergraduate degree.

This area includes subjects such as the following in the area of music theory. These are sometimes taught separately and sometimes in combination courses which may include several subjects.

A. Music Reading
B. Ear training and Dictation
C. Keyboard Harmony
D. Harmony
E. Eurythmics
F. Form and Analysis
G. Arranging
H. Counterpoint
I. Composition

The objective of these courses should be to develop sound musicianship, with constant emphasis on the usefulness of this material in the classroom teaching situation. The use of various mediums of performance in addition to the piano is encouraged as being beneficial in achieving this objective.

MUSICAL PERFORMANCE

MINIMUM requirement suggested:

33% of the total (120 semester hours) required for an undergraduate degree.

The following subjects are included in this area:

A. Conducting
B. Ensembles, Large and Small
C. Functional Piano Facility
D. Major Performance Area
E. Minor Performance Areas

II. Professional Education
MINIMUM requirements suggested: 20% of the total (120 semester hours) required for an undergraduate degree.
This area includes:

A. Music education, materials, observation and student teaching
B. Professional educational courses aside from music education

The objective is to prepare music education students to take their proper place in the total school program. It is also important that the students become well acquainted through study, demonstration, observation, and laboratory sessions, with the methods and materials for teaching instrumental and vocal music in elementary, junior and senior high schools. The student should do practice teaching on *both* elementary and secondary levels, and where he is qualified, in both vocal and instrumental music.

Professional education courses in general education and in music education (such as courses in Elementary Education and Elementary Music Education, Secondary Education and Secondary Music Education) should be integrated to avoid the duplication of areas which frequently exists and to prevent the resulting waste of the student's time.

Leadership Skills

Good music supervision requires skill in leadership. The essence of leadership cannot be prescribed, it is sensed. *A leader is best when people barely know he exists!* Leadership implies the existence of several persons and it depends upon relationships. It is a contribution that an individual makes to the group. A music supervisor, skilled in leadership, makes it possible for pertinent contributions to be made either by himself or by other group members. It is a quality that can be exerted when the music supervisor draws out the highest potential of other group members. The skilled leader sets the scene for other group members to lead.

Developing Leadership in Others

There is so much to be done in music education that the music supervisor alone can't do it all. His greatest strength lies in his being able to develop leadership in others. For example, one music supervisor had set up a series of vocal music festivals to give the elementary students the experience of singing for peer groups, and in massed choral groups. Local high school choral directors were called upon to direct these festivals, giving them leadership experiences which ordinarily would not come to them, such as

1. The opportunity to direct a large massed group of singers
2. The opportunity to get better acquainted with the abilities and programs of the feeder elementary schools; and the children from the elementary schools would have the opportunity to get acquainted with their future choral director (a desired asset for both student and director)

A new teacher with a fine musical background came to a twenty-teacher school where the teaching of music had been neglected. She could perform and sing very acceptably. Working closely with the supervisor she was shortly able to translate her ability into a very live music teaching program in her own room. This interest and enthusiasm of hers was contagious. It didn't take long before several teachers in adjacent rooms became interested in her music teaching. They began asking her to help them. Fortunately, the teacher remained at the school for several years. During this time almost all of the teachers learned to contribute something valid to the total music program. The young talented teacher was assigned to coordinate the program and become a sort of clearinghouse for the musical needs of the various rooms.

A good music supervisor is not the dominant group leader. He is, however, the change agent or catalyst in whichever teacher group he finds himself. His efforts are bent toward encouraging the best musical leadership in others to evolve.

Music leadership does not always necessarily begin with the supervisor. It can begin with the classroom teacher mentioned above. It can begin with anyone who causes ideas about music education or pertinent musical ideas to flow to other members of the group. True leadership is contagious. It is not jealous of prerogatives; it gladly relinquishes these for the sake of someone else's growth.

The New Music Supervisor

The new music supervisor faces numerous problems. In order to be successful he has to reckon with certain alternatives. The one promoted through the ranks must watch his own behaviour carefully in relationship to former peers. The one hired from the outside must find his way into the group. Both are on trial. The latter has an advantage—he can bury the mistakes of the past and start afresh. The supervisor who has been promoted to his post suddenly sees himself as he was at his worst and as his associates may choose to remember him. If there are other music teachers in the department, he must face this problem and resolve it. Teachers who were offended by him in the past, these he must also face.

The new music supervisor needs a great deal of help. Much can be provided by his predecessor if sought out and taken into confidence. Whatever changes are to be made ought to be the result of careful evaluation of the present situation, since it represents the best thinking of the people who were there before he came. He is the official leader and it is his job to help others in the group understand that the program is theirs, and that his function is to find ways to improve it. The new supervisor will be entrusted with the leadership role only in proportion to his ability to listen to the ideas of others. Leadership is not contracted for or assumed. It is given to him by the group itself after he has won the respect and confidence of the members of the group. More likely he will not be able to abandon or change an existing situation. He can merely modify it by rearranging certain aspects.

Some More Attributes of Leadership[4]

Leadership implies relationships with others, such as the teachers who are to be supervised. These are some connotations of leadership:

Loyalty: Teachers are loyal when the supervisor earns their loyalty by being loyal to them.

Building and maintaining morale: Morale is the emotional and mental reaction that a teacher brings to his assignment. It involves what the teacher believes and feels. If he has been led to believe that he is doing a good job of teaching a song, his morale may be high. His effectiveness as a classroom teacher will be affected by the status of his morale. Some of the outward signs of morale will be cheerfulness, promptness, enthusiasm, dependability, and cooperativeness. Morale has much to do with what teachers want from a job. Of less importance is what the music supervisor wants. The supervisor must contribute toward job satisfaction. He ought not wait for perfection before he nods approval or praise. There are many intermediate steps on the road to improvement that can be commended.

The teacher needs to feel comfortable and secure in what he is attempting. He needs pleasant working conditions. If the classroom teacher asks for, let's say, an autoharp, it behooves the supervisor to do something about helping the teacher to obtain one, and if it is not readily available, to be especially solicitous about making arrangements for purchase.

When the teacher goes out on a limb with a musical project and risks disfavor from both peers and administration, it is the obligation of the music supervisor to interpret this teacher to others. The teacher must never be left holding the bag, especially if his intentions are sincere. He must be made to feel that he is part of the in-group of the supervisors. Teachers need to feel competent, progressive, growing, important, and that they have a part in determining what they do. They need to be allowed self-respect and a right to live their own lives.

Supervisor's Attitude Determines Teacher Feeling

Well-meaning supervisors too often refer to the *insecure teacher*. This may give the music supervisor status; it also takes the props out from under the classroom teacher. A teacher is not insecure by himself alone. He has been made to feel insecure through his unfortunate group relationships. So much has been written about how to help the *insecure teacher* (such articles are usually addressed to the supervisors) that finally the classroom teacher, having got wind of this concept, has actually started playing the role of the *insecure teacher.*

Poor music supervision leadership perpetuates *insecure teachers.* Peculiarly enough, these same teachers were good enough to be hired for the position they hold. Somehow we missed the boat when we didn't provide leadership whereby they could grow and improve. How often have we taken the teacher where he is and showed him alternatives of action? From these he could have selected solutions that were in keeping with his frame of reference. A teacher need never *lose face* in the presence of the music supervisor. If he is insecure, have we contributed toward this state?

One new music supervisor addressed the classroom teachers in his schools thus: "I know you are very insecure about teaching classroom music. It's nothing to be ashamed about. You may not know how insecure you really are. Even the best of you are insecure. Those of you who think you can sing well, or even read notes, or, much better, play the piano, . . . I can easily show you how insecure you really are. But don't grieve over spilled milk! You can't help it! It's my job to help you overcome your insecure feelings about teaching music." This actually happened. Can you imagine the teacher's attitude after this?

An acquaintance returned from a college summer session where he took a course entitled Supervision of Music. These were his words, "I never realized how insecure teachers really are until I took this course from Dr. _____ . I really want to help these poor teachers."

Along with leadership go such perplexing concepts as authority, decisions, responsibilities, and deadlines. Surely, there is a time and place for everything. Someone must take the initiative to get a job done. These concepts can fall into their proper perspective when music supervisors allow teachers to grow in self-respect and confidence.

Music Supervision Needs Skill in Human Relations[5,6]

The important attributes needed by the music supervisor emanate from *how* the music supervisor uses leadership skill. The real HOW of leadership is the seasoned skill in human relations.

How leadership manifests itself determines whether self-confidence can be built. The supervisor needs self-confidence so that this quality can rub off on teachers with whom he works. He must display confidence in others. He must believe in the worth of others and recognize that people tend to live up to what others expect of them. By being blunt and undiplomatic he can easily destroy a teacher's self-confidence. A good teacher speaks out:

"I had to stay out of school yesterday. I was so ill at ease. I had to have a good cry. In all my eighteen years of teaching I never had as bad a day as when Miss A _____, our new music supervisor, observed me. I got more nervous every time I looked toward her—she was always jotting down notations and looking serious. Occasionally she shook her head in disapproval. I finally finished stumbling through a horrible music lesson. (The lesson would have been fair had she not been in the room.) To top it off, Miss A _____ came to my desk and said something about my not following the plan she gave me, and the song for the week. She also reminded me of my stumbling over the tune, and that I used the wrong method to teach the song."

It took a lot of doing before this teacher tried her hand at teaching music again.

There are many kinds of frustrations and difficult situations that even the best music supervisor experiences. He needs utmost self-confidence in his own ability to do what he should be doing, and he must be about deliberately building self-confidence in teachers.

Promoting Harmony Among Professional People[7]

Skill in human relations means also promoting staff harmony. Staff harmony is important in the small district where much transpires that involves face-to-face relationships of teacher and supervisor. It is no less important in a large system where the supervisor's relationship is more directly concerned with the various teaching specialists. The following example points up the supervisor's job to promote staff harmony.

This happened in a city school music department. The director-supervisor called a staff meeting with all the music personnel. Before the meeting could even be called to order, arguments about the use of materials and equipment ensued among the various instructors present. The arguments grew to such embarrassing proportions that the supervisor could barely call the meeting to order. His calling for order merely legalized the already existing hot arguments. It seemed that there was a great dispute raging about who got the lion's share of the music budget.

The first task was to establish harmony. Each person involved was jealous of his prerogatives, rights, privileges, and reputations. Each wanted to convey this to the supervisor in his own way. Each wanted assurance of no infringement on his *Lebensraum,* or psychological space. It appeared that they were trying to say, "We know you were hired for this job, but don't try putting over any new ideas—we are quite sufficient in ourselves." Fortunately, the supervisor understood the needs of human nature quite well. He was a good listener. He met regularly with the music instructors, always listening and watching for clues. After a number of meetings he discovered how he could be of real assistance to the teachers, but only after he had won their respect. It took some time, but gradually individual teachers came to him with some of the problems they previously hid. From these problems there evolved a common need. The supervisor set the scene so that eventually the group asked for the opportunity of setting up a time and place where they could examine their problems with an eye toward improvement of the total music program in the system. A college music professor was called in to organize this effort into a seminar for graduate credit. The supervisor acted as secretary of the group. He worked toward making it possible for them to solve their own problems more objectively than before.

Human relations is the lubricant that oils the educational machinery. It is the little kindnesses, the friendliness, the courtesies, and the prompt help freely given when requested. Wise practice of good human relations implies the relinquishing of personal prerogatives.

Human relations is an important skill needed by the modern music supervisor. The following operational habits will promote good human relations: being friendly—being cheerful—knowing and using people's names—showing interest—being interested in nonmusic activities of teachers—being available—avoiding taking privileges—being polite and courteous—avoiding delay—being prompt—keeping promises—seeing others' point of view—giving credit to others—praising others for work well done—showing concern for teacher's feelings—listening well—avoiding semblance of authority—relieving others of anxiety—avoiding arguments —offering assistance—being objective about problems—providing face-saving opportunities for people—giving people psychological elbow room —letting people grow by themselves—and many other actions and attitudes that build and uphold the integrity, pride, and dignity of the individual, above all, personal and apparent sincerity.

Music Supervision Needs Skill in Group Process[8]

There is strength in unity. The combined effort of a group is greater than the total efforts of individuals. The music supervisor needs the ability to coordinate the combined efforts of teachers. Much will be accomplished by this toward the achievement of the goals of music education.

GROUP POWER

The music supervisor may have power and authority over people or he may create a situation where the power of each individual teacher in the group is released toward the accomplishment of more and better music for more children. Group power is total capacity of the group centered upon the achievement of goals. The music supervisor must develop and utilize this power. The case cited above is one where group power, when it finally emerged, was focused on common goals. This did not just happen. The supervisor had to set the scene by (a) developing a framework within which the group could operate comfortably; (b) providing a time for the group to work and think together; (c) keeping the group informed as to its own progress; (d) keeping the doors open for any change of procedure; (e) assisting in the group's recognizing a mutual problem.

The music supervisor has to start where the staff is. His great strength and power lie in how he handles situations, and how he puts emphasis on *what is right* and not on *who is right*.

CHANGE BY CONSENT

Group process implies the ability to move from discussion to action. Not only teachers but most people fear change. If change is needed it must have the full consent of those involved in the process. It must have the full understanding of those involved. The concerned ones must know the specifics about the *what, who, when,* and *where* in the process of change. This may involve the relatively uncomplicated matter of introducing teachers to a new series of music books for classroom use. Unless the teachers, who are to implement the program, are included in the plans for introducing the books, and unless they have given their consent, no legislation or supervisory directive can enforce the use of desired materials.

Making staff meetings meaningful can affect the efforts of many teachers. Often the music supervisor is at a disadvantage unless he is in charge of a department of music teachers. Ordinarily, only when there is an existing common interest bond can he himself call a meeting. One does not call a meeting of the elementary teachers unless the building principal agrees. The administrator's office can do much to set the scene for an effective meeting of teachers. It behooves the music supervisor to develop a good relationship with him. He must build understanding and mutual confidence with him so that necessary arrangements can be facilitated easily. No one knows better than the principal how many meetings teachers are expected to attend. He also knows that such meetings had just better be good, because his teachers are very busy people.

This is all about consent—meetings by consent of the teachers, and meetings by consent of the administrator—decision by consent of those who are to implement ideas involved.

There should not be room for superimposed directives. Self-discipline and consent of the governed are virtues to be sought.

Music Supervision Demands Skill in Personnel Administration[9]

We have talked about the group: the faculty and the music staff. The group is made up of idiosyncratic and individualistic persons. Each one brings his own heritage, his strength, and his own peculiar weaknesses to the group.

The music supervisor's relationship with the administrative department should be of such a quality that he can suggest that a good balance of musically trained classroom teachers be employed. He should have the opportunity of looking over the applications to help the employing officer discover persons with musical background.

Even in large city school systems the director of music or the music supervisor does not always have the prerogative of hiring the full-time music personnel. This may be good. Teachers are hired for more than their specialty. Nevertheless, it is common practice for the personnel officer to send music applicants to the music supervisor for an interview and for the opportunity to receive his expert advice in the employment of special music teachers. He must be alert constantly to improve the quality of music instruction in the schools.

As official music leader in his school and community, he must bear the responsibility of helping to select, induct, place, train, and reassign music personnel whenever necessary. Some buildings, schools, or situations need certain types of musical talents or types of personalities in their staffs. The supervisor must sense this kind of need. The finest choral director can easily fail if placed in a school where he must accompany his own groups, especially if he can't play the piano well. Also, the finest band director can fail teaching beginners in a low cultural and low economic community. Even music teachers cannot be all things to all situations.

Personnel assignments can provide a balance of proper musical talent in the various buildings. If certain personality clashes cannot be resolved, reassignment may minimize the problem. If problems are actually solved or minimized, the individuals concerned are free to do a more creative job of teaching.

Music Supervision Demands Skill in Self-Evaluation[10]

Good music supervision also involves continuing use of evaluation. This means assessing the situation as it presents itself and constantly reviewing and examining the process of improvement in terms of goals. In the case of music education, goals are not only end results of a program of instruction, but also the process for fostering a continuum of musical growth at all levels.

Music supervision is helping others grow in their ability to teach music more effectively, and this job also requires skill in evaluation.

The conscientious music supervisor often becomes concerned about how well he is doing. He knows that others are constantly evaluating him. He feels that self-evaluation is the basis for his own improvement, and he wants his teachers to feel this way about evaluating themselves also. But self-evaluation is difficult because we do not see ourselves in the light of those who come under our influence. The following check-list contains important clues for the music supervisor:[11]

(Check the statements that describe your supervisory behavior)
"I

_____recognize that a program of music education cannot be accomplished without the help of others on the staff.

_____rely on the judgement of others on my staff and do not single out a few select music teachers for advice and consideration.

_____respect the opinion of all teachers, not only department heads and the especially talented.

_____back the teachers in their professional decisions, and try to give the feeling, "right or wrong I'll stand behind you," and allow for human error.

_____try to achieve loyalty through kindness I perform for teachers.

_____succeed in getting each one to feel responsibility for the success of the total music program.

_____make each teacher and specialist feel his job is important.

_____praise frequently, even in the face of unresolved situations.

_____emphasize the good aspects of a teacher's work.

_____am aware of the special talents and interests of the people that come within the range of my influence.

_____give proper publicity to the work being done by the teachers.

_____make all within my influence feel they belong and have worth.

_____let the teachers know I have confidence in them.

_____do not show favoritism to some in the district.

_____use "we" instead of "I" in referring to notable achievements in our district.

_____try not to impress others with my importance.

_____admit mistakes in judgment when results show I am wrong.

_____accept criticism and do not allow my feelings to be hurt.

_____am always available to those who need me.

_____am prompt and never keep those who need my help waiting for me.

_____do not become angry when suggestions are presented tactlessly.

_____keep a calendar of appointments.

_____encourage teachers to come to me of their own accord for advice.

_____draw on the intelligence and good will of all teachers to assist in setting goals.

_____allow staff members to make suggestions for replacements when a vacancy occurs.

_____consult with teachers in advance if they are to be affected by my decision.

_____orient staff members properly to their positions and responsibilities.

_____help prepare a proper climate for the teaching of music, by providing a reasonable budget for the specialist and the classroom teacher.

_____include classroom teachers and specialists in a program of self-evaluation and evaluation of the total music program."

Thus the music supervisor can evaluate his own effectiveness and relate these points to actual persons and situations. He should ask himself, "How long is it since you have been inside a classroom either teaching children or observing teachers?" One often gets involved in organizational activities rather remote from the true operational situations. Some of these involvements are in music professional organizations. These activities are time consuming but necessary. However, each day and each hour spent with such activities detracts from helping others to grow in their ability to teach music. Decisions about such things are also a vital part of self-evaluation.

Self-evaluation is the highest form of evaluation. After the music supervisor has thoroughly searched his soul he may come up with a residue of undone tasks and broken promises that can stagger one's imagination. These items form a pattern for the improvement of his own supervision program.

The evaluation of the supervisor ought to be in terms of not only what he does, but also how, when, and how often he does it in terms of how much is possible for one person to accomplish. He should be judged in relation to his effectiveness with the group. Do music staff members like him? Why? Do principals, teachers, and community members like him? And for what reasons? What effect does he have on children? Has he helped the program of music education to move forward in the particular school system? How does the school differ musically now from last year at this time?

A program of music education and the music supervisor are separate items. The program is dependent on the supervisor. He is judged by the effectiveness of this program. The following criteria for music supervision present clues by which a program and its official leader can be appraised:

1. Is there more voluntary and wholehearted participation of students, teachers, and community members in the improvement of the program?
2. Are there increased opportunities and activities for all students?
3. Are there more efficient learning situations that result in more rapid pupil growth? Is there less waste in the teaching of elementary school music? [Is the classroom music program made up of time-wasting trivialities that do not necessarily contribute to the improvement of music learning and to an increase in musical enjoyment?]
4. Does the school music program contribute to the improvement of community living? Has the ennobling influence of music as an art gone beyond the classroom walls? Is there more and better music in the home? Have church choirs improved? What is the status of independent community music activities?

Evaluation of the music supervisor must really be an evaluation of *program development,* with specific attention to how the development came about.

It is quite evident from the aforegoing that the supervision of music can be many things. To be sure, each of the blind persons of fable fame would have had a different view also of music supervision by merely experiencing aspects of it from his own vantage point and from his own frame of reference. They may each conclude, however, that music supervision is big (which it truly is); that it involves many skills; and that it appears differently to different people. But music supervision still has only one objective, and this one is in keeping with the aims of music education, that more children are more affected by more and better music. After all, the job was set up for *the improvement of all conditions that affect the learning of music.* The following eight points are concepts applicable to music supervision:

1. Instructional supervision is a dynamic, growing process that is occupying an increasingly important role in the schools.
2. The purpose of supervision is to offer leadership in the improvement of educational experiences for children and youth.
3. Leadership is centered in a group, not in an individual.
4. The type and quality of supervision are affected by the situation and the organization in which supervision exists.
5. The climate of human relationships within the group and the degree to which members are committed to group goals influence the degree of change in practice.
6. The way in which individuals perceive the problems and the tasks inherent in the situation affects their behavior.

7. The actual role of supervision—and of instructional leaders—is a composite of all the expectations held for the role by the people associated with it.
8. A primary goal of supervisory leaders is to foster leadership in others.[12]

Questions for Discussion, Thought and Study

1. Select a music supervision program in a nearby area and evaluate it in terms of process. Describe how this system works as expert technical service. List the good points of the program as you see them. What are some of the undesirable aspects of the program?
2. List some valid and objective criteria for evaluating a program of music supervision. What really makes for a good program?
3. Were you the school administrator, what items would you consider in an interview with a candidate for the position of music supervisor?
4. Imagine yourself a candidate for a music supervision vacancy, what questions would you ask of the administrator?
5. Give arguments for and against the music supervisor having been an experienced and successful teacher.
6. Devise a rating scale by which you would evaluate the music supervisor.
7. List the most important skills the music supervisor should be able to draw upon in the everyday working of his job and in the solution of the many problems that he encounters.
8. Why the focus on the *teaching-learning* situation and not on the teacher?
9. Do you agree on the importance of concentrating on the music supervision program as a *job to be done*? Explain.
10. How would you defend the concept of the importance of *program* and of *process*?

Notes

[1] Robert Choate, "Supervisor and the Curriculum," *Educational Music Magazine,* XX, (November 1950), p. 8-9.
[2] William Burton and Leo Brueckner, *Supervision a Social Process,* (New York: Appleton-Century-Crofts, Inc., 3d ed., 1955), p. 16.
[3] Commission on Accreditation and Certification in Music Education, *The Evaluation of Music Education,* (Washington, D.C., MENC, 1953), pp. 3-17.
[4] Neal Glenn, "Human Relation and Supervision," *Education,* LXXIV (September 1953), pp. 27-30.
[5] William Melchior, *Instruction Supervision,* (Boston: D. C. Heath & Co. 1950), p. 39.
[6] Herbert Thelen, *Dynamics of Groups at Work,* (Chicago: University of Chicago Press, 1954), Chapter 11.
[7] Melchior, *op. cit.,* pp. 109-128.
[8] Melchior, *op. cit.,* pp. 133-145.
[9] Melchior, *op. cit.,* pp. 209-245.
[10] Melchior, *op. cit.,* pp. 249-281.
[11] Melchior, *op. cit.,* p. 280.
[12] Reba Burnham and Martha King, *Supervision in Action,* (Washington, D.C.: ASCD 1961), p. 32.

Western Division Young Audiences, Inc.

Chapter 4

Recurring Problems in
Music Supervision

Many problems plague even the best trained and experienced music supervisors. And what is a good solution for one person's problems may be totally unadaptable for another. Solutions must be looked at in the light of the individuals involved, and in reference to the particular situation.

When problems persist, *it is not music supervision* (as a system) *that is wrong, or that causes problems, but it is more frequently the deliberate and unintentional acts of the music supervisor* involved. Had the music supervisor acted differently in the immediate situation or in the long-term interrelationship, things just would not have come to such a state. We do not mean to imply that the music supervisor is always *at fault* when something goes wrong, or when a problem arises. A different supervisory act could have averted or solved the problem.

Some problems are personal, others have to do almost entirely with promotion of a program. Still others reflect the maturity of the school community involved, or the experience, maturity, and understanding of the music supervisor. The following problems have been selected as representing two extremes of supervisory concerns. The first group is representative of beginning music consultants whose concerns had more to do with work load, budget, materials, and acceptance. The second group is representative of the thinking of a group of music supervisors who have been in the profession for a good many years.

A Beginning Music Consultant's Problems

1. Lack of a central office budget; how one gets a budget based on student enrollment

2. No time to work with teachers; must teach too many special music classes
3. Not enough equipment, such as autoharps, phonographs, rhythm instruments
4. Teacher who "knows nothing about music," and never intends to improve
5. Lack of direction in the music program; no goals or ideas for any particular grade level; supervisor has to grope in dark for materials
6. Lack of a sequential program K-8 or 9
7. Inadequate scheduling
8. Unsympathetic public
9. Fear of losing job if one stands up for certain educational principles

(These problems reflect a consultant's personal inadequacy dealing with a normal situation.)

An Experienced Music Consultant's Supervisory Problems

1. Making administrators and lay people aware of the educational values of music in the curriculum; music employs thousands of people throughout the world yet it has to struggle for a place in the school curriculum
2. Getting music teachers and administrators to realize that music at all levels must be broader than performing groups
3. Helping music teachers accept the music of contemporary composers; a musical diet of the three "B's" is fine but is not adequate
4. Educating the school and the public that a good school music program is possible when there is a basic classroom music program with performing groups in addition to it
5. Helping teachers and administrators realize that musical growth does not just happen—it must be planned carefully in a sequential way
6. Helping administrators realize that a developmental program in music needs the classroom teacher, the specialist, the director and the administrator
7. Convincing administrators that music must be part of the inservice education of teachers
8. Helping the administrator realize that effective classroom organization, a planned developmental program and a creative environment should be as obvious in a music class as in any other class
9. Convincing districts that a good music program costs money and that the budget must make adequate provision for it
10. Providing adequate time for music in the school schedule at all levels; daring to look at the old schedule critically and discarding the old patterns in favor of a new, more adequate schedule even at the expense of being different.

Music Supervisor's Problems—City School System
Average Daily Attendance
25,000

1. Can't cover all grades, kindergarten through 6 in 21 elementary schools besides working with 7 traveling music teachers who are assigned to three schools apiece; also 10 music specialists in 5 junior high schools
2. Poor music background of classroom teachers
3. Need clerical help; share a secretary and a clerk with four other consultants; most of the work comes from the music office
4. Have a budget of $5,000; this purchases music, recordings, and instruments for all of the schools; have to watch items too closely in case of special events
5. Too much time is taken up in central music library listing, stamping, and filing music, and dispatching music to schools
6. All forms must be kept up to date
7. Curriculum meetings take a lot of planning; I haven't learned to schedule my time properly to allow for this

The following problems, dilemmas, supervisory mistakes, sins of omission and commission, nasty situations, and frustrations make up a relay course through which many music supervisors race to attain a desirable program of music supervision. Wherever the situation resolved itself, there was evidence of a real effort to utilize good principles of supervision.

It was difficult to categorize problems in terms of prime concern, or in terms of affixing blame onto the transgression of a certain principle. For ease of consideration they were classified in accordance with the level or kind of situation in which they occurred. Consequently, the following six problem areas:

1. The supervisory level in a central school office
2. Working with the individual teachers and with groups of teachers
3. Working with school administrators
4. Working with various music specialists and special music teachers
5. Working with beginning music consultants, or with consultants in small cities
6. Facilitating the flow of materials and ideas

Solutions will be in terms of goals, that is, the improvement of the teaching-learning situation, and also in terms of how this improvement takes place.

The problems were taken out of the case books of numerous supervisors. At times they were related as they were felt. Solutions were not always available, and sometimes total situations had to be readjusted and personnel had to be reoriented. This happened when the total situation was educationally askew. To right all wrongs takes a dedicated educational team taking the initiative in the right direction. The music supervisor must lead in this process.

MUSIC SUPERVISION'S PLACE IN RELATION TO THE TOTAL SCHOOL ADMINISTRATIVE ORGANIZATION

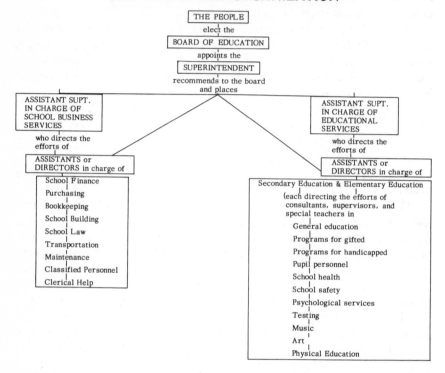

Problems Encountered in the Central Office at the Supervisory Level

The music supervisor works in a vast framework of interrelationships. These involve personnel at the supervisory level, such as supervisors for various grade levels and learning areas, consultants, coordinators, directors, department heads, assistant superintendents, associate superintendents, superintendents, governing boards, clerical help, and custodial help. Each of these and the total organization affect him and predispose him to function in certain ways. Each person and group look at the music supervisor in different ways. The small group views him more as an individual who can be of assistance and the total organization views him in reference to his *cog worth* and his *contributory value* to the total educational picture as it operates in that locale.

To appear as the ideal music supervisor just isn't simple. What one's colleagues have experienced with music supervision in the past as students, teachers, or as supervisors, determines, to a great extent, how the music supervisor will appear to them. There would be no problem at all if the music supervisor functioned in a role complementary to his colleagues' conditioned preconceptions.

He has three choices, each of which indicates his philosophy: (1) abdicating in favor of convenient acquiescence; (2) assuming dynamic leadership, regardless of the feelings of peers,and (3) constantly working at improving peer understanding and, at the same time, unobtrusively caring for the job exigencies.

The music supervisor has the advantage over his peers in that his job carries with it considerable *prestige*. He needs to learn how to carry this prestige with grace so that it does not become offensive to others. Many of the music supervisor's activities reap public favor. His effectiveness must not become warped and his judgment dulled by external praise.

The way others feel about music supervision, or what they think the music supervisor ought to be doing, can become a serious problem. If these ideas fall within a pattern of a good supervision program, fine. However, if they do not, someone must have the courage to say so. In the process of observing good human relations people can lapse into an appeasement kind of activity rather than the more difficult task of employing truth, honesty, and professional integrity.

These are some of the problems that can be bothersome to a new music supervisor. Many of these deal with feelings the old-timers on the staff have about music supervision's functions. For instance:

1. The impression that all educational services and needs are determined by general supervisors and coordinated through them leaves little room for the music supervisor to care for needs as he sees them.
2. The responsibilities of participating in many activities of a nonmusical nature can become so time- and energy-consuming that there is very little room to do much planning for music supervision.
3. Schools call the music supervisor after they have determined the need. However, often the administrator is not schooled in recognizing musical needs. And, too frequently, the call comes when the problem is beyond repair. ("On call" supervision may be an excellent device whereby a music supervisor is prevented from superimposing

his own program, but it can become a deadly device blocking communication and growth.)

4. Often the general consultant sees the music supervisor only as an aid to his own subject concentration. To him, the social studies program may be the core of all learning, and music must take its place as a contributor to this area, leaving little room for program growth in music learning. It is good to cooperate with generalists, especially if it results in the application of music to various learning areas. One must guard against sacrificing music as an art contributing to the enrichment of life.

5. The kindergarten supervisor feels that music is all rhythm and nursery songs. The physical education supervisor views the music program as contributing to bodily coordination and to the square dance program. The arithmetic supervisor feels that music is overemphasized if all children are not up to par in numbers. The speech specialist sees singing as something that will correct speech defects. Very few nonmusical consultants can interpret the music supervisor's stand.

6. The fact that music supervisors are called upon to provide music for educational and civic functions recognizes the organizational ability of the person, and utilizes music as functional value. These demands too often take precedence over a good program of supervision.

7. The many meetings in the office have their contributory value in developing necessary awareness and understandings. But there is an easier, a less time-consuming way of finding out about things. "Many a time have I sat in on meetings champing at the bit, waiting to get at the stack of things at my desk so that I could be freed to get out to the schools or just at the real business at hand."

8. The need for *trained clerical help*—someone who knows and who understands the specific things about which music supervision is concerned—someone who can do the desk work and intelligently answer the phone—is a problem that can be solved only when all persons involved or affected can see it from the viewpoint that it is a job to be done.

Problems Encountered in Dealing with Individual Teachers

The music supervisor meets many teachers that cause him supervisory problems. Advice that works for one teacher may be totally unadaptable for another teacher. Human relations skills give good clues for setting up effective working relationships. Presently, we are concerned with some of the typical problems teachers present. among them the following:

a. The teacher who just couldn't produce musical results. He had good musical training and a number of years teaching experience; is a good performer on several instruments; is a creative musician; is very personable; and is highly respected and admired by parents, teachers, students, and administrator. No one except the music supervisor and other musically trained people recognize that anything is wrong. Just how can this teacher be helped? He can't be fired and he can't be corrected easily. Clues for help:
   (1) befriend the teacher; (2) observe him frequently and give the impression that you are genuinely interested in the quality of his teaching; (3) arrange for him to attend professional meetings and to partake in clinics; (4) loan him better instructional materials; (5) provide him with materials that give him clues to improvement, and (6) give him many opportunities to exchange viewpoints with peers.

b. We remember one second grade teacher who became very concerned that her children did not seem to understand the circle of keys; after all, this was one of the first things she was expected to learn in her music fundamentals course in college. She was under the impression that this was what she was to teach.

c. Some teachers have rhythms on Tuesday for a whole hour. The children go outside during this period and play games to the tune of a phonograph record. This takes the place of several music periods. These children also get an hour's worth of hearing phonograph records playing. It is doubtful that they have been helped to listen purposefully.

   It is not always ignorance of music, or bad music teaching, or poor musical equipment. Ways must be found for teachers and supervisor to get together and try to explore the many possibilities that exist for enriched teaching.

d. Then there is the teacher who complains of not being able to distinguish one tune from another. It is difficult to show her ways of presenting music to children that are not dependent on her own ability to hear properly. Of course, if the problem is as serious as she indicated, it would be really very difficult for her to teach anything at all.

e. The supervisor-avoider type of teacher doesn't want you prying into her affairs. One such teacher opened her room door just a wee bit and said in a forbidding tone, "Oh, you are the music supervisor. Well, I teach by the phonograph method." It was discovered that she feared change more than anything else. The supervisor provided her with sufficient enrichment materials, rather unobtrusively, with which, after a while and of her own accord, she began to vary her classroom music program.

f. There was the teacher-performer who lined up her children into two straight rows, and had them sing at the top of their voices to the tune of her exaggerated piano playing. After they had finished singing for the supervisor, the teacher arose and asked, "Sir, what are your criticisms?" This certainly put the visitor on a spot where diplomacy was of utmost importance. No one could dispute that she was teaching music—the *how* was quite debatable.

g. One also finds the musical classroom teacher who is forever disciplining someone while you are observing; or the teacher, who when she sees you coming down the hallway assigns a drill-page of arithmetic or a page out of a spelling workbook to her youngsters. She explains that the children are so far behind that they have to use their music time for regular studies.

This fear of supervision can be overcome with the help of a discreet supervisor. If the problem is inability to organize learning experiences, and to control groups, she often recognizes her problem all too well and is desperately trying to save face while she is in the process of rectifying her trouble.

h. "One of the many extracurricular things they always ask us to do," and "children really get more music nowadays than a generation ago." No doubt you've heard this before.

Sometimes one has to work around recalcitrant people. Try to create a climate for the problem teacher so that he voluntarily seeks assistance.

i. Teachers may "clam up" during a meeting if the arrangements were made with the principal without their consent. The supervisor should ask the principal to take the teachers' needs into consideration.

There may be many reasons why teachers seem to be uncommunicative. Maybe they are just plain tired of meeting. To know the causes for ill rapport makes it possible to prevent a recurrence. But it is more important to know what to do when such a situation arises. The supervisor may have to exert salesmanship and drum up interest by (1) opening the meeting with a few lively songs, (2) get several teachers to lead off in discussing their own music program, (3) keep conversation on an informal level so that teachers will not feel uncomfortable participating, (4) get teachers to ask questions, and (5) get them to talk about immediate goals in terms of their abilities.

Teachers find life complicated enough without having their deficiencies pointed out. Most people, in the privacy of their own thoughts, recognize their own weaknesses but find it difficult to discover their strengths and capitalize on them. *It is more important for the supervisor to discover worth in the individual than to be part of even the mildest form of castigation.*

Case A: the principal who is concerned about his special music teacher. These are some of the complaints: (1) there are too many drop-outs in the instrumental program; (2) more students should be playing instruments, and (3) discipline is poor. Armed with this reaction, the supervisor wanted to visit with the music teacher. The principal arranged the meeting, but remained present so that teacher and supervisor could not talk freely. Only after the principal was called out to answer the phone was it possible to observe the teacher and to exchange a few words. These were some of the items noted:

1. The room lighting was poor
2. The few music stands in the room were each wired together with baling wire to prevent them from falling apart
3. Most of the horns were badly dented and in need of replacing
4. The music was archaic and not suited to the young students
5. Several of the folding chairs were unfit for use
6. An old cardboard box served as a music file
7. The school spent about $30 a year for instrumental repairs
8. No new instruments were purchased for four years; there was no budget allowance for this kind of expenditure
9. Half of the music teacher's time was spent in substituting for sick teachers.

Before leaving the school the supervisor reported to the principal's office. He entered the office and was invited to be seated. The principal, wringing his hands and shaking his head. asked. "Well, how did you find things?" The manner of this question implied that the principal was resigned to hear the worst.

The supervisor felt that he was put on the spot. He explained that he was not there to discuss personalities, but he was convinced that the music teacher was doing as well as could be expected of the best teacher under similar circumstances. The principal acted as if he were quite surprised at this but was interested in listening to suggestions for improvement. The prime suggestion was that all parties concerned engage in a thorough evaluation of the music program in the school, with particular attention to desirable goals, and the time, effort, energy, materials, equipment, and manpower that it takes to get there. This meant looking at the teacher in a different light, and respecting him for his know-how in music. It meant giving him a chance to make suggestions for the improvement of his own department.

The suggested improvements did not occur overnight, but these improvements took place over several years:

1. There is now a new music room with modern equipment
2. A sum of $500 a year is set aside for improvement of equipment and materials

3. Instead of sixteen ill-sounding urchins, blasting away through dented horns, there are now fifty-five members in his band
4. There is a seventy voice seventh and eighth grade chorus singing three- and four-part music instead of the eight girls trying to sing in two parts
5. The instructor is rarely imposed upon to act as substitute teacher any more

The one supervisory visit several years ago was not the total motivating factor in the improvement that took place. However, sometime after this visit things began to change. Even the teacher began to act as if he had a new lease on life. By providing him with the necessities, he was being released to do a job of creative teaching.

Administrators are busy people. They do not want to be known as laggards in providing for cultural things. When the administrator has all of the facts, and can see them in proper perspective, and can also see his own responsibilities, the right things are more apt to happen.

Case B: the unwilling principal who will not allow any supervisor in to see his teachers. In-service announcements are destroyed. Notices about musical events are not posted or passed on to teachers. The music supervisor is allowed to listen to the chorus only on graduation day. Other knowledge of the school's music activities that the supervisor had was through recordings of the chorus made by the principal. This administrator prides himself in protecting his teachers from supervisors.

Case C: the principal who sought help in finding a replacement for his elementary band teacher. His complaint was that the instructor received a low rating at the regional music festival. Also, he had poor classroom discipline, he screamed and shouted at the children when things didn't go right.

The community's expectations were very high. The new man was to have all of the virtues the incumbent lacked; besides this, he was expected to produce a very distinctive marching band that would develop an area-wide reputation for the school. No experienced teacher was interested, and new college graduates were offered higher starting pay with less job pressures elsewhere. The principal finally had to reconsider his own band instructor. Upon suggestion, a job analysis was made, with recommendations for improvement of the teaching-learning situation. The instructor, with some supervisory help, has grown in stature and respect in the community. His festival ratings even went up from "poor" to a "superior."

People can change when the total situation improves. Too often we want a person to improve right here and now, or we fire him. People can be salvaged when the total situation is improved or when ingredients making the situation are rearranged.

I don't believe the band teacher discussed here will ever lose his job. He has things to do with; and he has them located so that he can do them comfortably without violating his basic personality structure.

Case D: the music supervisor called in by the principal to evaluate the school music program. The twenty-four teachers in the system included a part-time instrumental instructor and a part-time vocal music teacher. The call was precipitated by complaints from several teachers that the school was overemphasizing music.

Upon arriving, the supervisor discovered that he was to appear before the faculty and answer questions about the music program. Fortunately there was time before the meeting so that the principal and the supervisor could discuss the questions that would possibly arise.

The two part-time specialists had developed a very fine instrumental and vocal music program over a period of six years. The vocal teacher had, besides classroom music and two choruses, developed a strong program of rhythmic activities through all the grades. A problem of proper distribution of musical efforts arose. There was concern that some of the more talented students were receiving as much as three-hundred minutes of music each week. Several new teachers wanted things like autoharps. Previously, musical equipment was the exclusive domain of the specialists. The new teachers also were quite concerned about the need for music for the upper grade students, the 70 per cent not in the chorus or band or orchestra. These students were usually assigned to shop and physical education.

It was difficult to give clear-cut answers to the problems posed. A boys' chorus and a trial music appreciation program were recommended to take care of many students who previously had no musical opportunity.

The principal through this meeting discovered that ten of his teachers in the first five grades taught music regularly. He became quite interested in hearing more about what is necessary to have a well-rounded program of music education.

This meeting was a culmination of several years working with the administrator. Previously he had been content and happy with the fine work of specialists. The supervisor had talked with this principal many times on this subject. But this was true, the principal did not hear until he grew in understanding. Outside help could be effective only after the school and administrator could internalize their dilemma.

A problem is not always resolved through one visit, or in a year's time. The job involves building up good will, confidence, initiative, and many other leadership qualities. At times the job just doesn't get done when the supervisor is seen manipulating the situation. Wisdom would dictate that he keep in the background, and be ready to assist. The supervisor must be the catalyst in the process of change. Teachers change and grow when the area about them is made "fertile" and ready.

Case E: the administrator concerned with the problem of tenure who asked his supervisors to rate the teachers for him. Most supervisors know that rating teachers can negate their effectiveness. He wanted to make sure that he retained the best teachers without overt effort on his part.

His request surprised and shocked the supervisors. They felt that he knew better. After discussing the matter with him, they also knew that he was under pressure from the board to present tangible evidence of an evaluative nature before it considered granting tenure to various teachers.

Unfortunately, the music supervisor couldn't get out of it. So she used the evaluative instrument, as it were, with a vengeance. She entered the classroom, took a seat in the rear of the room, proceeded to observe each teacher teaching music, at the same time jotting down notations on the rating sheets. Consequently, the teachers built up a resentment against her. When other teachers heard about this they refused to teach in her presence. Also her former friends on the staff began to avoid her.

She erred in that she let the situation deteriorate by observing the strict letter of the mandate. On the other hand, the general supervisor involved in this same chore chose to do the job in a much less offensive manner. She called in the teachers for informal conferences and explained to them the need of this procedure and asked them to evaluate themselves. The teachers recognized this as a job that had to be done, and they cooperated without developing any ill will toward the rater.

Problems Encountered in Dealing with Music Specialists

By and large music specialists, or special music teachers, encounter problems resulting from (a) their interrelationships with other teachers, students, and other school personnel, (b) their need for approval, and from (c) methodology to get musical ideas across effectively. The music teacher may be looking for a way to discuss his problems with the "outside expert" without losing face.

Case A: the classroom music specialist who insisted on using the stationary "doh." A previous supervisor tried to get him to change. When the new area music supervisor arrived on the scene, he was briefed by the administration and was warned that the music teacher was quite wary of supervisors because his ideas were rebuffed.

Several observation sessions later it was noted that there was very little emphasis on any method of music reading in his music classes. In fact, most of the music was learned by rote. The supervisor did, however, have other more immediate problems, like lack of room control. There was a lot of uncontrolled musical merriment going on. It was obvious (1) that he was an enthusiastic teacher and (2) that the students liked him.

The following year he was offered a job in a larger school; so he came to the supervisor for counsel. He wanted to succeed and at his stage of maturity he now had more of a personal motive for self-improvement. It was suggested that he take a few courses in music education so that he could couple his musician's viewpoint with that of education. A friendly supervisor probably gave him the initial confidence. Several years later he received a doctorate and is in a leadership position influencing many teachers.

Case B: A talented male singer who took a position as upper grade teacher in an eight-teacher semirural school. His assignment included teaching upper grade science and all the classroom music from grades five through eight. He was also supposed to develop a school chorus for special festival occasions. Musically he was most competent. He lacked adequate classroom control. It was reported that he used sarcasm in trying to control the students. This bothered the principal and some of the older teachers. The general supervisor was called in. Before long the senior teacher, the principal, and the general supervisor converged upon the teacher to observe him so that they could determine how they could help him most effectively. Failing in their mission, they called in the music supervisor.

Upon visiting several classes it was observed (1) that students were singing, (2) the lesson seemed to be planned carefully, (3) there were no overt student demonstrations, (4) the teacher was nervous (after all, there were official guests in the room), (5) the students seemed a bit timid (they had but scanty musical experiences prior to this year), (6) the senior teacher stood in the doorway nodding approval and disapproval, depending how things sounded to her, (7) the principal sat there with a concerned beam on his face.

A private conference with the music teacher brought out that he was afraid of the senior teacher, who had taught music the year before.

According to her, she never had this trouble. The supervisor however remembered that she had a very difficult time keeping together a small group of girls in a vocal ensemble. Her presence was a very disturbing factor to the young teacher.

The other teachers wanted him to teach only the songs they selected, and that were in keeping with the units they were teaching. He was disturbed that so many songs were requested, leaving him no choice of his own. Not being allowed to use his own individuality as a teacher, coupled with his inexperience, made a most difficult situation for him. The supervisor tried to interpret him to the administrator. But the situation had deteriorated beyond immediate repair.

Case C: *problems of coordinating teaching schedules of the several traveling music teachers, keeping them and their schools content.* Each of these traveling teachers has a different schedule because he teaches in schools with different needs and facilities. This results in different problems:

1. Each of three schools wants an instrumental teacher for a day and a half, but not on Friday (because of sports).
2. Teacher X had taught at the same schools for six years. A new principal curtailed his program to two half days at one of the schools, leaving him unemployed for a part of each week.
3. Each of four schools employing teacher Y had scheduled its Christmas program on the same evening. Each needed the music teacher for its program, but he could not be in four places at the same time.
4. When teacher Z comes to one of his schools once a week, teachers assign make-up tests and drill work to the band students during the band period. They can't go to band unless they finish the extra assignments. If they go, they get an *F* for the day in their other subjects. The administrator condones this.
5. A new administrator is unhappy about the old music teacher. He wants a new, more modern one next year. He doesn't realize that it is not easy to find a qualified teacher who will teach just for one and a half days. Neither does he realize that his old teacher is liked at his other schools.
6. Many communities with a limited instrumental music program want their newly formed (half-day-a-week) band to perform for P.T.A. before it is ready.
7. There is also the problem of finding legitimate performance outlets for the students in small schools. Area festivals to meet the needs of such small schools may be an answer.

Case D: the instrumental music teacher in a 200-teacher elementary school system is not permitted to take his students to the regional music festivals. In previous years his groups had received favorable comments and fine ratings at these festivals. This new administrative decision was a real blow to him. All of the neighboring towns and cities were sending their groups. He and the other directors had worked hard to make the festivals a success. Now he felt as if he had been pushed out of things. He was sure that his students were really more hurt than he was.

The administration had its own view of festivals. It argued that such festivals were educationally unsound. Besides, the cost of sending performing groups to these affairs and the breaking up of the school day was just not worth it. There were valid arguments on both sides. The music supervisor was called in to arbitrate. No change—too many rights and wrongs on both sides.

There are times when the music supervisor must serve as a crying towel for many music teachers who need to talk things out, or for those who have been hurt, and even for those who are in real trouble.

Case E: the high school choral teacher whose groups received low ratings at the regional festivals. It was not proper to say to her, "You certainly did well," or "You did as well as could be expected." There was really very little one could say. She lost face. She felt that she was a good choral teacher; after all, she had a background of fine choral teaching experience in grammar school. A music supervisor's job is to help pick up the pieces and to remember growth does not occur when the wounds are open—only after they begin healing.

Case F: the elementary instrumental teacher who favors only the very bright students. In this case, he had over twenty students in an instrumental class, but he chose to work with only five or six, leaving the others to their own devices. The principal didn't know what to do about it without offending or upsetting the teacher. Would suggested appropriate reading or observing others help?

These problems indicate that the music supervisor can be needed even by the trained specialist. Here he is needed in an entirely different role than when dealing with the classroom teacher.

Just the fact that the supervisor bothers about the special music teacher at all may be all that is necessary to give him the feeling that his efforts have worth.

Problem of Music Consultants in Small Cities

The status of music consultants in small cities is often very nebulous. It can be anything from classroom teacher to full-time music supervisor. There may be many reasons for this indefinite status, among which are (1) the inability or unwillingness of the district to hire and pay for an experienced supervisor, (2) the inexperience in teaching and supervision of the consultant, and (3) the lack of training in supervisory techniques of the consultant. Coupled to this may be added another reason, that of administrative ignorance of the function of music supervision. The responsibility for problems can be laid at the feet of the total evolutionary process of this kind of position.

In the following cases no situation was beyond repair; neither were any of the people responsible for the supervision program beyond help. The fault is often the school's, the administration's, or the community's. Even though the program failed, and the blame could be placed at the feet of many factors and people, the defeat of the music supervision program cannot be excused.

These are some of the factors that contribute to the success or failure of a music supervisory situation:

A. *The type of community has much to do with it.* It is represented by the board of education. What does it think of music supervision? Does it go for a nonteaching consultant? Or, does it feel that supervision can be done in spare moments between classes or after school? Since it expects the administrator to give leadership in curricular matters, does it assume that he is skilled in music education leadership, and that he also has the time to do this effectively?

B. *The school administrator has much to do with it.* What does he want from music education? Does he really know what is expected in a school's music program? Is he willing to relegate such leadership responsibility to the trained expert? Does he rely on the trained expert, or does he tell her what the program should be? Is the program mutually agreed upon? Does he tie the hands of the music consultant to the extent that the position eventually becomes one in name only? What does he do to stimulate leadership in his music consultant? Does he back his consultant? Does he prepare the teachers for the consultant's work? Does he let the teachers know where he stands in reference to the music program? Does he facilitate the acquisition of necessary teaching aids?

In recent polls 64.1 per cent of administrators, 60.3 per cent of classrom teachers, and 70.3 per cent of special music teachers preferred the classroom music specialist over the classroom teacher teaching music. Can this kind of statistic bias the administrator? Is such a statistic valid?

Administrators want a balanced music program, not always because they are convinced of its value, but more because "it's the thing to have." They can tend to take the fastest expedient to get the job done, even if it costs money. They may hire the specialist to do this, or assign the job to the band teacher. It's really less bothersome than having to worry about classroom teachers. After all, wasn't it the administrator who assured the new teacher when he hired her and she indicated that she didn't want to teach music "not to worry about it but please sign the contract and we'll figure out a solution later"?

The administrator is the key person in the determination of the music program. He may insist on a music specialist teaching the entire general music program in the elementary school, despite equally substantial evidence favoring the classroom teacher teaching music.

C. *The teachers in the school have much to do with it.* Have they been conditioned against supervision? Against music supervision? Do they know what is expected in the program of music education? What have they been doing about it? Do they feel as responsible for the music program, and for being conversant with it, as they do for the reading program, or the language arts program? Was her role as the classroom teacher explained to her when she accepted the job? What is she doing about filling in deficiencies in her musical background? Should she dictate what the music program of a school shall be?—If so, by merely being a teacher, does this give her the right?

D. *The music consultant has much to do with it.* He usually is an adequately trained musician and has had the necessary teacher training also. But what is his training and experience in assuming leadership roles? What is his personality makeup? How does he affect administrators, teachers, and children? Are the administrator and teachers far ahead of him in their thinking? Outside of being a competent musician, does he know music education materials so necessary to put across a program? How does he feel about the *self-contained classroom*? Does his idea of music education coincide with that of the district, area, or even the state? What about his pre-service training? Can he teach? Does he have the ability to talk with a busy administrator and solicit his aid in backing a program of music education?

In Cities from 10,000 to 16,000 Population

District A employed a full-time music supervisor for ten years. She was well liked by principals, teachers, and community, besides being a fine musician and a good teacher. Her mode of operation included regular classroom visitation and demonstration teaching. She received little response if she tried for in-service programs that went beyond routine classroom visitation. She was known outside her own community for her fine ideas on music supervision, but found it difficult to put these into practice.

When she left, it took a long time to find a replacement. The new consultant was competent but had no supervision experience. She taught an academic subject several hours each day, while the administration watched her and made up its mind as to her worth. She was frequently ill. She raced around each day demonstrating from classroom to classroom. While on the run she tried to correct papers for her junior high English classes. This arrangement lasted just one school term.

When she left, her responsibilities were shared by several musically inclined teachers and principals. About all they were able to do was to coordinate the musical affairs of the various grammar schools. Many classroom teachers began to teach of their own accord. A few in-service meetings well attended by interested teachers were set up.

In the meantime the administration was looking for a full-time music supervisor. They gave the position to a local high school choral teacher.

He had broad experience in both vocal and instrumental music and also taught music education years ago at a local junior college. The schools and community respected him. Many of the teachers in the system were in his high school music classes years ago. He had much in his favor, including readiness for in-service programs among the teachers. These were some of his more perplexing problems that he had to face in his first year:

1. Teacher apathy toward the music program
2. Administrative ignorance about the needs of the music program
3. The "old" teachers wanting nothing but phonograph records from him
4. Alarm expressed that he was interested in setting up a grade-by-grade program of music reading
5. Special music teachers trying to cause harassment
6. Being caught in a maelstrom of perpetual classroom visitation and demonstration teaching
7. Principals not being receptive to his ideas, forever referring to the wonderful supervisor of several years back
8. During his first year not being allowed more than a half-day each week for planning
9. A few teachers starting a whisper campaign against him and the principals doing nothing to help the matter
10. The schools having less than the minimum equipment and materials needed
11. No budget in his first year which he could use to get necessary demonstration materials
12. Having barely a place to put his brief case, and desk space only when the school secretary was not using the desk

The following items were in his favor. Over the years these helped him develop a pretty fair program:

1. The administration was understanding of his efforts during his first years. The leaders in this group displayed a real interest in moving music forward educationally speaking.
2. Neighboring supervisors were interested in his success.
3. He availed himself of seasoned professional advice through a professional supervisory organization.
4. He was sure what he wanted to accomplish. The chief problem was determining acceptable means.
5. Being overloaded with classroom visitations his first year was to his benefit. This gave him an opportunity to really get acquainted with the actual workings of classrooms at various grade levels.

He remained consistent. Whatever he stood for became recognized by all concerned. It is too bad that he had to play around an obstacle course for so long before the program could advance. This could have been avoided. He had to make his peace with each one separately in order to get at the job at hand. A person drawn in from the outside could have possibly avoided some of these problems. He might have gone where angels feared to tread. He probably would have taken the responsibility of actually setting up more positive communications.

District B had a program of music supervision for nearly twenty years. The first supervisor held the position for eleven years; the second one held it for eight years. After that, there was a succession of part-time consultants who stayed no longer than a year each. The program of music education had reached its peak here during the tenure of the second consultant. During her eight years a number of things happened that indicated that this school community had grown up musically:

1. The district eventually employed two full-time instrumental music teachers.
2. A full-time vocal music and upper grade general music teacher was employed.
3. An old building was rebuilt into an instrumental building, with private practice rooms, storage rooms, rehearsal rooms and a director's office. Also expanded budgets were approved each year for new music and equipment.
4. Quality of musical performance of both instrumental and vocal music groups was very high.
5. Eighty per cent of the classroom teachers taught the regular grade music.

When the music consultant resigned, the district was reluctant to release her. The music program was recognized far and wide. When the position was opened for applicants, there were very few who were interested, because (a) the salary for consultants was low, and (b) it was known that antagonism toward supervision had flared up.

Finally, a consultant was contracted for from an area where the classroom teacher did not take part in teaching music. However, she was quite eager to adjust to a new situation and to adopt a new philosophy. Realizing that she was following in the steps of a highly skilled supervisor, she became badly discouraged. Her background for the consultant type of supervision was very deficient, but she did avail herself of frequent professional help from the county music coordinator. With this help she set up series of in-service meetings, and worked out a system of providing necessary materials to the teachers.

These two problems hampered her work: (1) She was left without transportation, and (2) she took the advice of one of the old-timers too literally when she did not go into a classroom unless the school specifically requested her services. She left at the end of the school term.

Finally a beginning teacher was employed. Her assignment included teaching half-days—observation, demonstration, and supervision the remainder of the time in this 120-teacher system. The person employed was a competent musician and a charming person. She was so busy doing the many little things expected of her that there was no time to look at the instructional materials which were used in the classroom. She did indicate her plans to set up grade level meetings later in the year.

She taught from 8:30 in the morning until 3:00 in the afternoon. Her only rest period was a short lunch period at 10:30. Several of the principals felt very sorry for her. But that is as far as it went. It was very difficult to give her any professional help which would do any good at all because, (a) the superintendent was about to retire and wasn't interested in straightening things out, (b) the new department head was so busy getting the personnel to channel everything through him that anything special for the music consultant would upset his well-ordered routine, (c) the principals looked on warily, and no one intended to stick his neck out because of the transitory situation in the administrative department, and (d) she herself was too busy to take time for improvement on the job.

This whole situation was truly unfortunate because it represented 3,600 children.

District C has had an array of part-time music consultants coming and going for each of seven successive years. Their responsibilities were teaching the junior high choral groups and supervising the elementary classrom music program. *Supervise,* in this district, meant actual demonstration teaching for the classroom teacher. Each year's incumbent found teaching more pleasant elsewhere. Finally, the board asked the high school choral director to teach junior high choral groups and to handle the classroom music program.

This assignment was too heavy for him, so he proceeded to reorganize the pattern of the elementary music program. He had the respect of a miserly and musically disinterested administration, and they let him do what he pleased. He strongly urged, planned, and implemented a classroom music program that used all the teachers, even those with small musical background. His nonteaching time was spent working with teacher groups, helping to develop their own music-teaching potential. After a few months many of these teachers were not only teaching music to their own children, but had formed a network of "helping teachers" who were of assistance to anyone not able to teach classroom music.

Since his time there has again been a succession of people who left tired and frustrated at the end of each year.

District D has had a 40 per cent annual teacher turnover. The music consultant had a combination job, teaching junior high music and supervision. There had been an annual succession of consultants for many years. Each had either a master's degree or the equivalent of it. Most of them had some teaching experience. All of them were enthusiastic young people and eager to do a good job. It could be said that they failed in their mission because of not having the technical know-how of music supervision. But this is not the entire answer. They perhaps were guilty of certain errors of omission, but the ones who really should have borne the brunt of such accusations are the people in the administrative branch of this particular school district. After a number of years of misdirected music supervision, it doesn't make any difference any more which supervisor had which experiences. These were some of the situations and conditions:

Consultant No. 1

1. Well liked by teachers. They saw little of him because principals prevented him from setting up in-service meetings. Teachers were discouraged from requesting the consultant's services.
2. Very little time to train a performing group, but was expected to present groups whenever the principal wanted music for civic or P.T.A. programs.
3. In-service meeting contacts were made from his home since the principals discouraged such affairs.
4. He received only criticism from the administration. When he was up for tenure, he was released from his contract. The administration felt he was immature.

Consultant No. 2

The following year a husband and wife were employed. Each had a number of years public school music experience in another state— the husband, as consultant and instructor in elementary school music methods at a college. They had pleasing personalities and were eager to do a good job. They had the same experience as the previous consultant had. The principals and teachers caused them considerable consternation.

They visited several successful music supervisors and made a study of their systems and tried to adopt aspects of these programs. The administration was not ready. Circumstances developed that made it mandatory for this team to leave at the end of the school year. They were frustrated at every turn. But they had a driving zeal to do a good job.

Their need was more precise skill in human relations. They were not offensive, but they did not possess *the skill of making others less offensive*. In reality, the administration failed to assist them in achieving success. The administration ought to have shouldered the responsibilty for aiding and abetting failure. This trait of merely watching others fail is too common. In the excitement of seeing others fail it is so easy to forget the greater responsibility of helping.

Consultant No. 3

The following year a highly qualified young woman took the position. Because of her outgoing friendliness and her dynamic zeal, and because of the administration's remorse over previous debacles, much was accomplished within the next two years. Good relations were set up with teachers and principals. More teachers were interested in doing their share of music teaching. In-service meetings were re-established.

However, as time went on the consultant felt that much was left undone. She wanted freedom to set up in-service programs in the areas where she and the teachers felt the need existed. She wanted to set up grade level meetings. The administration indicated that she should be patient since the system was not ready for her ideas (the teachers were). Many of her plans were blue-penciled in the central school office.

Consultant No. 4

The position was filled by a female vocal music specialist from another area of the country. She had very little understanding of the school music program except in her specialty of teaching choral groups.

Many classroom teachers took it upon themselves to take night school courses to increase their music teaching effectiveness.

Consultant No. 5

It would have been rather simple to leave this district to its own ill-fated devices and advice. But supervisors are known to go where angels fear to tread. The area supervisor sat down with the local school administrative staff to discuss the newly established vacancy. Recommendations were made. The candidate referred for the position was without peer among all of the available candidates and was eager to accept this kind of challenge. However, during a period of administrative delay, an administrative assistant hired an affable young man "who was just traveling through looking for a band job," but was tired of hunting and was willing to settle for this. He seemed eager to adjust to working as a consultant. He did later upset the lethargic (music education-wise) administration. He lost his job because of ineffectiveness and because he complained about an overload. Consultants 6 and 7 were refugees from other departments. They had to divide their time and efforts in three areas.

District E represents a city of three thousand population. The district employs a full-time instrumental music instructor and a combination vocal and elementary consultant. A few years ago this position was held by a beginning teacher. He concentrated on teaching band and chorus and going to the various thirty or more grade rooms to teach a lesson in each room.

The instrumental department grew to such proportions that he began to neglect the classroom music program. He stayed only two years.

The new man had considerable band and vocal experience. He didn't keep the administration informed about his musical activities; neither did they communicate with him what they expected of the music program. Both parties apparently waited for the other to make a move; and one waited for the other to fail, without extending a helping hand. He became overworked and developed an aggravating health problem that caused him to become irritable. The administration blamed the irritability on unwillingness to get along. The problem was alleviated, but the administration still acted inconsiderately. He finally took a high school teaching job elsewhere.

For the following year the administration employed two people to handle all the musical affairs. The general music teacher-consultant was a man with many years experience in several states and in many teaching situations. He was very difficult to get to know. Because he had an austere personality he could have anything he wanted. Recently purchased materials were considered not worth using; so the school ordered several hundred dollars worth of music readers for all grade levels. The music supervisor (as he wished to be called) instituted a

rigid system of visitation. He visited each room once a week for observation, demonstration, correcting teachers and laying out their assignment for the following week. He reserved some time when he could
drop in on teachers without their expecting it so that he could check
on whether they were following his directions.

His own demonstrations were rigid and authoritarian. He required
absolute obedience of the children at all grade levels. He would single
out the perpetrator of an error and make him correct his error. Teachers
were also dealt with on the basis of extracting penance from wrongdoers,
and expecting an immediate change in their conduct after he "helped"
them. His choral groups deteriorated because of apparent mental cruelty.
There was more concern about exact seating arrangement, exact holding
of music, and exact following of directions than on transmitting musical
values.

The teachers became embittered. One elderly woman on the staff
said, "We at least learned how not to teach." Unfortunately, the administration was sold on the supervisor's activities and was not aware
of what was going on, so tended to disregard complaints.

The supervisor left at the end of the term. His reason was that he
was not guaranteed sufficient authority in his new contract so that he
could enforce his ideas about music teaching.

The following year an experienced female consultant was hired. She
inherited a situation not conducive to good work. Teachers were re-
sentful because she was asked to rate them on their classroom music
teaching performance.

A young man replacement was hired with several years teaching
experience. He had an outstanding educational and musical background.
He knew materials and procedures well. His personality breathed confidence. The administration was very pleased. The teachers became enthusiastic. The choral groups had a sense of accomplishing things. In
all this, everyone seemed to have a good time.

This district's dilemma was solved by getting the right kind of
person. Musical competence and supervisorial know-how are not the
only answers. The many aspects of leadership discussed earlier are
of utmost importance. Occasionally people come equipped with these
attributes. The skill to make others confident in your ability and judgment can be learned.

He was followed by a year-by-year succession of quasi-qualified
enthusiasts who had some of the necessary ingredients, but failed in
human relations. The last one year stand had all, but marriage took
her out of the community after a brief year.

District F had for years employed a full-time vocal music teacher
and elementary music consultant for its three elementary schools and

one junior high school. The system was known for the high percentage of teachers who taught their own classroom music. They received direction, guidance and concrete help from the consultant. The system broke down temporarily when the consultant became overworked because of an unduly heavy teaching schedule. Frustration and ill health finally caused her to resign and accept a single grade teaching assignment.

The following year an outside consultant was called in several times to hold teachers' meetings.

Later a local musician and former teacher was employed to serve as part-time consultant. No problems evolved. The teachers seemed happy. Some said, "She has a way of getting us to want to teach our own music; she helps us in such a friendly and interesting way that we want to do our share."

These were her strengths:

1. She was an excellent teacher
2. She was an excellent musician
3. She had a feeling for a good program of music education
4. She had the confidence of her administration and of the building principals; she always kept them informed
5. She had good organizational ability
6. She was able to lead
7. She furnished useful materials and aided teachers in whatever areas they needed help
8. She was ever friendly and complimentary to and about others

Subsequently a succession of music teachers were employed to serve in a triple capacity, choral, instrumental, and general music. The work load was so heavy that it precluded in-service activities.

District G represents an elementary school system in a town of 6,000 population. The music director's job included teaching band and choral groups and the supervision of music in the elementary grades. As the school grew he had less time to teach the classroom music. He depended more and more on talented classroom teachers. His schedule allowed him in each classroom weekly. He possessed a fine understanding of the elementary music program. Every minute of the day he was teaching or meeting with small groups of teachers, or observing and demonstrating.

Some of his chief problems were these:

1. The instrumental department had grown to the extent where it required most of his time. Frequent demands were made on him for assembly performances and parades.
2. The annual teacher turnover in the system was very high. This meant many special indoctrination meetings at the beginning of the school year, with allowances for follow-up.

3. He had little time for planning and working out new ideas.

The following tight visitation and teaching schedule explains the presence of problems.

SCHOOL A

TEACHER	DAY	TIME	1ST & 3D WK.	TEACHER	DAY	TIME	2ND & 4TH WK.
A	Mon.	9:35	"	H	Tue.	11:05	"
B	Mon.	10:05	"	I	Wed.	9:35	"
C	Mon.	10:35	"	J	Wed.	10:35	"
D	Mon.	11:05	"	K	Thu.	9:35	"
E	Tue.	9:35	"	L	Thu.	10:05	"
F	Tue.	10:05	"	M	Thu.	10:35	"
G	Tue.	10:35	"	N	Thu.	11:05	"

SCHOOL B

TEACHER	DAY	TIME	1ST & 3D WK.	TEACHER	DAY	TIME	2ND & 4TH WK.
A	Mon.	9:35	"	I	Wed.	9:35	"
B	Mon.	10:05	"	J	Wed.	10:05	"
C	Mon.	10:35	"	K	Wed.	10:35	"
D	Mon.	11:05	"	L	Wed.	11:05	"
E	Tue.	9:35	"	M	Thu.	9:35	"
F	Tue.	10:05	"	N	Thu.	10:05	"
G	Tue.	10:35	"	O	Thu.	10:35	"
H	Tue.	11:05	"	P	Thu.	11:05	"

Senior Elementary Band daily Monday through Friday 8 - 9 a.m.
Junior Elementary Band Mondays and Thursdays at 12:30 noon.
Beginning Instrument classes Tuesdays and Fridays 12:30 - 2 p.m.
Senior Elementary Chorus Tuesdays and Thursdays 2:30 p.m.
Junior Elementary Chorus Tuesdays and Thursdays 3:15 p.m.
Programming and special help to teachers on Fridays.

(Any apparent 'free-time' is compensated for by daily preschool time rehearsals.)

The Role of the Intermediate Unit

The problems in the eight systems described result from interrelationships with administration, teachers, children, and communities. They are also the problems of the music supervisor in the intermediate unit or county school department. His job is to help schools to grow in their ability to provide good programs. His problems are accentuated by the fact that he does not have the administrative license to enter a situation except by consent of those in charge. He can see and observe problems.

His strength may lie in forestalling problems by getting acquainted with personnel and situations long before a critical incident arises. He should serve as a guide to help others grow into such stature that they can handle the problems in their jurisdictions well.

These are some of the things the county supervisor can do in relation to district consultancies within his geographic area:

1. Orient new personnel
2. Offer assistance (only to the extent that such assistance provides proper growth opportunities for the consultants; but never to the extent of taking over for them); helping them develop a team approach, if such an approach seems feasible in the local situation
3. Provide research facilities—audio-visual facilities—supplementary materials
4. Provide outside consultant services to and for groups of consultants
5. Provide a system of personnel counseling
6. Doing many things that will help the consultant suceed
7. Provide professional growth opportunities for teachers

Problems in Dealing with Flow of Materials and Ideas

Much supervisorial time is consumed in doing "ant work." This little but necessary detail work should be done by secretaries, librarians, and technicians, relieving the consultant for creative and leadership functions.

Many central school offices employ pool clerk-typists who are assigned work by a foreman. By the time work reaches them its significance has been lost in the shuffle; or the particular worker has very little understanding of what is expected.

A music supervisor ought to be assigned a secretary who is able to answer the phone intelligently, type in-service bulletins, and transact necessary communications. If a teacher or an administrator calls in and asks for specific materials, she should be able to take the request and fill it. She ought to be able to disseminate information properly concerning the activities of the music supervisor.

The music supervisor needs to be released from the necessary daily trivia so time and energy can be devoted to the improvement of music learning in the schools, and so he can be free to do a creative and professional job of supervision. A good secretary is worth her weight in gold.

QUESTIONS FOR DISCUSSION, THOUGHT AND STUDY

1. List all the things you can think of that can make life difficult for the music supervisor. Still better, ask a music supervisor to give you a list of his problems.

2. Categorize these problems as to their origin. Whose fault was it that each of these problems occurred? At which level did each of these occur?
3. Give suggested solutions for each of these problems.
4. Explain when we say "it is not music supervision that is wrong but it is more the deliberate and unintentional acts of the music supervisors involved."
5. What are reasons behind some of the conflicts that arise between general education people and specialists in certain fields of education?
6. What is meant by "on call" supervision?
7. What are some typical problems that a supervisor faces in dealing with individual teachers?
8. Why has the administrator been regarded as the instructional leader in his school? Since this is so, how can you get him to assume leadership in music education?
9. Whom do we list as music specialists?
10. Each of five schools wants an instrumental teacher. Work out a schedule for one person if two of the smaller schools want merely a half-day a week and the rest of the time is divided between the rest of the schools. The schools are from ten to twenty-five miles from the home of the instructor.
11. Justify a school system employing 125 teachers supporting one full-time music supervisor.
12. What are the disadvantages of a combination teaching-consultant type of position?
13. What are some of the conditions that tend to contribute to the success or failure of a music supervisory situation?
14. List arguments for and against "the self-contained classroom."
15. Find a school that utilizes a music teaching specialist and one that utilizes a consultant. Compare areas of the music program in these schools.
16. List some of the reasons why some of the above mentioned music consultants failed, and why some succeeded.
17. List the many ways secretarial help cannot only relieve the music supervisor of details, but actually make him more effective.
18. If you have appointments in several schools and do not expect to be in the office for several days, describe an effective arrangement of taking care of necessary requests and calls.
19. Describe in words and diagram how you think the work space or office of a music supervisor should look. What should it contain? For what purpose should it exist? How can it be used most effectively?
20. What has skill in human relations to do with resolving many of the problems incumbent on music supervision?

Part II

The Music Supervisor
on the Job

... his routine life
... his interrelationships

Chapter 5

The Routine Life of the
Music Supervisor

The Full-Time Music Teacher Acting as Supervisor

As indicated previously music supervision can be found in many types of places under many kinds of labels or titles. In some places the band director of the high school doubles in elementary music supervision. In other places it is the responsibility of the vocal music director. In many places it is the musically talented academic teacher who assumes the kinds of musical leadership one refers to as supervision. In one particular community, the local piano tuner (a former teacher) serves as instrumental and vocal instructor in several schools and doubles as music consultant in the grades.

The *Music Educators Research Council Bulletin No. 18* lists numerous arrangements of music supervision. However, as inclusive as this bulletin is, it presents only cursory reference to supervision most prevalent in very small towns and large rural school districts, i.e., the almost-full-time music teacher in the local high school, or in the local consolidated high school and elementary school district.

Music Supervision in the Semirural Consolidated High School and Elementary School District

A three-ring circus, if you ever saw one! However, let's remember there are more positions like this in American music education than the sum total of all kinds of full-time music supervision posts. This is what they do! They direct bands on parade at patriotic events and at football games; their choruses perform at regional music festivals; and musical extravaganzas, like operettas, cantatas, and pageants, are performed under their direction. But very seldom does one hear about their assignment of elementary classroom music teaching and supervision. These people are the unsung heroes of the baton. They bring music to the smallest towns in every part of the United States. Besides their bands, choruses, orchestras, programs, class instrumental instruction, and ensemble instruction, they give time each week for elementary music supervision and occasional in-service meetings for classroom teachers. Unless you have been one of these, you cannot fathom the magnitude of their activities and the tremendous scope of their influence. The musical culture of the community rests in the palms of their hands. Without them the musical life of the community would be barren. They are the ambassadors for music. Community organizations depend upon them to provide music and to guide them in music. Civic and patriotic events almost always include some of the toils of this music person. The quality of local church music is affected gradually but surely by the music teacher having been there. They are the veritable *tastemakers*.

Schools in rural or semirural areas often make more provision for breadth and diversification than a large school system provides. The many musical choices or alternatives available to students in schools like this belie the efficacy of district unification. Students in such schools learn quite early to assume musical responsibilities and leadership. The instructor, doubling in many things plus supervision, has learned early how to delegate responsibilities to student leaders.

There are many challenges and frustrations the small town music director-supervisor faces. Many schools don't know what to do about music. Often the music educator seems to be hopping about willy-nilly, taking whatever time is left over just so more students can have musical experiences. More is expected of him than of teachers in other departments. The team loses games; the players in a cast may forget lines; students may sit through classes unnoticed and untutored—much of this is excused. However, the music department must produce results. Its public performances must be acceptable—it is the only music in town! The music department must be ready to serve the school and community on short notice. The band plays at all games—and often is expected to pay all or part of its admission. It must raise funds for its own support. Music periods are scheduled at inopportune times of the day. In one community the chorus met in two thirty-minute periods a week. When time came that the chorus had to become accustomed to the concert hall, it accomplished this during uninterrupted basketball practice. While the huge basketballs were bouncing off the heads of the youngsters, they were bravely rehearsing their "hallelujahs." The local music educator did not like such an arrangement. But there were four coaches to one music person. The show had to go on and there was no time or power to argue.

The local music educator must fight for music's place in a school system. He must sell music to the administrator and to the teachers. The community usually is quite understanding and insistent in wanting an agreeable music teaching arrangement. The following supervisor-director schedule evolved after several years of frustrations in a small

TIME	MONDAY	TUESDAY	WEDNESDAY	THURSDAY	FRIDAY
8:45- 9:30 a. m.	"A" BAND meets daily at this time (including students from grades 7 through 12)				
9:30- 10:30 a. m.	Music Consultant for Senior Social Studies and English core	Junior High General Music	Junior High Chorus — 10:00 Song Flutes in Elementary gr. — 10:30	Junior High General Music	Junior High Chorus — 10:00 Song Flutes in Elementary gr. — 10:30
10:30- 11:15 a. m.	Music Consultant for Junior Social Studies and English core	Music Consultant for Social Studies and English core Sophomore	Music Consultant for Social Studies and English core Freshman	Music Consultant for Social Studies and English core Eighth Gr.	Music Consultant for Social Studies and English core Seventh Gr.
11:15- 12:15 a. m.	Clarinet Class Beginner Intermediate Advanced (each 20 minutes)	High School Mixed Chorus High School Girl's Chorus each 30 min.	Advanced Voice Girl's Vocal Ensemble. Boys Vocal Ensemble each 30 min.	High School Mixed Chorus High School Girl's Chorus each 30 min.	Cornet Class Beginner Intermediate Advanced (each 20 minutes)
12:15 1:00	NOON LUNCH with varied music activities as the need arises				
1:00 2:00 p. m.	Class instrumental music instruction				
	Trombone and Baritone Eb reeds (30 min.)	Horns Percussion 30 min. each	C Woodwind Bb sax 30 min. each	Strings Bass 30 min. each	Instrumental Ensembles
2:00 3:00 p. m.	ELEMENTARY MUSIC SUPERVISION				
	Grades 4 5 3	Grades 6 1 2	Grades 4 5 3	Grades 6 1 2	Elementary School Band
3:00 4:00 p. m.	Special program ensembles	Music Appreciation and Theory High School	Consulting with individual elementary teachers	Special programming problems	Consulting with individ- ual elemen- tary teachers

school system. It attempted to provide for the varied needs of a total elementary and high school student population of 450 students. It was the feeling that students ought to have available the same rich choices in music as would be available to them in a large city school. In looking at this schedule one can notice there just wasn't time for a "free period." Noontimes the music person ate hurriedly, had marching band practice almost daily during football season, did special work with small ensembles, helped sell popcorn, pop, and candy to support his department, and straightened out the music room for the next class.

This schedule points out that much music supervision is carried out along with such a teaching assignment. Many of the ablest music supervisors came up through the ranks with such an experience background. This arrangement includes every type of music teaching, at all grade levels. It includes in-service teacher training experience in such a capsuled form that every word and activity has to have significance. These people are, as it were, holding up music education's frontiers in the thousands of little communities all over the country.

The specifics of music supervision are applicable to anyone providing music education leadership in a community. The problems, qualities of leadership, and the specific leadership skills needed to put across a program or to solve a problem are the same universally. The small town music director must be a thoroughly trained musician and diplomat in one neat package. He must be able to direct a group with one hand and plan in-service programs with the other. He must jump from a chorus rehearsal to the first grade room with barely enough time to get from one place to the other. His job satisfactions supercede the frustrations and inequalities he has to meet daily. He becomes a symbol of music to the community and its musical conscience.

What the Music Supervisor Does

A Typical Day in the Life of the Music Supervisor

No day in the life of the music supervisor can be repeated. Each day is part of the total supervision pattern. The following extracted from the diary of a music supervisor in a semirural area depicts a typical taxing day, with its compensations. The supervisor lives just a three-minute drive from his office. So if he rises at 7 A.M. he can get to his office by shortly after 8 A.M.

Music Supervisor's Calendar
Friday 13

A.M.
7:00   Alarm clock!
7:20   Breakfast and packaging materials for junior high classroom teachers.
8:15   At office.
8:20   Phone calls
      1. Teacher A requesting a two-part arrangement of a song out of print. Promised to find a substitute.

2. Kindergarten teacher called asking for rhythm band scores to prepare her children for a P.T.A. program. Promised to help her for this occasion, but will add materials to encourage more educational activities.
3. Administrator called about an autoharp. He never heard of it. Wants explanation and assurance that it represents a wise purchase. Where can it be purchased? How is it used in the school music program? Would supervisor come out to show them how to play it and keep it in tune?
4. Secretary of local Music Educator's Association called to get help in setting up details for a dinner meeting.

8:45   Checked mail.
1. Looked for new suggestions to pass on to teachers.
2. Read letter asking supervisor to promote a new patriotic hymn to replace the standard songs. (Filed letter in "to be tactfully answered" file.)

9:00   Placed materials packaged at home on delivery truck. Checked on publisher of song requested above. Made out purchase order for them.

Wrote thank-you letter to administrator and music director for hosting a music education meeting.

9:45   Coffee break referred to as "individual and small group conferences." Discussed articulation problems with several consultants. Social Studies consultant wanted quick "run-down" on ideas for fifth grade music to go with a Latin-American unit. Suggested recordings listed in Audio-Visual Center, and apropos songs in currently adopted music books.

Received reminder from department head that last week's work sheet is overdue. "Also, please check mileage report; it's only twenty-seven miles to school Z, not twenty-nine miles." (Two cups of coffee . . . black.)

10:15   Returned to office. Call from business office regarding research information on music building plans. One of the high schools in area plans to move its music department out of abandoned school shop into a new building. Hope the band director lives to see the day! Checked out Music Educators National Conference research materials on music buildings and rooms. Discussed building plans with business office.

Suggested better arrangements of proposed practice rooms. Made notations on architect's plans.

10:50   Called high school asking for a meeting with music department personnel, administration and architect—to discuss music building plans in terms of present and future needs. Promised to provide materials and recommendations for consideration.

Noted pile of unfulfilled requests and unanswered mail. Bundled up stack to finish at home in evening. (No, tomorrow evening. Choir rehearsals this evening!)

11:15   Sent out special recordings to teachers to correlate with unit they are teaching.

Call from Audio-Visual Center to preview three new films on music teaching. Dropped off films at local music educators' meeting for preview and evaluation. Arranged to spend a day in the Center to evaluate noncirculating films and recordings to help determine whether they should be "pushed" or discarded.

P.M.

12:10 Signed out for school thirty-five miles away.
Mental notes while driving:
1. Problem at school: Local consultant asked to rate teachers according to an officious-looking rating sheet. My responsibility to talk the superintendent out of this procedure? How can the consultant be properly advised?
2. Must find materials for illustrations in a new music bulletin.
3. Public Relations Department left word they want a quick radio program. Would I provide music from some of the schools. (Luncheon on the run!)

1:00 Met consultant entering her choral room. Saw damage caused by pranksters a few nights ago. (Why they should pick the music room is beyond me!) Listened to her problems. Tried to piece together a pattern in order to determine solutions. Suggested I talk with the principal about this rating business. Noted that special group was assembling. Discipline problems: If she'd only place her piano in a position so that she could see the students while accompanying. Too bad an accompanist wasn't available! Suggested such a rearrangement. After hearing a fine choral group, left with reassuring remarks and a host of mental notes. It really isn't entirely the school's fault, nor entirely her fault.

2:00 Met with curriculum specialist to get her reaction. Found out that the administration is really more interested in cooperative evaluation with supervisor and teacher conferring with each other. Rating sheet merely intended as a point of departure. The real problem was noticeable friction between the music consultant and the instrumental teacher. The consultant has a Master of Arts degree, whereas the band director was still trying to complete his first degree . . . (his only sin was that his work showed up more favorably).

2:30 Left school hoping to have been of some help.

2:50 Arrived at neighboring school to discuss in-service meeting with principal and music teacher. Plans included inviting teachers from several surrounding schools. Worked around local calendar conflicts caused by preset social studies meetings, track meet, and P.T.A. Council meeting. Finally agreed on day and time of day.

3:50 Left school.
Made mental notes during return trip to office. . . .
Type of materials to be prepared for this new series of in-service meetings. Noted lack of enthusiasm of music teacher. Seemed as if the principal was making all of the decisions for him. There are problems in connection with publicity for the in-service meetings. Will the local school carry out its end of the bargain?

4:40 Arrived at office:
Two urgent phone calls:
1. A high school band director wants special film on marching band maneuvers. Wouldn't talk to anyone else. Made arrangements for immediate delivery.

2. Administrator called, "We're having a lot of scheduling problems —can you figure out a decent schedule of instrumental lessons? Our fourth, fifth, and sixth grade teachers are crying about too many students out of class too often."

5:00 Checked mail.

5:15 Arrived home. Tired . . . !

6:30 Left for evening meeting (must take preview films, sound projector, and screen).

10:30 Returned home.

Not all days are like this one. At times weightier problems present themselves (less time consuming, but more energy consuming). The music supervisor really wants to meet with each teacher more frequently, and be of greater service to the music specialists. He also wants schools to purchase a minimum of musical equipment hoping it will be used. He does find it difficult to see how much can be accomplished in terms of goals after such a hectic day. However, after many days a pattern and trend emerges from the problems that present themselves, daily.

The Monthly Report (Patterns and Trends)

Monthly reports do not reveal the dynamics of the supervision program. But each month does point out its own problems and highlights: *September* is the time of the year to become acquainted with new teachers. The turnover of teachers may vary each year. New teachers are not all beginning teachers, but they need to become aware of their classroom music teaching responsibilities, or their expected contributions to the total music education program. Most beginning teachers need direction and encouragement. Experienced teachers often come unprepared to teach their own music. It may take some time to help them find a comfortable spot in the total music education picture, i.e., a point of departure from which they can begin to get their feet wet. Typical September problems may include a full-time music specialist who may need a bit of orienting; or the new principal who just doesn't know what this music education business is all about. It may also be the month to assimilate new ideas for the benefit of many teachers; or to take some time for quiet research work to prepare in-service aids.

October and November mean many things to the busy music supervisor. He may be concerned with the band playing at home football games. Around this time teachers are in a mood to enrich their instructional program (what with Columbus Day, Armistice Day, Halloween, and Thanksgiving). The supervisor must be ready with all sorts of ideas to put more meaning to the music program—and into other learning programs.

Schools have been accused of fostering only holiday-centered music and art programs. One should make sure that such music programs have real significance.

The music supervisor ought to utilize these stopping-off places to provide inspirational materials that do not lend themselves to the ordinary ways. October and November contain several events that could easily stimulate the utilization of special music. These can easily be the crest on which rides musical growth.

December presents its own problems and genuine pleasures. Many teachers are searching for ideas for Christmas programs. Christmas is part of life and culture involving the school. Its artistic observance needs help. Plan ahead for spring activities.

January and February present many opportunities for seasonal holiday music. It also is a rather bleak time in the school year. Teachers may welcome timely in-service meetings about this time.

March, April, and May bring Easter activities, spring festivals, concerts, May Day celebrations and graduation activities. Many schools plan pageants for their graduation programs. The supervisor is very frequently asked to find source material for such programs. He may find himself organizing an instrumental ensemble to play a processional and recessional at some four- or five-teacher school far off the beaten trail.

Despite these seasonal activities, phone calls and the mail remain the inescapable stabilizers and realities in the life of the supervisor. Neither of these can be stopped nor can the responsibility of fulfilling them be escaped. A promise made over the phone is a sacred commitment. An unanswered letter from a teacher or an administrator is an indictment against any supervisor who otherwise may be known for his outstanding contributions. One can describe the efficacy of the music supervision program in terms of the many little fulfilled requests. They add spice, meaning, and quality to the "big" supervisory program, especially when they come at a busy season.

Semester Progress Report

A *semester report* does not always present a minute picture of the many activities. It does list the larger categories reflecting ultimate goals and an approximate percentage breakdown of types of music supervision services:

High schools 15% of time
Elementary 85% of time

Total coordination activities 60%
Supervision 30%
Administration 10%
100%

The music supervisor's semiannual report, sketchy as it may seem, begins to portray a picture of service to schools, teachers, and education. Since there are about 175 days in a school year, this means that in one semester the music supervisor would have received at least 250 pertinent phone calls and 100 to 150 mailed requests. One hundred twenty-nine teachers were seen as individuals in a face-to-face relationship. About thirty were met in small staff meetings; while about 400 teachers were met in in-service meetings of an area-wide nature. Not included in any records, but elicited from conversation with music supervisors was that at least three or four teachers a day came directly to the office for help, ideas, or suggestions. This usually occurs between 3:30 and 5:00 P.M. daily.

A County Music Supervisor's Annual Report and Summary in Terms of Goals

1. Organized and conducted twenty-seven area and countywide in-service meetings in music education; approximately 900 teachers in attendance; four sessions conducted by outside consultants
2. Prepared bulletins as follow-up suggestions for in-service meetings
3. Assembled and edited teacher-made unit plans on teaching classroom music utilizing new instructional materials
4. Assisted consultants in area in setting up their own in-service programs
5. Visited all but ten elementary schools—however, served all through in-service meetings, phone calls and correspondence
7. Provided on-the-spot aids through phone calls and correspondence
8. Assisted schools in buying music equipment for elementary school music
9. Lent instrumental materials such as autoharps and song bells
10. Distributed in-service bulletins
11. Promoted music education programs in all schools
12. Planned with large districts to set up consultant positions
13. Visited and observed music programs in all the county high schools
14. Helped organize three city music festivals and one rural elementary band festival; about thirty schools involved with about 1,800 participating music students

15. Organized and directed four regional elementary vocal music festivals, involving over thirty schools and nearly 2,000 students
16. Coordinated activities of seven traveling music specialists in thirty schools
17. Developed rotating library of instrumental methods for the traveling music specialists
18. Made recordings of forty elementary and high school vocal groups for school radio broadcasts
19. Previewed musical recordings and music films. Arranged for previewing sessions for teachers
20. Arranged for musical presentation at county educational meetings
21. Served on central office agenda committee (setting staff meetings, acting as clearing house to screen items to be presented before staff, and to schedule staff presentations)
22. Aided school districts in screening candidates for music positions, interviewing them, and arranging for local school administration interviews
23. Assisted in placement of personnel leaving the area, or district; writing recommendations and making contacts
24. Made arrangements for music educators clinics
25. Conducted music clinics held in other areas
26. Set up music reading clinic for area
27. Chaired regional music supervisors association. Three official meetings plus three planning meetings
28. Assisted with regional festival arrangements, area music educators organizations
29. Assisted full-time music directors in the county with projects
30. Served on board of regional music educators association and on regional festival board
31. Worked with music department of nearby colleges for articulation purposes
32. Worked with state-wide music education groups in developing in-service aids for the classroom teacher
33. Worked on the production of cooperatively planned music education materials
34. Advised local civic concert association
35. Advised civic groups on community music projects
36. Promoted concerts for children through local symphony orchestra
37. Arranged for music education radio programs
38. Arranged for television programs, utilizing music departments of various schools
39. Worked actively on a Mass Communication Committee toward the improved use of mass media for educational purposes
40. Retained opera company to present a standard opera to students
41. Cooperated with the federal government in obtaining Title I and III funds, and funds through NDEA Humanities Division

Justifying These Activities in Terms of Goals

This itemized report does not indicate how each activity took place, or how often, but it definitely points up the variety of activities of a full-time supervisor. Most of these activities actually contributed to the desired *goals of music education.* A system's approach to music supervision would categorize these activities in order of relevance.

Some educators may question the contributory values of items such as public performances, festivals, radio and television appearances, frequency of nonmusical meetings, and efforts to foster community music projects. Festivals have been advocated as a means for providing self-evaluation by students and instructors. Performing groups receive the opportunity to hear other groups. Such occasions can be pleasant learning experiences for all.

Participating in radio and television programs is a good stimulus for excellence. The school community's attention to the fine work of the music department can thus be highlighted.

Attending nonmusical meetings with a central office staff and with other groups responsible for implementing the educational program in general is a vital and necessary activity in that it promotes understanding of other disciplines and tends to assure music a fair slice of the educational pie. Fostering and promoting community projects helps assure a place for musical enjoyment and participation outside of school.

The annual report contains in-service programs for teachers; individual visits to schools and with teachers; preparation of teaching aids for teachers; development of teacher-made materials; assisting teachers with immediate problems; consultation with administrators to develop better supervision programs; promotion of large group music activities; articulation with higher education; promotion of valid music equipment; professional upgrading; and many other items relevant to improving music instruction in the schools. All these music supervisory activities are important if they contribute toward accepted goals.

The Five-Year Resume

The hundreds of daily and weekly details, when summed up over an entire year, present a picture of goal-seeking activities for the year. They are in terms of teachers contacted, schools visited, and kinds of in-service programs. The number and kinds of requests fulfilled and the sum of the many other activities also form part of the total picture. From this one can determine which proportion of these items is part of an educational picture and reflects desirable goals. The annual report lists the many things the music supervisor initiated or did. But a summary taken every few years will tend to reflect what actually happened in the schools. It will highlight significant concepts and generalizations that label the supervisor and leave their mark on the schools. Is it the things that personally affect people or is it the concepts that have lasted? Is it the ideals for which the music supervisor stands that wend their way into the thinking and acting of others who are more directly connected with the teaching process?

A "before" and "after" tally can show up change in desirable areas. This change may not be because of a program of music supervision. It certainly could have been aided by such a program. The following taken from a music supervisor's records shows certain changes that reflect a planned program in

1. the administrator's understanding of the music program;
2. classroom teacher participation in teaching music;
3. improvement in the taste for music as reflected in the programs for public performance.

The changes that were listed were in terms of *more of or better than before.* To measure improvement accurately is hazardous, since

CHANGES OVER A FIVE-YEAR PERIOD
REFLECTING A PLANNED PROGRAM
OF MUSIC PROMOTION
BY THE SUPERVISOR

	Five years ago	Now
Student population	45,000	44,600
Number of districts	90	70 (decrease caused by consolidation
Number of teachers	1,842	1,876
Number of special music teachers		
high schools	18	23
elementary	41	52
Number of districts with music programs employing qualified specialists	43	57
Number of choral departments		
high school	12	12
elementary	32	41
Number of instrumental organizations		
high school	14	17
elementary	38	50
Teachers attending in-service meetings	268	over 900

items that are remotely related to the essence of what we are after are really the only things that are measurable. For instance, the number of instruments used, the number of student-owned instruments, the number of minutes per week spent in music, or the total number of programs per year.

To measure the effectiveness of a program of music supervision in terms of goals, one should look into the community for change in musical interests, feelings for and participation. These may be a few of the questions one might ask:

1. How many more pianos are in the homes now?
2. How many more other musical instruments are in the homes now?
3. How many more people take private lessons now?
4. What changes in listening habits of the people are evidenced in the purchase of hi-fidelity equipment and recordings?
5. Does the school music program affect the home listening habits of the community?

These and many other questions could be asked to determine change over a several years' period of time. It is important to ascertain whether the school music program uses and controls change in a community's habits, or whether changes come about because of good advertising of musical merchandise.

Statistics do not present a vibrant, dynamic picture of what really transpired. Change showing improvement is not always registered in increased numbers, but more often in the quality of what happened. For instance, is there a change in the quality of the music listened to? Or, is there a change in the quality and degree of difficulty in the music performed? Progress can also be measured by what individuals do to improve a total situation around them. Such improvement is a reflection of their improved insights. Recently a principal told me, "Do you remember the time you talked to our administrators' group? Well, we bought two pianos for the school this year, and I want you to know that each room has a phonograph. Now you have to tell me what records to buy."

Questions for Discussion, Thought and Study

1. Justify calling some full-time music instructors, supervisors of music. What are they expected to do that entitles them to this recognition?
2. List some of the frustrations and perplexities that a small-town music director has to face.

3. Ask the music director who is responsible for the total music program in a rural district for his schedule. Out of a thirty-hour work week, how many hours are devoted to each of the instructional aspects of the program? How much time is allotted to the in-service program?
4. List a number of the music supervisor's activities that he engages in each month of the school term. Justify these in terms of goals.
5. How can one properly judge a year's activities of the music supervisor? What would determine one year being quite different for the music supervisor than previous years?
6. How do the forty-one items listed square away with acceptable goals of music education and music supervision?
7. What can a five-year résumé reveal? What is its particular value?

Chapter 6

Interrelationships Affecting
the Music Supervisor

The music supervisor depends on the good will of many other people for the effectiveness of his program. His ability to get along with others and to understand and appreciate the total educational program is an important force controlling effectiveness of the program.

"The many fields of knowledge that we have are but windows through which the human soul can look out upon a significant and beautiful universe. As fine as music is, it is only one window, and a good life calls for a broader vista than one single direction. I claim that music always has been a highly significant emotional and aesthetic stimulus in human life and that to weave it into the fabric of American life will do much to create a thrilling and hopeful dawn for humanity in this new world."[1]This statement gives recognition to the many other disciplines, and admits that they each contribute to balanced growth. It implies that the people responsible for the promotion of these areas are equal to the music supervisor in the respect that each contributes a vital part toward successful happy living. Music without the others provides an unbalanced education.

In order to appreciate the contributions of the many disciplines it is important to establish relationships with people representing other learning areas. These may be his own peers in supervision, other music instructors, administrators, classroom teachers, students, board, and communities, secretaries, librarians, and even custodians.

Important Music Supervisorial Relationships

1. With peers, but in other learning areas
2. With superior officers

99

3. With the school principal
4. With the teacher
5. With the student in the classroom
6. With the community
   a. As a citizen
   b. As an organizational worker with service groups
   c. As a leader in civic music affairs
   d. Cooperating with music dealers and music industry
   e. Working with private music teachers
   f. Using school public performances as sound public relations media
   g. Working with community representatives for the school—the board of education
7. With peers in music supervision

The supervisor as a human being; the supervisor as an expert; the supervisor as one skilled in leadership attributes—all these aspects have been documented. His relationship to those who come within the scope of his influence needs to be dealt with specifically as it pertains to music education. Another aspect relating to supervision deals with the supervisor's relationship to his peers in supervision, or how does he get along with the persons in the central office?

The Central Office

Good relationships are of critical concern at the administrative and supervisory level. It is here where the "educational pie is sliced" into its various parts and parceled out. The home base and starting point for many supervisors is at this level. He gets his mail and his phone calls here. Many teachers call on him here. He may even have an office equipped for the effective dispatch of his varied obligations.

A good share of his supervisory life is spent in and about the office. In fact, the office often becomes so synonymous with supervision that anyone wishing to speak with the music supervisor just calls the office —and is quite frustrated when the music supervisor is not there. Often the caller is dismayed to find out that the person wanted is thirty miles away in a school. He is still more dismayed when he finds out that the supervisor is "in conference." Patience rubs thin when he discovers that the person answering the phone is not able to provide the right answers. How often have you had this happen?

Operator: Good morning, City Schools.

Caller: I would like to speak with the Music Supervisor. We found a note in our box this morning telling us about a children's concert in Civic Auditorium. I would like to know . . .

Operator: Sir, if you please hold the line, I will ring the Music Supervisor's Office . . . there you are, sir.

Caller: Is this the music supervisor?

Other end: I am sorry . . . I just heard his phone ring so I came in and answered . . . can I help you? . . .

Caller: Well, I really wanted to speak to the music supervisor privately . . . . but maybe you can help . . . you see, this morning we found a note in our box . . .

Other end: From which school are you calling, sir?

Caller: Anyhow, we found a note in each of our boxes telling us about a children's concert in Civic Auditorium . . . what I really wanted to know. . . . I really would like to speak with the supervisor personally . . . With whom am I speaking?

Other end: I am the health supervisor . . . I'll switch you over to someone in the instructional division. They may know . . .

Caller: Well, it really isn't that important. You see, I am just a substitute teacher . . . and when I saw this note . . . you see, I really don't want to complain . . .

Other end: We are here to help you, sir. I am sorry that I can't give you the right answers—but while you are waiting for the music supervisor, we may find someone who can help you.

Operator: I am ringing the instructional division . . .

Secretary: Good morning, Instructional Division, City Schools Administration Office, Office of Dr. K., Associate Superintendent of Schools in Charge of Instruction. May I help you?

Caller: Well . . . I just wanted to . . . see, I was calling to get hold of the music supervisor . . . about a personal problem.

Secretary: Sir, we are only eager to help, I will connect you with Dr. K. . . . (Dr. K., a gentleman on the line . . . he seems a bit upset . . . I guess a complaint about the music supervisor . . .)

Dr. K.: Good morning, sir. I just didn't get your name?

Caller: Bill Tomkins, from Lincoln, substitute . . .

Dr. K.: Oh, Bill, it's good to hear your voice. I remember seeing your papers the other day. How did you like substituting at Lincoln? I hear you had a bit of a problem with our music supervisor . . . well, don't let it bother you . . . I don't think he knew you were a substitute . . . what?

Caller: No, you get me all wrong, sir . . . all I wanted was . . . you see this morning we found a note in our boxes telling us about a children's concert in Civic Auditorium . . . and I was asked to check the children on the busses . . . two parents came in and wanted to know whether the music supervisor would be at the concert to talk to the children a bit about the music. I know this is a silly question.

Dr. K.: Why, no, Bill, it's not a silly question . . . now let's see whether we can get in touch with him. . . . Let's see where he is . . . hm.

	I don't see. . . . Oh, yes, here it is. He is checked out . . . to Civic Auditorium. He won't be back. Now I don't know whether we can contact him there. . . . Wait a minute . . . here is the Art Supervisor—say, do you know? . . . Oh, you heard, you don't know . . . he didn't say. . . . Well, say, Bill, it seems no one here knows much about it. Needless to say, I was glad you called. Good you're working in at Lincoln. Anytime you have a problem be sure to call. Goodbye.
Caller:	Goodbye.

This conversation points up the real need for communication. Had the people involved in this phone conversation made it a point to develop basic understandings about the need for maintaining open channels of communication, the caller would have left the phone with an intelligent answer.

This implies a deliberate effort from each one in the organization. Communication has been perfected technologically. The phone is there; it works well. The mails seldom err. The newspapers, publications, radio, and television respond quite accurately to the human touch. The unresolved problem is the human factor that uses these media as part of the process of getting the educational job done. Miehl[2] identifies two problems that deal with communication, each of which is applicable to successful music supervision: (1) the problem of making constructive use of technical inventions, and (2) the problem of capitalizing upon opportunities for face-to-face communication.

The phone call was an example where the people behind the machine fell down on a job. Politeness and solicitude were apparent, but nothing happened that satisfied the caller. Channels were set up, but no communication occurred. All these are no cover for inability to convey the right answer at the right time.

The incident could happen at any level of education. The secretary receiving the call should have had a schedule available within arm's reach. She should have known whether the supervisor was engaged in an activity from which he could be called without interrupting something. If he is busy, she could have found out whether he is able to leave long enough to answer the phone. Still better, she should find out the nature of the problem and give the exact answer, assuming she had been given proper information.

An Attempt at Better Communications

Some schools have set up a huge screen in a conspicuous place where all concerned could see it. On it are flashed periodically the announcements that are of concern to most of the teachers who have occasion to pass by. The daily, weekly, and monthly bulletins which traditionally are placed in each person's mailbox frequently fail to do the job because they are so common. They are read perfunctorily. The truly perfect attention-getting device has not been devised.

Paper, mimeographing machine, typewriter, ink, and stencil all seem to function properly. But communicating through these needs to be cultivated constantly. Music can easily be lost in the shuffle of the educational system if the music supervisor fails to convey to his peers the purpose of his program and the particular devices he hopes to use in order to develop excellence in his area.

The music supervisor may be striving to develop more creative teaching. He may be trying to get across the concept of a developmental program. Or he may be trying to implement a new series of music books in the various grades. If he has not been able to communicate these ideas to his peers, he must exert more than ordinary effort to get these concepts across to teachers.

Central Office Staff Meetings

Too often central office staff meetings lose themselves in the discussion of routine problems. Communication is neglected. One music supervisor told me, "The people in the schools are more interested in the things I am trying to do than the home office. The office espouses projects, like NDEA, titles I, II and III ESEA, Headstart, NYC, Preschool, etc., leaving no time to get some of my ideas across. They say they will try to set up a time where all of us who have a need to be heard can have a chance. . . . This is certainly not an answer."

This may sound like an indictment against existing modes of communication. In reality in this case it is a way of saying ". . . we are desperately seeking a better way of communication . . . because we all feel the need for it in order to put on a good educational program." It is important that one hand knows what the other is doing. In many systems the only accepted communication vehicles are the notice, the directive, and the calendar.

Too frequently the music supervisor is an entity in himself. Other supervisors are vaguely aware of what music education is all about. Also, too frequently the music supervisor displays little interest in the workings of the other educational consultants, even though they are friends and they have coffee and dine together. They respect each other's subject by keeping a respectful distance.

Channels of communication are needed as a way of promoting a good educational program and *not as a favor to an individual*. Personalities and disciplines must get together to understand each other and each other's programs so these can be interpreted properly wherever needed.

In one office a music supervisor shared a large room with four other supervisors, Kindergarten, Art, Physical Education, and a General Supervisor. The five spoke together very frequently . . . each expressing views . . . also discussing problems and projects. Each one could interpret the other quite well. And each was sympathetic to the program of the other. The music supervisor said: "I never saw any sense to physical education; now I understand there is a developmental program. I had notions about proper musical activities for the kindergarten, but felt rather uncomfortable whenever I would have to demonstrate with a group of kindergarten children. I really found out I needed my colleague so that I wouldn't go off half-cocked. I also found out that most of the kindergarten teachers in this area were fairly skilled as musicians. Our new industrial arts supervisor and I can work together a lot. We are planning a series of workshops on making musical instruments. Incidentally, the art supervisor and I are working together on developing creative art through listening to music. I guess we can each help each other put our subject across."

By working together and talking out their problems and aims, they had developed a solid and mutual respect for each other. They developed a mutual understanding and can communicate and interpret or answer for each other. If either one of these had answered the phone call (a few pages back), a more satisfactory answer could have been given. These are attributes that contribute toward effective educational communication:

1. Knowledge of the total program
2. Knowledge of the plans and objectives of the system
3. Knowledge of the individualistic contribution to the program—the individual as a person and the discipline he represents
4. Understanding of the aims of the separate areas and of the total area; understanding of the supervisor's role in the total picture
5. Accepting the *responsibility* and *promoting* the opening of many avenues of communication

By taking things for granted one can become remiss in taking personal responsibility for opening avenues of communication. Never assume that the right things will happen just because you are on a staff. Act as if you are part of the educational pie, not the whole pie. Music people ought to show more genuine concern for the entire educational program; the other disciplines may have an edge on methodology and on clarity of goals.

The central office ought to be a small United Nations: a place where each subject is ably represented; and where each subject representative is responsible for understanding, interpreting, and creating an awareness of the needs and contributions of his own area to the others on the staff.

The failures of communication are more glaring and are longer remembered than the hundreds of instances of good communication. Mackenzie and Corey[3] make this observation: "Even when concern about professional security is not involved, communication may greatly influence a staff member's feeling of being liked and accepted. The individual who knows he is well informed about policy, program, and budget realizes that he, as an individual, is held to be important. His sense of involvement in the activities of the school and in the educational profession as a whole tends to increase. When staff members participate actively in making decisions, communication, of course, is greatly facilitated."

The complexities of present-day organizational structure demand open lines of communication.

Effective relationships break down when the individual music supervisor does not communicate information to co-workers. Withholding communication may even be for reasons such as (1) fear of having information misused; (2) fear that it would not be understood anyway; (3) fear that it may be used to lessen the influence of the supervisor; (4) or the attitude, "give the boss only the information he wants."

Small group meetings provide better opportunities for free face-to-face discussion. Job satisfactions increase when face-to-face communication is part of the operation of a supervisory staff. Such a relationship is accomplished when a small group becomes accustomed to working together and talking over problems and goals together.

One staff was concerned with a breakdown of communications. To remedy this, meetings were set up so that no more than five persons met in a group. Each of these groups discussed aspects of a common problem. People in each of the subgroupings got to know each other. Later they were shifted into other groups. After a few months each staff member had the opportunity to get well acquainted with all the other members. There evolved a freer exchange of ideas, opinions, plans, and information.

The music supervisor's effectiveness is improved in direct proportion to the amount and kinds of communication channels he utilizes.

If there are no official channels set up, it is for him to initiate setting them up.

The Music Supervisor and the Principal

The music supervisor cannot do effective work in an individual school unless he uses the right *key* to get into the school. It determines success or failure of a program. This key in this case is the key person in the school—not the key music person—but the school *principal*.

Never walk into a school and superimpose a program without the permission, support, or understanding of the principal. The principal must know of the program of music education, for he is charged with the responsibility of implementing the entire educational program. He is recognized as the educational leader of his building. He has been hired because of his facility or talent for understanding the particular community in which the school exists; or he may have a special talent for guiding the particular staff of this school. This is a common-sense reason.

The principal usually understands the community, the patrons, the children, and he is aware of their socioeconomic situation. He knows the minority groupings, and the dominating factors controlling the community. He knows the strengths and weaknesses of his teachers. He tries to provide a balanced arrangement of desirable teaching talent. He knows that very few teachers are equally talented in all things.

The music supervisor must learn to see the situation in the same light as the principal looks at his school. He needs to discover that the principal really wants good music for his children. Most principals would be delighted if all of their teachers could teach music equally well. However, they would be quite concerned if these teachers did it to the exclusion of other valid subjects.

The music supervisor's initial visit can set the tone for future working relationships. It can easily determine whether he will work effectively with the staff. Because the principal has so many and such pressing responsibilities, he may be quite unaware of the need and the importance of music in the program. This does not mean that he is against music; so it is up to the music supervisor to set up friendly relations with the principal. Their first meeting must be the opportunity for the principal to orient the music supervisor as to the entire situation.

Some years ago I visited a six-teacher school in a poverty area. Mr. Green, the principal, welcomed me in by motioning me to sit down.

He asked what he could do for me. (Music supervisors don't really come out to poor schools unless they want something badly!) I expressed an interest in finding out how his music specialist was accomplishing her job—and whether the school was lacking certain musical materials that I could help them get. I also inquired about facilities and provisions for the teaching of classroom music. Mr. Green took me aside telling me, "What I am going to do with you will be more important to us and you than what you want to do." He proceeded to take me on a tour through the community. After not more than a block he pulled his car to the side of the road and called a big barefooted man in torn overalls to the car. This man was introduced as the Reverend Mr. _____, minister of a local church. The principal introduced me and the purpose of my visit to the minister. As we drove on, he explained that the minister is very much interested in the welfare of the community and wants to be assured that all is well at the school. We drove up to a church (a small barnlike-looking structure). The third grade is housed here. He pointed out another old church building across the field, saying that that is where the first grade is. As we drove up to a dilapidated store (the kind found in typical ghost towns), we heard various noises emanating from this structure. This old store was used for a band room. Proceeding on a tour through the unkept village, he pointed to improvements made over the past years. "Five years ago this row of unpainted shacks was not here; they replaced an open-air camp made up of burlap sack tent shelters, heated with old oil drums. Most of the people, when they came here, were unemployed. There were no job opportunities. They stopped here because their cars broke down enroute. . . . They couldn't get jobs because they didn't have transportation to drive where jobs were available." Farther down the line he pointed to another row of homes inhabited by the "employed elite." Some of these had little fenced-in yards and a few flowers planted conspicuously. The sides exposed to public view were a gleaming white. He implied a process of evolution that is constantly at work in this transient village. Most of the people here started with nothing . . . now they are at varying stages of poverty. Later we saw a group of women sorting clothing and shoes intended for the more unfortunate children. This was my basis for music supervision here.

Another principal, whose school had just been condemned because of earthquake damage, maintained office space in a protected corner of the ruins. Teaching went on in barracks and tents. It was a dismal rainy day, and he was a first-year principal. The feeling of catastrophe was overwhelming. He had so many problems that just letting him talk gave him a better feeling.

The principal of another school informed me that Mr._____ coordinated their music program . . . and that anything he and I made out was all right. Had I not been made aware of this, I could have run into trouble.

One supervisor went to a large elementary school on request of the principal. The principal entertained him royally, and at the same time explained his philosophy of music supervision. He believed that the local consultant was to relieve the teacher of her music teaching responsibility—as he put it, "so she can get her coffee break and have a smoke." He did not want any of his teachers present when the music supervisor was in the room.

The music supervisor could have gone into this school without the principal's approval and started something that would have reaped the resentment and long-term distrust of the administrator. However, by getting acquainted with the principal and seeing his view, but not necessarily agreeing with it, an acceptable working relationship evolved.

In the light of his many responsibilities and concerns, and teacher backgrounds, the principal promotes as much as his situation will permit. Beyond this, he cannot be prodded. He wants to be known as a principal who does right by his school; this the music supervisor must understand. It may be wiser to move slowly but surely. A point is made when the principal leads and the teachers set up their own program and solve their own problems.

An effective way to get the principal to assume leadership in the school's music program is to involve him directly in in-service programs.

One consultant stated that she holds a meeting each year with all the building principals. At this time she explains the music program to them and is prepared to answer any questions. Besides this she displays many materials her teachers ought to be using. Many of her principals have been reported to conduct their own in-service meetings for their teachers. Some of them would call in the supervisors just to be on hand in case a difficult question arose.

The Music Supervisor and the Teacher

Teachers are not all alike and these differences are not entirely because of training and experience. Two classifications of teachers that concern us here are (1) the classroom teacher and, (2) the special music teacher. Since teachers have been good enough to be hired by the local principal and board of education, it can be assumed that they possess the minimum preparation needed for doing a respectable job of teaching. Now, not all teachers are superior, but all are worthy of respect because of their responsibility.

Since the principal needs diversification of talents on his staff in order to bring valid, authoritative, and yet varied experiences to his students, it can easily happen that a teacher is unmusical. The music supervisor not only will be dealing with the musical and the unmusical teacher; he will deal with a vast variety and degrees of strengths and weaknesses that can either enrich or detract from the educational program. These are some of the kinds of teacher situations to be expected in the typical school:

1. The musical teacher
2. The unmusical teacher
3. The fully trained teacher
4. The person teaching on a substandard certificate
5. The teacher at each grade level
6. The combination grade teacher
7. The multigrade teacher
8. The teacher for atypical children
9. The new teacher
10. The teacher protected by tenure
11. The ready-to-retire teacher, and others

Bartky[4] classifies teachers into many categories, depending upon the situation that confronts them. He prefers the Havinghurst and Taba classification that emphasizes normal behavior. He suggests identifying these types of teachers:

1. The self-directive teacher
2. The adaptive teacher
3. The submissive teacher
4. The defiant teacher
5. The unadjusted teacher

He also notes that culture can be a teacher-personality determinant. Even though he feels that this was a frivolous attempt at categorizing teachers, nonetheless, it is a phenomenon that seems more true than funny. He lists these cultural categories:

1. The kindergarten-primary teacher personality
2. The middle-elementary grades teacher personality
3. The upper-elementary grades teacher personality
4. The high school teacher personality

Each category has its overtones in terms of specific kinds of teacher behavior. One must remember that whatever teacher one encounters and no matter how she appears to the supervisor, she deserves to be treated with utmost respect and as a mature adult. Her personal or professional concern may be so all-encompassing that she is not tuned-in, and her thoughts may be miles away.

Snygg and Combs[5] summarize this by saying, "It is impractical to think of the learner (teacher) except in terms of his own need, his own desires, and his own point of view." One must find ways for her to see herself as others do, then she can modify her music teaching behavior, and still retain her individuality. The music supervisor has the mandate to work with the teacher, helping her see herself, helping her enlarge her musical horizons, and helping her become effective as a classroom music teacher or as a music specialist, but always within the framework of her own point of view.

The music supervisor must put himself in the position of a diagnostician. And beyond this he must be a therapeutist. The relationship of the music supervisor is never a simple one. If he could predict with some degree of reliability what any teacher's behavior in reaction to any music educational stimulus would be, his position would be relatively simple. He could then standardize his supervisory techniques, and his job would become a routine process.

The Musical Classroom Teacher

The musical classroom teacher can be of tremendous help in implementing a program of music education. The extent of her help is in direct relation to the faith exhibited toward her by her principal and by the music supervisor. The supervisor must help her assume musical leadership. She can become a valuable resource person for others on the staff. She can be an effective liaison between staff and supervisor. She can help the school to maintain its own musical integrity—using the supervisor as a counselor, advisor, helper, or coordinator.

The Nonmusical Classroom Teacher

The nonmusical classroom teacher probably was hired because of certain special talents she possessed that would enhance the total educational program of the school district. The music supervisor needs to capitalize on this teacher's otherwise fine teaching ability and present her with compatible alternatives so that she will gradually undertake teaching some aspect of the music program. These are some considerations in working with the unmusical classroom teacher:

1. Does she believe that music is every child's heritage, and that public education promises the child a complete program of music education?
2. Does she herself enjoy music, but is unable to perform?
3. Is she willing to try devices, such as the phonograph in her teaching?
4. Will a tailored in-service program whereby she can acquire certain skills be of help?
5. Is she aware of the many teaching aids available so that she can give her children a minimum program of instruction without sacrificing quality?

The Teacher Who Has Had No Previous Formal or Informal Training in Skills Necessary to Produce Music

There are degrees and kinds of musicalness. The teachers under discussion may indeed have had certain kinds of musical experiences which were probably of such a nature as not to be directly relatable to school music.

When the teacher comes to the point where she wants to teach music, only then can she be helped effectively. One teacher approached the writer some years back with, "Sir, you made an interesting presentation, but other music supervisors have vainly tried to get me to teach music . . . and have failed utterly. . . ." We will always have these with us. The time spent at trying to work with her kind could be more profitably spent with the teachers in the rooms on either side of her room and across the hall.

Music supervisors are helpers, and not judges. It is far better if they place no value judgments on actions, but proceed unperturbed to try to fulfill their task.

The Teacher Whom Everyone Knows Is Tops

Her training may be as good as that of the supervisor and ideas may be more alive than the supervisor's. She is busy teaching daily from nine to three o'clock for one hundred seventy-five days of the school year. In-service must be given to her when she can implement it without much delay. Since she is a good teacher, she serves on several committees. Everyone wants to use her talents. In this case— let's not pity the poor teacher—but *pity the good teacher*. She is wanted in many places. She adds intelligence to deliberations. Now we want her to come to many in-service meetings in music so she can do better what she already does pretty well! The music supervisor ought to be pretty nice to her. He ought to do everything in his power to free her for more creative teaching.

The Educationally Unqualified Teacher

The music supervisor must be careful how he works with the teacher who is struggling to teach and at the same time is trying to complete her educational requirements. She may need much encouragement and help in music, but with proper consideration of the educational hurdles she is trying to cross while teaching full time.

The music supervisor must recognize that all teachers cannot be placed in the same mold. He must be ready to be very specific about his help so that it is readily applicable to several ability levels.

Each teacher should be treated in a manner reflecting respect for her particular situational problems.

The New Teacher

The new teacher requires a sympathetic and personalized approach. She may have come from an area where the specialist did all the music teaching. Possibly she came from a system where an entirely different series of music books was used. She needs to be welcomed into the sorority of classroom music teachers. She may want specific help, and doesn't appreciate that some supervisors are nondirective. Give her the kind of service she wants at the time. She may be one of the future leaders.

The Permanent Teacher

People say that the teacher on tenure resists changing her ways of teaching or employing new ideas. This may be true. The music supervisor ought not to make this assumption, however. He should accord her the full respect her status merits. Her stability may do much toward adding respectability to a music program. This also holds for the *ready-to-retire* teacher. She may not be in the race any more, and is fondly looking to the other side of the fence. This is often far from the truth. This teacher deserves the respect her years of faithful service connote. She can contribute immeasurably to the music program of the school if she is included in the deliberations. All efforts should be bent toward helping her feel wanted and useful.

The about-to-retire teacher has sixty-five years of exposure to music to offer. The supervisor needs to encourage this person to contribute out of her accumulated sagacity. One can also be musical who can't perform, even though the odds are in favor of the performer.

The music supervisor's greatest success is in discovering where people are, and then leading toward objectives. The music supervisor is the "greatest" when he has built rapport with even the meekest or the most cantankerous, and when he recognizes that even they serve, who stand and just hold the music. There are many clues for dealing with teachers. The answers lie in the direction of good human relations.

The Music Supervisor and the Learner in the Classroom

Music supervision and music as a curricular consideration exist because of the child. The Music Educators National Conference expressed the responsibility of the American public schools for the teaching of music in the following pronouncement:

The Child's Bill of Right in Music[6]

I

Every child has the right to full and free opportunity to explore and develop his capacities in the field of music in such ways as may bring him happiness and a sense of well-being; stimulate his imagination and stir his creative activities; and make him so responsive that he will cherish and seek to renew the fine feelings induced by music.

II

As his right, every child shall have the opportunity to experience music with other people so that his enjoyment shall be heightened and he shall be led into greater appreciation of the feelings and aspirations of others.

III

As his right, every child shall have the opportunity to make music through being guided and instructed in singing, in playing at least one instrument both alone and with others, and, so far as his powers and interests permit, in composing music.

IV

As his right, every child shall have the opportunity to grow in musical appreciation, knowledge, and skill through instruction equal to that given in any other subject in all the free public educational programs that may be offered to children and youths.

V

As his right, every child shall be given the opportunity to have his interest and power in music explored and developed to the end that unusual talent may be utilized for the enrichment of the individual and society.

VI

Every child has the right to such teaching as will sensitize, refine, elevate, and enlarge not only his appreciation of music, but also his whole affective nature, to the end that the high part such developed feeling may play in raising the stature of mankind may be revealed to him.

This pronouncement speaks for itself. It spells out the school's responsibility for the teaching of music to every child. It implies the utter impossibility of one person alone doing this teaching effectively, and it implies the responsibility and help of each classroom teacher.

The supervisor helps toward this end but never replaces the teacher. Whenever he demonstrates with students, these contacts must result in (1) enriching what the classroom teacher is doing musically, and (2) illustrating a fine teaching technique. He must build rapport with the children—but not the same degree or kind of rapport as the regular classroom teacher has already developed with the same children. It should be a wonderful time for all, but not the kind that detracts from the loyalties the children have for their own teacher. The relationship should be one that strengthens the fine feeling that exists between the teacher and her students. A word of praise about the teacher to the students works wonders.

One cannot talk about the supervisor's relationship to the children unless one also considers the physical teaching locale, or arrangement. It is here where the children meet their instructor in a learner-instructor relationship. This relationship must be built up in order to dispose the learner to more effective learning. The supervisor's role ought to be to see to it that the atmosphere for the best possible relationship exists.

Public Relations and the Music Supervisor

Public relations takes into account the supervisor's out-of-school musical influence. The best PR program is what students tell their parents about their musical involvements.

> *As a citizen* he lets people know what a good job the school is trying to do for the children and community in musical matters. A favorable climate will have been set in the community for the continuation of good school music activities.
>
> *As an organizational worker* he may speak for music education to the Kiwanis Club, the Optimist Club, the Women's Club, or the many other organizations found in most communities. He may lead a community sing for some public function, or he may direct a community choral or instrumental group. No matter where he is, and no matter for what else he is known in the community, he still is regarded as the music leader. This regard and trust by the community must be encouraged in such a manner as to place the music program in a favorable light with the community.
>
> *As a Civic Music Leader.* One music supervisor is commentator for a well-known symphony orchestra. Another is known for his leadership in improving choral conducting through special clinics. Many supervisors serve on regional arts commissions, on civic music boards and on local symphony and opera boards.
>
> *Music Industry* represents a profession eager to extend its services to school and community, not only for personal gain, but for the promotion

of music ideals in the community. Many valuable services are performed by local firms for the promotion of music education. The music supervisor's dealing with them and the way he speaks of and for them can be of estimable influence on the program of music education in the local school district. In many areas they expend huge sums of money to benefit the music departments. In several areas well-known music firms stage week-long clinics each year to which teachers and students from the entire state and from several surrounding states are invited. Such clinics have in the past rivaled the finest music education sessions or workshops sponsored by universities and teachers' colleges. Music industry is noted for its research that affects many aspects of music learning.

Relations with the Private Music Teacher stand in much need of upgrading and professionalizing. This may not be within the immediate realm of the music supervisor. It may be within his province, however, to set up friendly relations with private teachers since each is trying to bring music to more people. Many indirect techniques can be used to encourage professionalization. The private teachers' best students are our soloists and accompanists.

Mass Media, the Press, Radio and TV are able to publicize what the school is trying to do. They are especially eager to highlight musical affairs of a school community. The news items, the radio reports and music programs, and the television programs including school music are only as good as the school wishes to make them. The newspaper. the radio station, and the television station all convey ideas. They edit them and put them into form, but they cannot inject educational thinking when there is none apparent. They cannot add quality to a performance. This is the place for the music supervisor. It is his responsibility to assist schools to present various aspects of music education in their best light. He needs to build goodwill with communications agencies. The picture that mass media presents can influence public support for music in the schools.

The Board of Education represents the school, community-wise, and represents the community to the school. The board must be kept informed, must be deferred to, and must be taken into confidence about music educational goals, ideals, and needs. At times, the supervisor may be asked to appear in person at a board meeting to explain the program and to answer questions. . . . The board is in a unique position to interpret the music education program to the community. It can also be a fairly valid sounding board of the community so that the music supervisor can know and better evaluate the program of music education as it appears to the people.

Relations with Peers in Music Supervision

It has been said by John Donne and in a modern song that no man is an island. The problems that confront the music supervisor are so many and varied that a single individual, no matter how esteemed and how qualified, cannot fully solve them. He must rely on the help and advice of others in similar positions. No music supervisor can assume that he is a better supervisor than the person in the next city or area. He may take a different approach to problems, since he deals with different people and different situations. Music supervisors need to know each other personally. They need to develop mutual respect. And they need to find ways of exchanging ideas so that each other's program is improved.

The many relationships in which all music supervisors are involved are keys to the success of a program. None of these can be ignored. The levels and areas of relationship necessarily do not carry equal weight; however, each is very important.

The teacher is the one who executes the program. All avenues of communication should point directly to the teacher. Nothing should be permitted to block a wholesome interchange of in-service ideas between her and the source. It is never a one-way street. No matter who the teacher, he or she is worthy of the music supervisor's most discreet consideration, because *it is at this level where the music program is made or broken.*

The wise supervisor does everything possible to keep all music learning channels open, all the way from the main office, the principal, and the teacher to the child.

QUESTIONS FOR DISCUSSION, THOUGHT AND STUDY

1. List the persons a music supervisor must contact before he can effectively work with a teacher.
2. What can happen if you work with a group of teachers from a school and no one tells the principal?
3. Devise a foolproof system of communication in a central school office.
4. Why is it necessary for professional consultants to know and to understand each other's work?
5. What is the role of a secretary in providing good communication?
6. How does the public interpret poor communications?
7. What is the role of the principal in the modern school?
8. Outline a program of working with principals that can elicit their support for the music program.
9. How would you get teachers to cooperate on the elementary music program?
10. Describe the prima donna kind of specialist and devise ways of getting his support.
11. What is the supervisor's relationship to the children in the classroom?
12. How, in your community, can the various musical and civic agencies contribute toward the school's music program?
13. What can you do in your area to get music supervisors to work together? Of what value is it? Do you believe in sharing ideas? Do you believe you have something good to offer? Do you really believe each

of your music supervision colleagues can offer something to you that you didn't think of?

NOTES

[1]Russel V. Morgan, "A Forward Looking Program for Music Education," from *Music, a Living Power,* (Morristown, N.J.: Silver Burdett Co.), 1954.

[2]Alice Miehl, *Changing the Curriculum,* (New York: Appleton-Century-Crofts, Inc., 1946), p. 110.

[3]Gordon Mackenzie and Stephen Corey, *Instruction Leadership,* (New York: Bureau of Publication, Teachers College, Columbia University, 1954), p. 64.

[4]John Bartky, *Supervision as Human Relations,* (Boston: D. C. Heath and Company, 1953), pp. 58-96.

[5]Donold Snygg and Arthur W. Combs, *Individual Behavior,* (New York: Harper and Brothers, 1949).

[6]Music Educators National Conference, Source Book No. 2, *Music in American Education,* (Washington, D.C.: MENC, 1955), p. 298.

Part III

The Music Supervisor's Responsibilities

...the music program
...the curriculum
...the learning situations
...the flow of materials

SYMPHONY no. 40 in G MINOR

First Movement

Molto Allegro

W. A. Mozart 1756-1791

Pat. pending

Donald Barra

Chapter 7

Administering
the Music Program

Program Administration, the Job of Music Supervisors

Music supervision is a growth-implementation program that must be administered. It presupposes that administrative responsibilities go with promoting a good music supervision program. There is no separation of function or philosophy in administering and supervising a program of music education.

Music supervision must grow out of the needs experienced at the teaching-learning level and should return to this level if learning is to be affected and improved. In order to set up a program that emphasizes a *job to be done* and goals to be reached, these are some basic considerations:

1. Obtaining base-line data in terms of where we are going.
2. Setting up realistic educational objectives and finding the program and means to get there. This means: finding out areas to be improved: personnel, instruments, music, music equipment or grade by grade articulation, etc. Where should the immediate emphasis be placed? And what should be the long-range emphasis?
3. Determining the additives needed to improve the program. Let's say you want twice as many string players in the ninth grade who are able to perform at a year higher level than present string players; are you going to settle for the chorus teacher getting them?
4. Developing better ways of working together to streamline the means so that one may realize the projected goals. This means improving communications.
5. Putting into operation the best possible music education means that give assurance that objectives will be reached.[1]

The effective administration of a means program must be expressed in terms of end goals and a complementary process. Musically speaking, how do we want second graders to act when they become sixth graders? What do we want on a national basis, on the state level, the county level, the city level, the medium-sized city level, the small city level, and in the rural school, in terms of over a period of years? And, what are the *immediate* steps that need to be taken at each level in order to assure these expectations?

Short-term goals must complement and feed into the great *long-range* goals.

One must keep in mind that *the classroom is the basic unit in a school system. The teacher is the basic operator.* What the school recognizes and determines as its need, is, for the time being, vastly more important than what the supervisory organization determines. Music supervision will be ineffective to the extent that it ignores the felt and expressed needs of those who are on the firing line—the teachers. Administration is that implementive aspect that steers the program to pre-set goals.

Coordinated effort is needed to administer a means-program of music supervision prudently. Those responsible for the program and those responsible for teaching must have a good understanding of the balance between the *immediate* and the *long-range*. This involves simultaneous moving in certain directions. Spear's[2] suggestion for a coordinated program, adapted for the area of music supervision, may have value here:

A COORDINATED MEANS PROGRAM OF MUSIC SUPERVISION

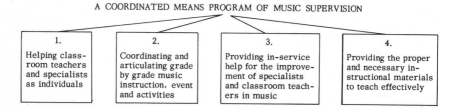

1.	2.	3.	4.
Helping class- room teachers and specialists as individuals	Coordinating and articulating grade by grade music instruction, event and activities	Providing in-service help for the improve- ment of specialists and classroom teach- ers in music	Providing the proper and necessary in- structional materials to teach effectively

The Four Overlapping Fronts of Music Supervision

Helping classroom teachers and specialists, coordinating and articulating grade music instruction, providing in-service help for all concerned in music instruction, and providing instructional materials are four special kinds of supervisory overlapping services with each dependent on the other. Together, these services form a coordinated supervisory front when channeled through the regular program. Separate, it would be difficult for any of these to stand alone and still be effective.

If each of these services is objective centered, there will be less opportunity for random activity on the part of the music supervisor. This coordinated front is the supervisor's program. The many activities of the supervisor must reflect the direction of the means and directly affect the goals. The one hundred listed activities maintain their validity as facilitators of the means as long as they fit into the *total coordinated program* and lead to the goals. (See page 124-129 ff.)

A coordinated program prevents even the best of us from going on a one-track binge. The following diagrams point up what we are talking about. In the first illustration each of the music supervision services of means-facilitators act independently on each school and on the learning situation, causing a goal-less activity. On the second chart all the facilitating services are channeled through the *coordinated way* as part of the total effort to serve the schools of a city or county.[3]

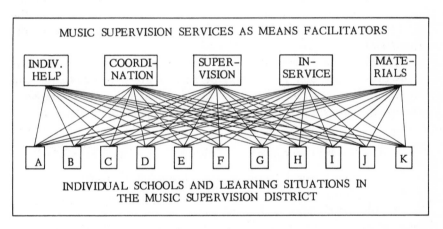

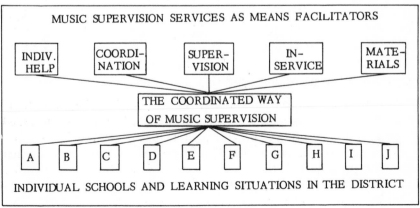

The diagrams place the emphasis on means, and point out the importance of moving forward with facilitating services through a coordinated effort on to the operational level. Planning around the work, thinking, attitudes, and needs of the individual teacher and school will help to draw supervision into perspective, but only through coordinated effort. Supervision thus remains the handmaiden of general and special music programs, originating from teacher and student needs and desires.

Coordination is the process that funnels the facilitating services through a single organized front. It is the aspect of the music program which is initiated at the local level, evolving from the needs of the teacher and the school. All complementary talents, materials, and devices can then be focused on the means. Thus resulting action will be close to the local situation where it is to do some good, and can have a better chance at reaching goals.

The most important cog in the machinery of good music supervision is *planning with the school principal and the teachers.* Planning will avoid the traditional pitfalls resulting from calling teachers together for trivialities.

A music supervision program must be administered by someone. It is of the essence that this person be sufficiently *product-oriented* that the irrelevancies of the maze of misguided and ill-conceived processes do not obscure the *program* and fail to affect the *objectives.*

The Administrator of the Music Supervisory Program[4]

The administrator of such a music supervision program must be performing tasks that are goal seeking in nature. These tasks need to reflect the needs and desires of those at the operational level, the teachers themselves.

Wherever a good music supervisory program has been accepted, the emphasis is on filling such needs as facilitate the means in the direction of the objectives. This is a *job to be done* regardless of who does it.

These are some of the things that the music supervisor-administrator can be doing:

1. Help to organize ways to achieve the goals of music education
2. Contribute corroborative ideas at faculty meetings
3. Assist schools with formulation of ground rules that will facilitate the program
4. Help schools utilize proper supplementary materials from a central library

5. Advise with administrators as to selection of special music person-nel and musically trained classroom teachers
6. Keep teacher informed on new materials that will facilitate the program
7. Encourage teachers to list music teaching problems
8. Help teachers to organize extracurricular music activities
9. Plan with teachers for the use of music resources in other learning areas
10. Advise schools in the selection of evaluation devices and in their proper use and interpretation. Do they fit the objectives?
11. Help teachers evaluate growth in musicality of children; and de-termine interim goals in light of progress
12. Search for new and better procedures to reach goals
13. Make music enrichment materials available to teachers
14. Arrange for outside experts to help teachers
15. Prepare radio and television programs interpreting aspects of the total music program
16. Assist in preparing materials designed to help the beginning teacher teach music
17. Prepare and disseminate suggestions and directions for use of teach-ing materials
18. Prepare notices and announcements relative to music programs, items of music interest to either teachers, students, or specialist, or notices about concerts, special programs, or in-service meetings, etc.
19. Guide teachers toward better insights through study of child and adolescent psychology as it relates to musical growth
20. Demonstrate music teaching techniques with students for teachers' groups
21. Help teachers utilize to best advantage undesirable teaching situa-tions such as crowded facilities and unattractive quarters. This does not mean to encourage satisfaction with poor conditions, but to help utilize these so teaching can go on uninterrupted
22. Arrange opportunities for teachers to observe work in other schools
23. Serve as a resource person to schools in the promotion of musical resources such as films, records, special enrichment books, and many other aids
24. Work closely with building principals in soliciting their participa-tion in implementing an effective program of music education
25. Work with Parent-Teacher groups for the promotion of music in home and school
26. Give teachers clues on how to watch for musical growth in an individual child. Clues should be in terms of objectives
27. Help teachers devise continuous evaluation instruments to de-termine whether they are still headed toward the goals

28. Prepare exhibits pertaining to various aspects of the music education program for presentation and availability to teacher or lay groups
29. Arrange for teacher-student trips to large musical events, for instance, to see an opera, or a ballet
30. Prepare periodic activity reports for the central office in terms of goals
31. Prepare in-service bulletins to assist different aspects of classroom music teaching
32. Help teacher groups to reexamine their daily schedules in order to include music instruction as a regular consideration
33. Help classroom teachers plan activities in music that will contribute toward continuous musical growth toward goals
34. Confer with teachers and administrators in a process of "taking a look at what we are doing at this point," and review "where do we go from here?"
35. Help schools establish individual guidelines that can be a gauge testing the quality of progress and process toward a desired music education
36. Encourage use of audiovisual materials to the extent that they contribute toward a desired goal
37. Encourage schools to set up music shelves in their library containing supplementary and enrichment materials
38. Encourage the development of grade or interest level study groups to improve aspects of the music program
39. Develop program of public relations for music in the community
40. Attend educational conferences to bring back new ideas
41. Serve as liaison between local district and nearby college
42. Find demonstration teachers to present new techniques in teaching various aspects of the music program
43. Help teachers set up experimental programs utilizing new ideas in their own classrooms (purpose: to find better means to achieve objectives)
44. Prepare resource reading lists around topics that meet individual teacher needs
45. Promote interclass visits of students so that, for instance, a fifth grade can observe a second grade doing some play-party games.
46. Arrange for parent visits to schools to observe interesting musical activities
47. Prepare news releases about aspects of the music program
48. Provide for exchange assembly programs and exchange classroom visitations between neighboring schools
49. Assist the local district with materials such as records, autoharps, song bells
50. Help teachers find library materials

51. Urge membership in music educators groups for special music teachers
52. Make presentation before the local board concerning the program
53. Help administrators evaluate the process of music instruction in terms of goals
54. Help set up music in-service meetings for teachers
55. Contribute to the preparing of courses of study and teaching guides so that music education is represented on an equitable basis with other learning areas
56. Work with civic and professional music groups to extend their programs to schools
57. Help orient new teachers to teaching classroom music
58. Promote music instruction in the special classes of the school. (M-R, gifted, etc.)
59. Help teachers in proper use of audiovisual equipment
60. Help administrators screen candidates for music positions and aid them in placement of musically talented classroom teachers and specialists, so that the various buildings or schools can maintain a balanced music program
61. Arrange for area clinics and workshop programs to care for the needs of both specialists and classroom teachers
62. Help in setting up music festivals
63. Work with other educational leaders in supervision and administration to coordinate the entire educational program
64. Allow time daily to take care of routine matters such as phone calls, mail requests, salesmen, and private conferences with teachers about specific music problems
65. Help teachers become conscious of a good physical atmosphere for the teaching of music
66. Promote school consciousness of the value of general music education
67. Speak to civic groups and service clubs about the school music program
68. Help organize teacher study groups around specific music teaching problems
69. Introduce teachers to newly adopted materials and music guides
70. Assist teachers in finding a program of music education in a new series of books
71. Make surveys of the use made of music educational materials to determine future needs
72. Help new music teachers adjust to teaching situations
73. Obtain teacher opinion on their desires as to in-service program content
74. Advise teachers to take evening and summer school courses to build up musicality

75. Assist teachers seeking employment elsewhere. Advise them, and help them
76. Help special music teachers evaluate their physical needs in the music program. Suggest a several-year plan of financing purchase of instruments and equipment
77. Help schools outline needs when contemplating the building of a music department
78. Advise in teacher transfer in order to assure a balance of music teaching talent in the schools
79. Provide periodic reports as to the progress of the program. Such reports ought to be process-centered in terms of product
80. Survey current educational literature and music education writings
81. Sift newly acquired knowledge into usable form for teachers
82. Let teachers know about other teachers' successes in using new techniques
83. Conduct orientation workshops for principals to inform them of their role in music education
84. Serve on committees of music education organizations. Such working committees can tend to be time- and energy-consuming though most valuable to the job
85. Assist large educational agencies survey city- and area-wide music education needs, especially through new developmental centers
86. Assist formation of educational policies at local, regional, state, and national levels
87. Assist a teacher so she can be free to do a creative job. Can this mean taking over her class while she runs to the stock room for some bit of needed material?
88. Assist in developing an area-wide coordinated school music program by working closely with several music consultants
89. Prepare guidelines on screening students for special performing music classes
90. Interpret school, regional, and state policies to teachers in the local schools. This is a necessity because of teacher mobility
91. Serve as a liaison officer between specialist and professional music organizations
92. Assist in developing leadership in especially talented teachers
93. Assist teachers in developing student leadership (allowing students to organize small ensembles)
94. Provide opportunities for teachers to share music teaching ideas with others
95. Promote professionalization of teachers by encouraging them in graduate work
96. Encourage potential music supervisors by providing them with leadership opportunities

97. Develop television programs for student learning at various grade levels
98. Promote multimedia in-service programs for teachers in various areas of music education
99. Provide rotation of materials to facilitate certain kinds of musical experiences
100. Preview music teaching materials and devices

These one hundred activities are among the many things a music supervisor is called upon to perform. Each of these contributes toward the total program or means if it has the goals in mind, and if it originated from the needs of the teaching situation.

These items can be categorized, some as administrative and some as supervisory; many items belong to the overlapping areas of the administration and supervision of the music program.

Administrative or Supervisory?

1. Personnel
2. Budget
3. Building
4. Rooms, rehearsal, office, storage, etc.
5. Materials, music
6. Equipment
7. Program evaluation
8. Personnel evaluation
9. Progress evaluation
10. Curriculum development and implementation
11. Direct supervisory services to teachers and schools
12. Indirect service to teachers and schools
13. Coordination service
14. Promotional activity
15. Public relations activity

If these activities arise from the local teaching situation and are guided by a goal-centered philosophy of music education, then they become part of a path making up a coordinated program of music education. Each of these categories and activities is a significant part of the total program. Operated as a coordinated effort such a program exerts greater strength than is ascertainable in the individual activities listed.

These are among the many kinds of activities that can take place at each of the supervisorial levels. *Supervision is the means; administration is the implementation of the means.*

The humble man in the unknown school does the same things in order to present a coordinated program of music education as does his big city colleague. The chief difference is in the climate and in the complexity of the particular school community.

Music's slice in the educational pie is ideally the same in every kind of community. The actual difference is in the quality of leadership that administers the program. Quality is not necessarily the exclusive property of bigness.

We know of a man who administered a music education program in a small town in the Midwest for over thirty years. He had a band, an orchestra, and a choral group in the local high school. He taught and supervised the music program in the elementary grades. Years ago he taught most of the parents of the children he had in school. The music education of the children began at the cradle, because the parents of these youngsters had been embued with musical ideals. When they entered school they had what is frequently called readiness for music. Music played a prominent part in early childhood, in the elementary grades and throughout high school. When they left school they either married a miner or worked in the mines. At night they played in the civic band or symphony orchestra. The community music activities were also directed by this man. He directed the total music program. He administered it, and he supervised it from cradle through adulthood. The factor in that community was this one man. As the local music teacher and the music administrator, he gave to this community a musical heritage that has lasted for over a generation.

The center or hub of the program is that part of it that directly affects music learning by boys and girls. This illustrative diagram depicts the focus of a supervisory program on the teaching-learning situation, or the hub of the educational wheel. It also points to the objectives as goals to which the total program must be guided.[5] The direction of the total hub within the *teaching-learning* cone toward the target indicates a nonstatic situation. (Something that is *objective-directed* must happen.)

What actually occurs at the hub, and what emanates from it is important. A good program of music supervision grows out of the classroom and returns to enrich it. It is easy for us to be active around the outer rim of a program without ever affecting the learning situation in a positive way. It is easy to engage in many music activities and still not affect the classroom. If supervision is to count it must take place in and close to the learner. The music administrator has the obligation to point the effort toward the objective.

The pattern of American music supervision as revealed in various sources does not reflect an ideal program. *MENC Research Bulletin No. 18* relates things as they are, and as various writers have found

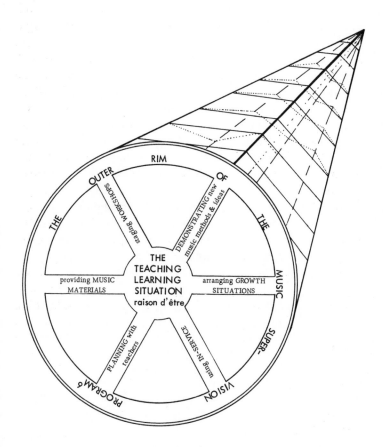

them to exist in various situations. Music supervision is on the run. Districts are dissatisfied with status jobs that do not affect goals.

As of 1952 no more than fifty-one per cent of city schools over 2,500 population employed a music supervisor[6]; and no more than 21 per cent of rural superintendencies employed the services of a music supervisor. However, music supervision positions do occur with greater frequency than any other supervisory positions. While 51 per cent of city schools employ a music supervisor, only 4.5 per cent of city schools employ a supervisor of curriculum, and 6 per cent employ a reading supervisor. Even though much leadership in music education was discontinued during the post-Sputnik era, there seems to have occurred a rethinking of the function of the music supervisor, and positions are being reinstated in many areas as of 1967.

The administration of the music program is a two-way road. Its failure in many places is because one or the other way had been blocked. Its success is dependent not only on musical understanding and prowess, but on the educational thinking and leadership of its own leaders. Music supervision must see and reckon with the total educational picture. It must understand education, its principles and its goals, so that it can remain part of it. However, in the process it dare not become engulfed by temporary educational theories.

The music supervisor must know the process of education so well that he can apply it to the musical growth and development of the child. He can let music contribute toward understandings in other learning areas; however, he dare not let it be swallowed up by other areas just in order to perpetuate a notion of integration of subject matter.

> Music is an integrative force that can enrich lives wherever it is used, and in whichever connotation it is applied. So—in order to administer a program of music education, top consideration must be given the concept that music takes its place in the curriculum only "when the integrity of its own status as an art is maintained."[7]

Only true music educational leadership can bring this about. And only when music is placed in the curriculum for its unique contribution toward the good life will it become most effective. When this is accomplished, it will not matter so much in which vehicle it presents itself; it will matter that it is there in its magnificent effectiveness.

The only answer for accomplishing this ideal lies in the direction of leadership. Until leadership effort is unified and coordinated, music supervision, even in its present relative state of esteem, is but a handmaiden of transitory whims. Currently, not much more than two-thirds of the state departments of education have considered music of sufficient importance to have it represented with a leadership position at the state level. Its influence will be limited as long as music's uniqueness in the educative process is not officially recognized.

Direction for Modern Music Supervision

United States Office of Education

The Arts and Humanities Division in the United States Office of Education maintains a special office fostering the position of Music Specialist. This office ought to attract the finest music education leadership available in this country. The music specialist can be a genuine stimulant and a unifying agent for a nationwide coordinated program of music education. Such a post could assure similarity of philosophy but diversification of application in the various parts of the country. It should have at its command the means to initiate and continue much needed basic research. It can also assume leadership in working closely with the large universities, encouraging them to set up research projects. Part of its mission could conceivably be in such areas as setting up nationally financed music education programs televised to the many schools for whom music is not available on a regular basis. These and many other projects could be originated and encouraged by the Music Specialist in the United States Office of Education. With the current national thrust this office can carry much weight in encouraging use of federal funds and encouraging cooperative research aid.

State Supervision

As of 1966, state departments of education of 34 of the 50 states list a supervisor of music on their staffs. The number of positions has almost doubled during the past seven years; nevertheless, some of the largest states are still without state music leadership. Before such a position is set up in a particular state, it would be well for the state to consider most seriously what the sphere of influence of this post should be; what peculiar orientation its leader ought to have; and what freedom its leader would have in doing the job as he sees fit in the light of its being a positive contributory factor toward, not only improved instruction in music, but also, increased acceptance of musical values of life. Its ideal should be to promote music education in each town, in each distant rural community, and in each classroom of a large city school so that the effects of music will be a potent force operating to the full development of the child throughout the entire school system. These are some of the suggested areas of influence and some of the lines of communication that such a state music director could utilize (see p. 134).

A National Conference to Improve the Effectiveness of State Supervision of Music was sponsored by New York University and the United

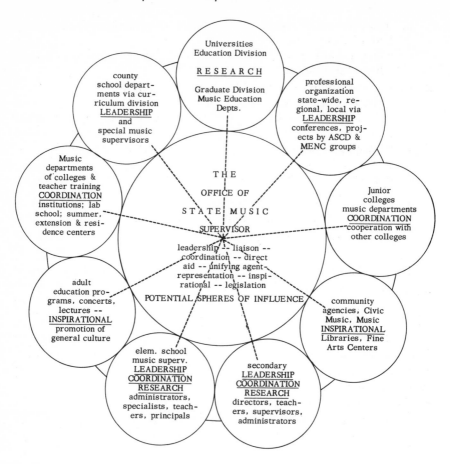

States Office of Education in 1965. The resulting research project was terminated in January 1966. Its director was Roger Phelps. Chapter II of the research report contains significant findings relating to both elementary and secondary levels.

1. These were considerations for the elementary level:
   a. teaching of musical concepts through learning experiences
   b. giving more attention to musical needs and capacities of children
   c. curriculum guides should be flexible and adaptable to changing social and cultural needs of individuals
   d. the teaching of musical skills so children grow in musical understanding
   These were considerations for the secondary level:
   a. encouraging teaching music history through performing groups

b. utilization of flexible and modular scheduling to bring about better music programs

c. wider use of humanities courses as a way to relate music functionally to the other arts

2. Responsibilities of state supervision of music were listed:
   a. assisting in the selection of textbooks
   b. helping local districts to institute, expand, and improve music programs
   c. serving as liaison between lay and professional groups
   d. promoting state art councils
   e. organizing and assisting with in-service workshops and clinics for classroom teachers
   f. maintaining legislative reference and vigilance
   g. assisting in the certification of music teachers
   h. transacting communications as needed to keep the field informed

Eleven implications for further study were approved. These ranked all the way from finding better ways to teach through more effective ways to supervise. It is hoped that in future years this group will attack the problem of leadership.

Where there is no state music supervision, music supervisory groups have developed their own leadership. Their network of supervisory organizations interests itself in many of the legitimate projects about which the state music supervisor be concerned.

This chart shows a feasible function of the music supervision members of the Association for Supervision and Curriculum Development and its affiliates in the absence of state leadership. In some states this leadership is assumed by the state music educator associations and its network of officers. In several states both the A.S.C.D. and MENC state groups have joined forces to fill the void (p. 166).

It is admirable that these adjustments have taken place. At least a minimum of leadership is guaranteed thereby. This leadership is given by people who already have full-time positions. In some states the influence of these various arrangements has been outstanding, but its affectivity value could be still greater if an official state leadership position existed. There are many things that organizations alone can't do. For instance, in one very large state less than half of the counties employ a full-time supervisor of music education. A task for a state music supervisor would be to work with such areas to promote the employment of proper music supervisional personnel. If some of the counties are too small to support one person in this position, then two or three counties could contract together for such service. Arrange-

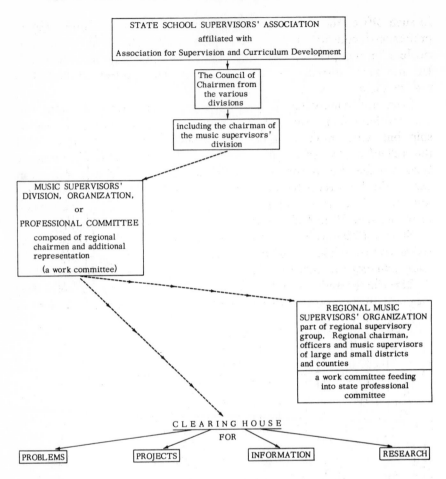

ments of this sort, and such things as course of study development, promotional bulletins, and myriads of other vital things could be handled through one state office. The need exists, and it ought to be met.

County

All county education departments ought to employ a music supervisor. Such a position would guarantee equality of musical opportunities to all children. It could coordinate the music educational efforts of the many districts by providing inspirational leadership. The position of the county music supervisor has grown in stature over the past many years in several states fostering large county school central offices.

In such offices the music supervisor is part of a staff of thirty or more professional educational consultants. He speaks for music in the curriculum in the places where the curriculum planning is being done. He also helps districts to determine their own musical needs and to resolve them.

State and county music supervision has a somewhat different role than the individual district. It is a position of music educational leadership but with emphasis on service, especially over and above what the individual district is able to supply. It can be a unifying influence tying together the music programs of the many individual schools. It can do this because it has the total picture of the *state of music education* in a given area, and from this point can determine what needs to be done to fill in lacks or improve a total program.

State and county supervisors are more able to analyze local supervision problems because of the experience of seeing and working with many situations in other districts or in other areas of a state.

The county and the state officer has the freedom to promote ideas that will further the total music educational program. He has less to

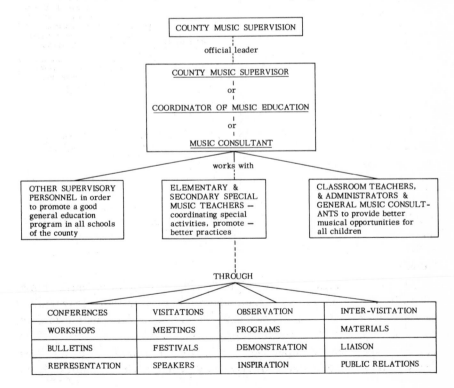

CONFERENCES	VISITATIONS	OBSERVATION	INTER-VISITATION
WORKSHOPS	MEETINGS	PROGRAMS	MATERIALS
BULLETINS	FESTIVALS	DEMONSTRATION	LIAISON
REPRESENTATION	SPEAKERS	INSPIRATION	PUBLIC RELATIONS

do with the line and staff administrative arrangement because his central office is essentially set up as a service center. But he is in a position to initiate new ideas and to promote action research. He deals chiefly with *long-range* goals. It is the nature of his job.

The District

The district supervisor exercises his administrative prerogative best *in leading toward* instead of in *seeing to it that*. Many districts have the grave problem of very frequent consultant turnover. It appears that failure of the consultant often is the result of lack of communication between various branches of the school system. The administrator, when hiring the music consultant, does not always give a clear picture of the expected scope of responsibility; and the consultant tries to assume something for which the school is not ready. These are among the many problems:

1. Now we have a music consultant, what do we do?
2. The principals have not been told, and the consultant is expected to make her peace with each one separately. This often takes several months, if at all.
3. Some districts want a relief teacher only, but are willing to call her a supervisor.
4. Some want a demonstrator.
5. Some want an in-service program operator.
6. Others want a combination.
7. Others don't want anything.

Each school district of forty teachers ought to have the service of a music teaching specialist. For every one-hundred-fifty classroom teachers, there ought to be a full-time nonteaching music consultant. In large systems there ought to be a part-time public school music specialist in each unit of fifty elementary teachers. In still larger systems there ought to be a music director and several supervising assistants: (See chart on page 139.) A formula could be developed based on (1) what needs to be done, and (2) how many people does it take to do the job?

A very large city can expand on this idea proportionately in its many categories. Some of the ideas spelled out here are intended principally for those in the process of setting up music consultancies and for those wanting to become consultants. The music administrator of the large city school system or of a state or large county usually has had many years' experience in many kinds of programs. His organizational structure can serve as a model for other systems.

No organizational structure can serve as an ideal model unless it spells out the dynamics of the individual and of the situation at work within its framework.

These are suggested frameworks and suggested activities that go into administering a program of music education and a program of music supervision. It is a job to be done with infinitesimally many small activities and tasks. A real concern is to find ways of implementing such a program.

The suggested ratios are merely relative figures. No one can devise a proper teacher-music consultant ratio that would be apropos for all situations. There remains the conflict in educational thinking whether a music specialist should do the classroom music teaching or whether the classroom teacher should do this with the help of a specialist, consultant, supervisor, or what you will. Of greater importance is to find effective ways of reaching teachers. And these cannot always be measured in terms of half time or full time, or in hours or minutes.

(This may be a basic structure for many large city schools; it is expanded by the utilization of additional special supervisors, possibly

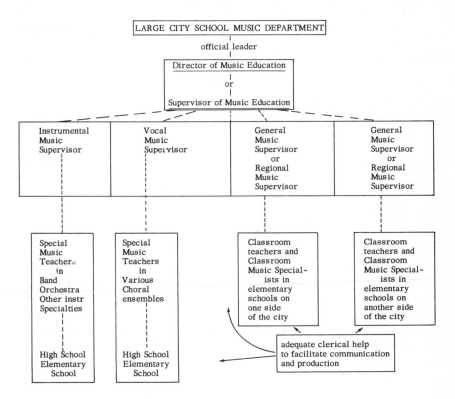

some assigned to the elementary schools only, also others assigned to the secondary schools. In several large systems there is a core of elementary consultants, each assigned four to six elementary buildings. The director or supervisor in charge works primarily in the area of developing unified program and in coordinating city-wide music efforts.)

QUESTIONS FOR DISCUSSION, THOUGHT AND STUDY

1. Differentiate between the role of music supervision and the role of administering a program of music education. Where does one leave off and the other take over?
2. What is meant when one says that music supervision is a job that needs to be done?
3. Do you agree with the five listed considerations about music supervision? What considerations would you add to this list?
4. What is the difference between long-range and immediate goals? In what ways can they be related? When are they not related?
5. Defend the stand that the classroom is the basic unit in a school system and the teacher the basic operator.
6. What are the four overlapping fronts in music supervision? How are they part of a coordinated program?
7. Classify the one-hundred activities in which the music administrator engages. How can these activities reflect a coordinated program? How do they contribute to goals?
8. Name a number of typical supervisory activities that can easily detract from the job at hand. How can a coordinated program prevent this from happening?
9. How can the federal government in its Education Division give leadership to the fine arts?
10. In what ways ought individual states provide music education leadership? Give reasons for and against official state leadership, that is, the position of state supervisor of music education.
11. Write to several state departments to obtain information about their music education leadership status. Find out what those who maintain a music supervisor do in regard to leadership to the various types and levels of music education within the state.
12. What is the emerging role of a county music consultant? Write to several counties that have a music supervisor to get complete information on activities.
13. Devise an equitable music supervisory distribution for various-sized districts. Take into account the many necessary activities besides classroom visitation and demonstration.
14. What part of a supervision program should be the classroom demonstration and visitation kind?

NOTES

[1]Harold Spears, *Improving the Supervision of Instruction,* (New York: Prentice-Hall, Inc., 1953), p. 149.

[2]Spears, *op. cit.*, p. 150.

[3]Spears, *op. cit.*, p. 159.

[4]Spears, *op. cit.*, p. 172 ff.

[5]Spears, *op. cit.*, p. 269, adapted from.

[6]CMEA and CASCD Committee, *Teachers Guide to Teaching Music in the Elementary School*, (Sacramento: Calif. State Dept. of Ed., 1963).

[7]Roger Phelps, "Resume of Final Report National Conference on State Supervision of Music," *MENC Journal*, Vol. 53, No. 1, Sept. 1966, p. 131.

M. Hohner, Inc., Hicksville, L.I.

Chapter 8

Administering
the Music Curriculum

Music Curriculum

What Is the Music Curriculum?

The music curriculum represents the many experiences, facts, and knowledges that are known to contribute positively toward the development of attitudes, habits, skills, feelings and activities of persons recognized as possessing musicality.

Music curricula are based on the best we know now of how people become musical. We are merely at the threshold of understanding human behavior and learning, also of understanding the intricacies of musical learning, musical behavior, and musical development. It would be preferable to establish the signposts identifying a *musical* person and then find the best process to attain the goal.

There are certain indispensible ingredients that are known to translate an orderly sequence of musical events or experiences from a written course of study into an active curriculum. They are:

1. The course of study, facilitating the process in terms of product
2. The people—personnel—music supervisors, administrators, teachers, children
3. Ideas—program—the content that points to the product. The sequential music learning program
4. Materials to illustrate and facilitate the plans and ideas—books, music, equipment, and instruments—(things that help the process)
5. Space—place—to carry out organized plans—buildings, rooms, stages, storage room, office, studio, practice rooms—(the incubator and nursery for the product)

6. Wherewithal—money—to buy and pay for each of the above aspects of the music curriculum—(the external stimulus, the "carrot," the pay-off, the materialistic incentive).

The above ingredients mixed together in proper proportion, with due care for the *goals* results in the *curriculum*, the teaching-learning-situation or the total interaction between teachers, students, ideas, materials, facilities, energizers, facilitators, and the affected territory (community)—to the extent that a "musical" person evolves (the product).

These are also effective in *changing* curricula, and in their improvement. Consequently, these questions are important considerations:

1. How do we arrive at a music curriculum?
2. How do we implement the accepted music curriculum?
3. How do we change the music curriculum?
4. Why do we change the music curriculum?
5. How do we improve the music curriculum?
6. How do we go about putting the proper value on the effectiveness of the curriculum?

The American public, the fathers and mothers, want the finer things in life for their children. They want to dress up their communities, adorn their churches and public places, and to gladden their hearts with music. They turned the problem of their desires over to the schools, saying, in essence, "We will buy this product—you furnish the process that achieves this."

The community's demand for music in the curriculum explains why the many and varied types of music programs exist in the schools today. (1) There is a demand for *culture for all.* (2) There is a need to develop artistry, in order to delight the supporting community and to impress neighboring communities. Hence the two types of music curricula in the schools.

The Music Curricula in American Elementary and Secondary Schools

These are the two types of music curricula found in both the elementary and the secondary schools:

1. The general music program—intended for all children, especially for nonperformers
2. The special music program—intended for those who can succeed and benefit from specialized music instruction

A program of general music for the elementary grades is rather universally accepted in most states, even though such a program or course of study may not be implemented fully. Nevertheless, there is a positive awareness of its existence.

To the same degree is the special music program accepted and practiced in the secondary schools, whereas the general music program (or the program originally intended for all) leaves much to be desired in its implementation.

The General Music Curriculum in the Elementary Grades

There are two probable answers to how we arrived at a general music curriculum in the elementary school:

1. Music enthusiasts like Lowell Mason started the trend over a century ago to see whether music, as a school subject, was feasible and to find out whether children in schools could profit by instruction in music.
2. The writers of graded music books have been responsible for general music programs in use in the elementary schools. The presence of graded books alone implied a sequential learning program of acceptable scope.

Ideas which seemed to have produced marked musicality after careful and prolonged application were arranged in logical sequences. It was supposed that if the contents of the books were taught in proper sequence, there could evolve a generation of musical people. Observed flaws led to further search by consecrated music educators, so that now we have the elementary music curriculum broken up into the various *activities* or *skill areas*. These activities presented as a unified whole contribute toward bringing the child closer to music. The activities are the course around which the modern elementary music curriculum revolves.

1. *Listening activities,* or skill in—is of prime importance because there is no music unless it is heard and listened to. *Music is transmitted to the person who listens actively.*
2. *Rhythmic activities* are of importance because all music moves in regular and irregular fashion. Also, man tends to respond to music's rhythm by sympathetic bodily movement responses.
3. *Singing activities* are of importance because more people sing than do any other musical activity; also singing is produced by the most universal of all instruments, the human voice.
4. *Music reading activities* are important because they involve the intellectual process of translating the visual symbolism of music into sound. These activities are also of prime importance in the production and reproduction of music for posterity.

5. The activities involving the playing of musical instruments are important because they involve a mechanical process or skill of producing music from other than the human instrument. Playing on musical instruments reinforces learning, kinesthetically.

Skill in these activities is recognized as contributing positively toward a desired growth in musicality. The integrated application of all of these activities is a more positive influence toward musicality than is each of these activities. Thus, in the presentation of a single song the instructor utilizes all the activities simultaneously with the assurance that each will reach out to make music more meaningful.

Note the several activities involved in the presentation of songs:

Suggested Song Sequence
Grade Two

Song Title	Page	Record		Activities Involved:							
		Teacher's Book	Album JS	Music Reading	Singing	Instrument Playing	Rhythm	Listening	Creative Response	Parallel Listening
September-October:										
Wake Up	2		8251	X	X	X			X	
Breakfast	5		8251		X	X	X		X	
Telling Time	36		8253	X	X	X	X	X	X	
Clocks and Watches	3			X	X	X	X	X		X
Leaky Faucets	6		8251	X	X	X	X	X	X	X
Will You Play with Me?	20		8252	X	X	X			X	
Jumping Rope	8		8252	X	X	X	X	X	X	
This Old Man	88			X	X	X			X	
My Kitty	13		8251		X			X	X	
It's Hallowe'en Tonight	113			X	X				X	X
Boo!	114		8259	X	X	X			X	X
Shake My Hand	46		8254	X	X			X	X	X
November:										
Trees in Autumn	110		8259		X		X	X	X	
Like a Leaf	111				X	X			X	
Who Can It Be?	19		8252		X	X			X	
Mr. Duck and Mr. Turkey	116		8259		X	X	X	X	X	
Harvest	107		8258		X		X		X	
Making Cookies	10		8251	X	X	X		X	X	
We're Going Round the Mountain	47		8254		X		X	X	X	
Ally-Galoo-Galoo	102				X		X		X	
Over the River	114			X	X	X	X		X	
Thanksgiving	111				X					
I'm Going to Sing	46				X	X	X		X	

Most publishers of graded music books prepare scope and sequence charts indicating grade level expectations; also the various kinds of activities that can be engaged in at various levels.

SCOPE AND SEQUENCE CHART BASED ON RECOGNIZED GROWTH PATTERNS[1]

	GRADE I HOME AND SCHOOL	GRADE II SCHOOL AND NEIGHBORHOOD	GRADE III NEIGHBORHOOD, STATE, REGION	GRADE IV UNITED STATES	GRADE V WESTERN HEMISPHERE	GRADE VI WORLD
Learning to Use the Voice to Sing	Unison songs----	simple two note ostinati----	two-part rounds; simple descants----	harmony tones; simple descants----; 2, 3, and 4 part rounds and canons; descants and ostinati; 2-part songs		Three-part songs
Learn to Respond to the Rhythm in Music Through	Free, rhythmic movement and simple patterned dances----	dramatization of songs and program music----	creating dance steps and simple folk dances----	square dances----		polka, waltz and other national dances----
Learning to Make Music on Instruments Such as	Rhythm instruments; bells, triangles, ----drums----Indian drums----	Autoharp, 1&2 chord songs----three-chord songs	Keyboard instruments; piano, organ, resonator bells, melodica----; Song flutes----recorders----	Latin American percussion--ethnic percussive instr.----; diminished chords--new ways of strumming----zither--folk instruments----ukele----simple guitar chords; band and orchestra instruments----		
Learning to Respond to Music Creatively By	Creating verses and new tunes; responding to musical questions and phrases----	adding introductions and codas----	improvising ostinati and descants; creating rhythmic patterns in movement----; making up word to melodies	making up melodies to fit mood of poems----; making up pentatonic songs--using simple harmony--applying simple A B, A B A and A B A C A D A--making up accompaniments and second parts		
Learning to Make Music Out of Representational Symbols By	Dramatizing tonal contrasts.. drawing melodic contours**; Relating sounds to notation----	Recognizing symbols, relating text to notation; rhythmic and melodic patterns:	1-chord, time signatures; dynamic markings----	recognizing phrases; identifying notes; sight-singing--; Key of F and G; uneven rhythm patterns; minor scale----; Key of D, Bb and e minor; construct minor scale; understand 6/8; study V and V7; know key signatures--	G clef; home tone; scales in tunes; relative note values; recognizing simple	Irregular meter and phrase construction; 1-chord in minor; g and d minor; intervals; melodic skips; accidental triplets; sequences, interpretative directions--
Learning to Internalize Music By Listening	Environmental music----		broadened regional music and simple music of significance with easily noted form----	U.S. Composers; recognizing harmonic, melodic and form content----; Latin American and Canadian m----understanding; more complicated rhythms; Great composers of the world		

The Specialized Music Programs in the Elementary Schools

The specialized music programs in the elementary school require specially trained and skilled teachers. The acclaim the special music programs receive is justifiable only to the extent that it is the outward manifestation of a good general music program.

The specialized music program revolves about these three major music organizational activities: (1) the band, (2) the orchestra, (3) the chorus.

The following could well be a format for organizational instruction, which includes regularly scheduled (1) full band, orchestra, or chorus; (2) sectional practice with like instruments or voices; (3) basic technique; (4) solo classes to develop poise and musicianship as an individual; (5) performing or singing in small ensembles.

No standardized schedule can be set up that fits each type of school community. The following is a minimum schedule for small schools with limited scheduling flexibility:

Monday	Wednesday	Friday
separate instrumental classes for all divided according to type and student proficiency	separate instrumental classes for all divided according to type and student proficiency	full band or orchestra experience for all students. Possible division of "A" Band and "B" Band, etc.

Tuesday	Thursday	Friday
grade level mixed choruses or girls' chorus and boys' chorus	grade level mixed choruses or girls' chorus and boys' chorus	select mixed chorus

The size of the school and the complexity of the community determine various rearrangements of suggested organizations. All special activities ought to emanate from a vital general music program.

Lack of Supervisorial Specificity Kills the Music Program

Unless something musical and educational happens that makes consistent sense, efforts are of no avail. Music supervisors need to spell out quite exactly and without compromise what it takes to make a good music program in a particular school. The following are such considerations:

1. The kind of schedule that will guarantee good musical results both in the general music program and in the special music programs
2. The kind of teacher who is able and equipped to teach the special programs (who has a thorough acquaintance with instruments and technics, etc.)
3. The kinds of learning materials that will present general or special music in such sequences that the average good teacher can make sense out of it and "get it across" to the students; materials must be goal-centered
4. The kind of equipment and facilities needed to make music instruction effective (stands, proper chairs, instruments, phonograph, chalk board, staff liner, etc.)
5. The kinds of rooms and buildings that will facilitate music learning (lighting, space, storage, practice, office, communication systems, etc.)

The best facilities, materials and personnel cannot do the job unless adequate time is provided. The word *adequate* does not imply *how much* a school district is willing to sacrifice in the way of schedule. "Adequate" is based on *known experiences of school districts that have been successful in developing good musical programs.* It is a good idea to ask several schools of similar size and conditions to submit their schedules for review.

Dynamic and *human* considerations revolve about the total feelings of what is *really* wanted, in relationship to the personalities who can implement what is wanted. *Supervisory specificity is necessary as a reliable gauge against which all of these factors can be squared away.*[2]

Specificity and professional honesty is badly needed in spelling out even the general music program in the elementary schools. This could imply that the music supervisor induces a school through its administration and board to adopt a resolution recognizing minimum standards for the various programs in music education, and that a definite minimum time must be spent at it. Also, that all teachers understand that they are to share in the responsibility of teaching music, leaving the more technical areas to the especially trained.

The General Music Curriculum in the Secondary Schools

A conscience-stricken professional organization has looked at itself and found itself wanting in the implementation of its avowed ideals, that of providing *music for all* at the secondary level.

In the elementary schools the general music program is an established and accepted right and a must for every child, and the specialized programs are ideally offshoots from the general program. However, in the secondary schools of America, pretty much the reverse is in evidence. The general music program is not general but is, in reality, a specialized program of more advanced listening for those who can take it. In many places a special general course in music appreciation is offered (too often to fill out the music director's time, or as an expiatory symbol of a school's or a director's remissness in not having provided musical opportunities for all high school youth). The total music courses offered in secondary schools do not serve much more than 20 per cent of the high school student bodies. And these 20 per cent are enrolled in the special courses.

Music supervisors need to exert professional influence to make general music for the 80 per cent a reality. The mandatory physical education programs for all students are thoroughly enmeshed with graduation requirements. These programs exist beside and independent of the specilized sports programs.

General music in the high schools is needed. Music supervisors need to meet with curriculum planners and administrators to determine the following:

1. What constitutes a proper general music program at the high school level?
2. How can such a program be geared to the interests and aptitudes of the 80 per cent not currently participating in the specialized programs?
3. If it is for all, does it have to be watered down music activities?
4. What constitutes a desirable scope of musical learnings?
5. Do these experiences need to be arranged sequentially? Do we consider principles of growth and development at this level?
6. How can content be determined?
7. What type of teacher can teach a general music course to nonperformers?
8. Should there be maturity level classes, and desegregated classes?

These and other questions need to be cleared away by the curriculum planners before a general music program can be implemented for the 80 per cent.

With the inroads of flexible and modular scheduling it may be possible to set up time each week for general music in the various high school grades. Such a course could be part of a learning area embracing the fine arts. This lack has been noted in official circles. Now these things remain to be done:

1. Setting up a course of study (which could logically follow the sequence of units in English classes or units in the history courses)
2. Setting up the proper unit credit
3. Selecting the proper teacher
4. Making proper scheduling provisions
5. Selecting and having on hand the necessary materials and equipment
6. And, of course, getting the necessary agreement to carry out such a course

The Specialized Music Programs in the Secondary Schools

It is not necessary to dwell at length on these programs, since they are so well established no matter where one looks. These are some of the activities that symbolize this curriculum:

1. The advanced band
2. The second band
3. The beginners' band
4. Instrumental classes
5. The advanced orchestra
6. The intermediate orchestra
7. Special string classes
8. The concert choir
9. The boys' chorus or glee club
10. The girls' chorus or glee club
11. Freshman general chorus
12. Vocal and instrumental ensembles of varied combinations
13. The pep band
14. The dance band
15. The parade or marching band
16. The general student chorus
17. Music appreciation classes
18. Theory classes
19. Voice classes
20. Piano classes.

Arriving at a Music Curriculum in the Secondary Schools

One thing is certain: It would be folly for the music supervisor or the administrator to superimpose a music curriculum on to the high school. It is the administrator's responsibility to make provisions for and to care for such needs by planning with those who are to implement the program. In order to make such provisions these ought to be provided:

1. the necessary personnel
2. materials and equipment
3. budgetary allotments
4. space—buildings, rooms, etc.
5. scheduling—adequate time

Music in General Education[3] refers to the core of musical experiences that should have been provided all high school graduates. The authors believed that the following eleven content areas *could* lead to desired outcomes. These areas were selected as being most representative and inclusive of the vastness and complexity of the total potential involvement of music:

1. Elements of music
2. Form and design in music
3. Interpretive aspects in music
4. Science of sound
5. The musical score
6. Historical considerations
7. Music and man
8. Music as a form of expression
9. Types of musical performance
10. Relationship of music to other disciplines in the humanities
11. Music today

These content areas will be approached through four aspects of the music program:

1. Experiences all music classes should provide. This assumes that significant aspects of each of the eleven content areas should be part of the course for all students, regardless of the classes they take.
2. Special experiences for nonselective music classes. This assumes that all students even in non-performance-centered classes should be taught some of each of the eleven content areas, however apropos to their "consumer-type" of understanding.
3. Special experiences for instrumental classes. These content concepts should be a significant part of the learning in rehearsal classes.
4. Special experiences for vocal classes. This assumes also that students in choral and vocal classes should pursue a broader content than the traditional rehearsal.

The music teacher in implementing such a program makes adjustments in light of his training, experience, special talents, and proclivities, and in the degree he sees his challenges as teaching responsibilities.

The supervisor ought to be available as a stage hand, preparing the stage with proper settings, drops, props, and other accoutrements that make it possible for the real actor, the teacher, to do the job. His role should also be that of a catalyst and a conscience prodding the busy special music teacher and administrator into planning for more positive musical and educative values.

Personnel

It Takes People to Make a Curriculum Work

The school music teaching profession requires a personality endowed with the highest of attributes in several areas. The standards of admission to the profession should be (1) identification of desirable, interested, and talented prospective school music teachers, and (2) selective admission into institutions preparing school music teachers (see Chapter II of MENC report "Evaluation of the Music Program").

In many places potential music teachers are being identified in the early high school years. This is accomplished through a program in which likely music teacher training candidates are apprenticed as *teacher helpers* to the regular music teacher for certain periods each week. This is the function of a Future Teacher's Club. Student officers in the school music organizations are also likely candidates for potential music teachers. Such offices provide early experience in many activities and attributes needed to implement the music curriculum. The training for future music teachers ought to begin early in childhood, with deliberate exposure to music and opportunities to participate in music activities.

The Future Teachers of America (FTA) and the student chapters of MENC, with their planned programs of involving students at the collegiate level in professional activities, are a real force in determining the quality of future music teaching personnel.

Other Factors for Retaining a Music Teacher

These are some of the factors relating to the immediate situation that need to be considered in hiring a music teacher:

1. *Age.* This is especially important if it is important to maintain a proportion of the total teaching staff in each age bracket.
2. *Sex.* In some areas it is thought sound to maintain a balance between men and women teachers.
3. *Marital status.* Some communities prefer a good share of their teachers married for the reasons of stability and emotional maturity. Others prefer the majority single.
4. *Place of training.* This is a consideration in some communities. The assumed philosophy of the music department of certain teacher training institutions may be a consideration for or against hiring a person from that institution.

5. *Amount of teaching experience.* Some school communities require a reasonable balance between experienced teachers and so-called "new-blood."
6. *Home of the teacher.* Whether or not the teacher is local may be a consideration. Does localism promote inbreeding? And, if so, is that bad?
7. *Special talents, musical or otherwise, and special personality traits.* These may be considerations also.

The music supervisor rarely hires the music teaching personnel. His role is most important in determining the quality of instruction. And his judgments are apart from the general considerations just listed. They reflect the needs, projected plans, and strengths and weaknesses of the music department.

These are preferred procedures in selecting teachers:

1. A school employee should be nominated by the professional head of the school system.
2. The staff, including the music supervisor, should actively participate in the selection.
3. Music teacher selection policies should be in harmony with state laws and local policies.

Procedures for the selection of special music teachers include these:

1. Establishing qualifications based on current and projected needs
2. Seeking candidates.

In these two areas there are seven basics to be considered along with previously listed considerations:

1. Can the prospective music teacher manage a classroom full of students along with all the other job expectations?
2. Does he have adequate instructional skill?
3. Is personal fitness for teaching in evidence?
4. Is there sufficient evidence of professional preparation and scholarship?
5. Does the candidate show inclination toward professional improvement?
6. Has he manifested real zeal for the job at hand? Is this reflected in a genuine interest for the students, for the community, and for the particular aspects of the music program to be taught?
7. Is the candidate willing to cooperate with others?

These basic concerns can be taken care of by observing recruitment procedures that set up a frame of reference assuring satisfaction, such as advertising an accurate job description that includes

1. Name and location of school system.
2. Exact description of position to be filled.
3. Salary range.
4. Brief school calendar.
5. Specifics of work expected in terms of student numbers, extra responsibilities, and results expected.
6. Working conditions (including type of room, equipment, and other important facilities).
7. A brief description of the type of community and special living conditions.
8. The exact academic and professional training, experience and certification.
9. General cultural background of the candidate.
10. Personal and social qualifications. This may include a list of specialized skills needed for this particular job. The school may need a band director who is also a skilled string teacher.
11. Name and address to whom application should be made.

This information should discourage those whose qualifications do not match those listed.

The prospective candidate needs to make known what his special skills are and the type of music teaching position he needs in order for him to do his very best:

1. Types of position wanted—vocal, instrumental (orchestra, band), high school, elementary school, college, supervision, department head, theory, etc.
2. Name and address of applicant.
3. Personal data—age, marital status, place of birth, hobbies.
4. Educational—dates, institutions attended, major and minor subjects, and degrees held, also specialized music training, including that from private artists, teachers or conservatories.
5. Experience—schools, positions, dates, other types of work experience that would tend to qualify the applicant for the desired music position. Symphony experience, or the many kinds of community music that may predispose the applicant for the desired position.
6. Travel—places visited, to indicate breadth and versatility.
7. Talents other than music that would dispose one favorably for leadership positions.
8. Statement of interests.
9. References.
10. Physical examination record.
11. Proof of certification.
12. Recommendations.

COUNTY SCHOOLS
Office of Superintendent
Court House

Attach copy of recent photo or snapshot here

APPLICATION FOR POSITION

I. PERSONAL DATA:

Last Name   First   Middle   Maiden Name If A Married Woman

Place of birth_____ Date of birth_____ Age _____Height_____Weight_____

Present Address_____Telephone _____

Permanent Address_____ Telephone_____

Marital status (underline):   Single   Married   Widow   Separated   Divorced

Are you a citizen of the U.S.A.?_____Ages of children _____

What is your church membership or preference?_____

To what other organizations do you belong_____

Vision_____Hearing _____Physical defects _____

II. PROFESSIONAL PREFERENCES:

For what position are you applying?_____

Can you teach: Art?_____Music?_____ Physical Education?_____
for your grade

         Dramatics?_____ Rhythmics?_____ Speech Correction?_____

What California credentials do you hold?_____

III. REFERENCES:

Give name and address where confidential papers can be secured _____

List four or five superintendents and principals not included in the above who know of your professional qualifications.

NAME	POSITION	ADDRESS

IV. EDUCATIONAL PREPARATION:

	INSTITUTION ATTENDED	State	DATES ATTENDED		GRADUATION		SUBJECTS	
			From	To	Date	Degree	Major	Minor
High School								
Normal School								
College								
or								
University								
Graduate								
Work								
Summer								
Sessions								

V. EDUCATIONAL EXPERIENCE:

List ALL paid experience in chronological order.

Years Experi- ence	DATES		NAME OF SCHOOL	LOCATION		Grades, Subjects, or Position	Annual Salary
	From	To		City or County	State		

VI. MISCELLANEOUS:

Did you serve in the armed forces?_____If so, give branch, length of service, and rating_____

What work experience, other than teaching, have you had?_____

Have you ever worked with youth groups such as Boy Scouts, Girl Scouts, etc?_____

Where and how long?_____

To what extent have you traveled?_____

_____ Do you have an automobile?_____

I certify the above information to be an accurate statement of my personal and professional history.

Date_____Signature_____

Applicant interviewed by_____

Some districts require written examinations; others require some form or other of recommendation blank filled out by responsible persons from previous employment.

Among written examinations, the most widely used is the Teacher's Examination of the American Council on Education, which presumes to test for (a) professional information, (b) mental abilities and basic skills, and (c) general culture.

After perusal of an array of written material, usually several candidates are called in for an *interview*. The music supervisor may be called upon to interview a candidate. Interviews of this sort can be subject to prejudicial judgment. Of interest are the findings by the Research Division of the National Education Association

> that over a period of nine years, of those teachers . . . who were selected by correspondence alone, 75 per cent were not rcommended for reappointment. Of those chosen after an interview, 24 per cent were not re-elected; while those teachers selected after OBSERVATION OF THEIR TEACHING, none failed to be reappointed on account of unsatisfactory teaching or discipline.[4]

A later study revealed that for many reasons observation of the candidate was not used for more than 39 per cent of teachers hired.

The Teacher Selection Flow Chart adapted from the bulletin brings into focus a sequence of steps to observe in selection of music teaching personnel (p. 159).

After the aforegoing processes have been utilized and two or three candidates remain, it may be well to compare their scores in the various areas by plotting them on a graph similar to the one below. This is a visual means of determining who the top candidate is.

Once the final selection has been made, the actual placement and assignment takes place. This is a job of putting the right person into the right position. The problems of properly placing and orienting new personnel is within the province of music supervisors. A former president had occasion to refer to "the tragedy of hiring the wrong person . . . and the responsibility to bypass considerations like age, youth, seniority, etc., to get the right person."

These are some of the problems of new music teachers which the music supervisor can help solve:

1. Assisting in arranging for proper housing
2. Helping the new music teacher become part of the group (the framework of his acceptability). Sometimes conformity to group can be a detriment!

CHART INDICATING NECESSARY PROCESS
INVOLVED IN HIRING DESIRABLE
PROFESSIONAL MUSIC TEACHERS[5]

DISTRICT POLICY OF SELECTION OF MUSIC PERSONNEL

JOB DESCRIPTION BASED ON ANALYSIS OF DISTRICT NEEDS

RECEIVING APPLICATIONS THROUGH USE OF REGULAR FORMS

unsatisfactory
personal data

FILING TRANSCRIPTS, CERTIFICATES, RECOMMENDATIONS

unsatisfactory
record

WRITTEN EXAMINATIONS FROM INTERESTED CANDIDATES

unsatisfactory
test scores

INTERVIEWS WITH PREFERRED CANDIDATES

unsatisfactory
indications

OBSERVING CANDIDATES ON THE JOB

obviously poor
teaching

REPORT OF PHYSICAL EXAMINATIONS

physically unfit
for particular job

SUPERINTENDENT RECEIVES PREFERRED
CANDIDATES

selects
best candidate

SUPERINTENDENT NOMINATES--BUT
BOARD ELECTS

CANDIDATE PLACED BY SUPT.

CANDIDATE ASSIGNED BY MUS.
DIRECTOR OR SUPERVISOR

REASONS FOR
REJECTIONS

PREFERRED PROFILES &
ELIGIBILITY LISTS

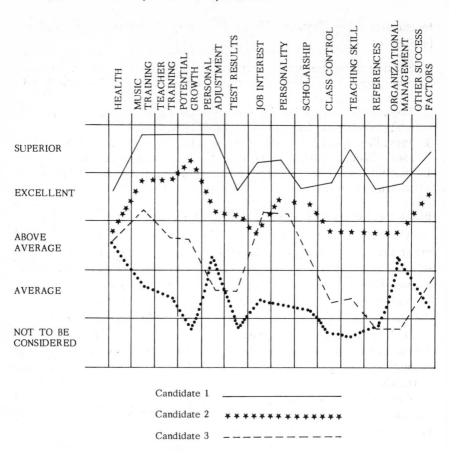

| | | HEALTH | MUSIC TRAINING | TEACHER TRAINING | POTENTIAL GROWTH | PERSONAL ADJUSTMENT | TEST RESULTS | JOB INTEREST | PERSONALITY | SCHOLARSHIP | CLASS CONTROL | TEACHING SKILL | REFERENCES | ORGANIZATIONAL MANAGEMENT | OTHER SUCCESS FACTORS |

SUPERIOR

EXCELLENT

ABOVE AVERAGE

AVERAGE

NOT TO BE CONSIDERED

Candidate 1 ——————————————

Candidate 2 ★★★★★★★★★★★★★★

Candidate 3 – – – – – – – – – – –

Candidate 4 ••••••••••••••••••••

3. Making sure that the new teacher gets acquainted with the school's philosophy (the framework of his planning)
4. Making sure the new music teacher gets to know the school's rules and regulations (the framework of his functioning)
5. Helping the new teacher get acquainted with the community (the framework of his affectivity)
6. Orienting the new teacher to the available professional affiliations
7. Making provisions whereby the teacher can enjoy job satisfaction and can grow professionally

It is the responsibility of the supervisor to assist the administration in making provisions for certain adjustments in order to obtain a better teaching-learning climate. These kinds of adjustments are, at times, justifiable:

1. Shifting personnel to a different building where certain talents are more needed, or where they are in a position more compatible with their personalities
2. Rearranging the work load of certain music teachers in order to make allowance for energy-consuming responsibility
3. Providing special teacher help for classroom teachers who find it most difficult to teach music in their self-contained classroom
4. Placing a seasoned, strong music teacher in a so-called trouble spot to remedy a situation

Bases for Retaining the Special Music Teacher

The music supervisor may be called upon to evaluate the special music teachers and regular classroom teachers in an effort to discover whether desirable musical outcomes are in evidence in the total teacher-learner situation. This type of administrative activity must be performed. Continuation of a music learning climate, or the improvement if it is dependent upon *how the process of evaluation is carried out.*

A total evaluation program ought to include evaluation by (1) school administrators and supervisors, (2) the teachers in question themselves, (3) pupils and parents, and/or (4) cooperatively by combinations of these groups.

One of the most discriminatory modes of teacher evaluation and one that is but little short of police action is letting things ride until near report time, then observing the teacher in action, and basing judgments on this very brief slice out of a teacher's life.

Evaluation must be continual and centered around goals, desirable processes, and the relationship of authorized persons in relation to these goals.

The following teacher evaluation forms are applicable to music teaching personnel. Musical acuity is not being evaluated in any of these. Candidates with lacks in musical skills were supposedly eliminated in the preliminary screening. Of major concern in evaluation and self-evaluation forms is *the teacher's general skill in teaching, his teacher-pupil relationships, and his professional attitudes and personal qualities.* Other areas of concern should have been cared for in any preliminary investigation (p. 162, 164-165).

A good teacher can be compared to a good electrical transformer whose purpose is to transform available electrical energy into usable

OFFICE OF DEPUTY SUPERINTENDENT
DEPARTMENT OF PERSONNEL

TEACHER CHECK SHEET

Teacher_____ School_____

Classification: Probationary_____

Long-Term Substitute_____

* *

For the purpose of checking, a five-point scale shall be used for staff members with one (1) as the highest rating and five (5) as the lowest.

	1	2	3	4	5
Teacher's Control of Class — Pupil Behavior					
Teaching Methods and Techniques					
General Housekeeping and Classroom Mechanics					
Cheerfully Accepts and Carries out Suggestions					
Adequate Planning					
Knows Content of Grade Level and Uses Curriculum Guide to Advantage					
Sympathetic Understanding of Children					
Adaption to Individual Needs					
Pupil Response					
Personnel Relationships					
Personal Characteristics (Voice, Appearance, Professional Attitude, Tact, and Judgment					

* *

At the present time, do you feel that the teacher will meet standards for re-employment?

Yes_____No_____Questionable_____

If the answer is "no" or questionable," what steps have you taken to help the teacher to improve?

What further suggestions do you have for helping this teacher?

What do you consider this teacher's greatest asset?

Initialing or signing the check sheet does not necessarily mean that the teacher concurs with the rating, but does show that he has actually seen the "Teacher Check Sheet." Teacher shall examine and sign at time of the conference.

Date_____Time_____

Teacher_____

Principal_____

form for humanity. The teacher transforms the vastness of curricular considerations into usable form for his students. *Teacher selection and retention is a real concern in administering a music curriculum* (pp. 164 & 165).

Budget

It Takes Money to Make the Music Curriculum Work

If music is to take its rightful place along with all other curricular considerations, it must be allowed to share in budgetary allotments on

a par with other learning areas, with just considerations for its con-
tributory value to the total educational scene, and to the improved
living of its participants.

No one can presume to set down what ought to be an adequate
music department budget for all types of school situations. Proper budget will vary with the type and size of school district. There are im-
poverished communities that have put small fortunes into their music
programs, while, at the same time, some wealthy communities deal
their music program very sparsely. The reverse can also be found.

A budget ought to reflect thoughtful planning. It should be a positive curricular consideration. The people who are connected with the
operation of the school and of its music instruction should be in the
position to ascertain the needs and determine what should be purchased to do the job. This involves making a check list of all of the
necessary personnel, materials, instruments, equipment, space, etc., and
for this check these questions under each category: (1) What do we
need? (2) What do we already have?

The budget is not only a *reflection* of the curriculum, but in reality,
a projection of the curriculum. A budget takes the curriculum out of
the smoke-filled planning room into reality. It is the practical application of the curriculum.

Communities have been willing to pay a high price for including
music on the regular school program. Think about these facts for a
moment:

1. For the price of a bass horn more than two-hundred children could
   be each supplied with a school book
2. For the price of a bassoon two classrooms of thirty children in each
   could be supplied with all of the books to carry on normal school
   operations
3. For the price of a baritone horn several phonographs could be
   purchased that could bring music to hundreds of children.

I am sure that no just formula could be set up that would make
adequate provision for each aspect of the music curriculum. It is im-
perative, however, to look at the total twelve-year or fourteen-year
music curriculum of a school district and from it determine the needs
and the amounts to be spent each year.

These are certain considerations in discussing music department
budgets, viewed in terms of curricular needs:

1. The particular lacks of this school system
2. A *long-range* plan to develop the music department; like—a five-
   year plan

SELF-APPRAISAL GUIDE SHEET
FOR THE SPECIAL MUSIC TEACHER[6]
(Who Evaluates Self and Her Teacher-Learner Situation)

Only record situations and conditions since July 1, 19___	Satisfactory progress	Unsatisfactory progress
What improvements have been made in the musical space facilities in our school?	☐	☐
What has been done to improve the quality of music teaching in our school?	☐	☐
Has the quality of music instructional materials improved?	☐	☐
What can I point to as real evidence of my improvement in teaching music?	☐	☐
What has been done to enrich the musical offerings in our school?	☐	☐
Have the music activities reached into the students' activities and enriched them?	☐	☐
Has our music department reached into the community to add to the cultural level?	☐	☐

	Satisfactory progress	Unsatisfactory progress
What adjustments has our music department made to meet the needs of the exceptional child?	☐	☐
Has our total school's music program been improved?	☐	☐
What has been done to improve the musical atmosphere in our school? (displays, music centers)	☐	☐
What has been done to conserve time in rehearsals and other music periods?	☐	☐
Have we more classroom teachers (elem. or h.s.) with a good musical background? Also other increases in music personnel?	☐	☐
In what ways has the community shown interest in the music program?	☐	☐

In your estimation... list NEXT STEPS IN THE IMPROVEMENT OF THE TOTAL MUSIC

PROGRAM _____

3. A *short-range* plan to provide a minimum of immediate music learning. (Such a plan ought to be in keeping with the total projected growth plan)
4. A financial provision for a minimum of *unforseen special music events*
5. Certain principles, such as need, equitableness (as differentiated from equality and equalness), and reasonableness
6. The elementary and secondary general music program, and the special instrumental and vocal music programs

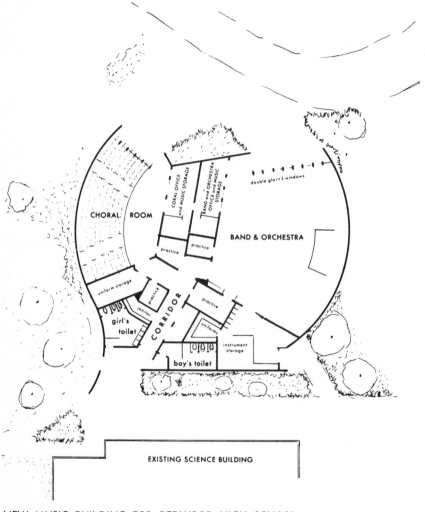

NEW MUSIC BUILDING FOR REDWOOD HIGH SCHOOL
James P. Lockett, Architect

Materials and Space

It Takes Building, Equipment, Materials, Rooms to Implement a Music Curriculum

See pages 000-000 for a listing of minimum material needs for the general music program in the elementary grades.[7] A list of this sort can be expanded or contracted to meet individual school needs. At best it is a guide toward the realization of a balanced music program.

The following are recommended lists for facilities and equipment of a band program in a school system:

A. Music Room and Building
   1. The rehearsal room should be isolated, if possible, in a separate building. It should be near the auditorium stage and easily accessible to the athletic field.
   2. Standards of adequate heating, lighting, ventilation and water facilities should be self-understood.
   3. Acoustical treatment should be provided to properly reflect true tonal quality and cut down on noise.
   4. There should be provided at least 18 square feet per person.
   5. There should be a director's room with desk, file, and storage cabinets.
   6. There should be library space with storage cabinets and sorting racks.
   7. There should be permanent risers so that the band will be elevated, giving a better balance and blend.
   8. There should be blackboard, piano, and a high quality phonograph in front of the band.
   9. The rehearsal room should contain movable chairs, 18 inches in height.
   10. Proper instrument cabinets should be built along the walls for safe storage of the school instruments.
   11. There should be provision for a series of small practice rooms, for practice or individual lessons.
   12. A good tape recorder and a high quality microphone should be available.
B. Basic instrumentation
   1. Orchestra (instrumentation around which an orchestra of symphonic proportions can be built) for thirty players:

6 first violins	2 B♭ clarinets
4 second violins	1 oboe
2 violas	1 bassoon
2 cellos	2 French horns
2 string bass	3 B♭ trumpets
2 flutes	2 trombones

percussion

2. Band (those starred are ordinarily listed as school-owned instruments

    a. for a thirty-five (35) to forty (40) piece band:

3 flutes	1 E♭ alto saxophone
*1 C piccolo	*1 baritone saxophone
*1 oboe	1 B♭ tenor saxophone
*1 bassoon	6 cornets
10 B♭ clarinets	*2 baritone horns
*1 alto clarinet	*2 sousaphones
*1 bass clarinet	*3 percussion
*4 French horns	

    b. for a forty-five (45) to fifty-five (55) piece band:

3-4 flutes	1 B♭ tenor saxophone
*1 C piccolo	*1 baritone saxophone
*1 oboe	8 cornets
*1-2 bassoons	3 trombones
13 B♭ clarinets	*2 baritone horns
*1 alto clarinet	*3 sousaphones
*2 bass clarinets	*3 percussion (including
*4 French horns	tympani)
2 E♭ alto saxophones	

    c. for a seventy-five (75) to eighty (80) piece band:

6 flutes	*1 baritone saxophone
*2 C piccolos	*1 bass saxophone
*2-3 oboes (or substitute an	8 cornets
English horn for one)	3 trumpets
*2-3 bassoons (with one a	*6 French horns
contra bassoon)	*5 baritone horns
2-4 E♭ alto saxophones	6 sousaphones (include
20 B♭ clarinets	a recording bass)
*2 alto clarinets	*1 string bass
*2 bass clarinets	*4 percussion (with
*1 contra bass clarinet	tympani)

C. Care and Maintenance. Among these considerations are items that require budget allotments:
1. Yearly repair work on instruments, music and equipment
2. Major overhaul of instruments every three to five years
3. Good storage cabinets will prolong life of instruments, equipment, music, and uniforms
4. Pianos tuned every six months

D. Budgetary and other sources of funds:
1. The board of education
2. Community booster organizations

3. Special music organizational projects
4. Cooperation with other school organizations
E. Principles for determining budget
   1. Only high quality material
   2. Develop a definite purchase plan

(See *Five-Year* plan developed by Clarence Sawhill, Director Bands, University of Southern California, published by LeBlanc Music Instruments Mfg.[8]) The Preplanning suggested here can easily be translated for use in other segments of the music program.

SAMPLE FIVE-YEAR PLAN

FIRST YEAR	Budget of $4680
20-Music stands—$9 each	$180
40-Pre-band melody instr.	
$1 each	40
1-Bass drum (34"x16")	85
2-Snare drums (8"x15")	
$60 each	120
1-Pair of Cymbals (16")	50
1-Sousaphone	500
1-Baritone	200
2-French horns $270 each	540
1-Baritone saxophone	350
Music	250
35-Uniforms $65 each	2275

SECOND YEAR	Budget of $3115
1-Oboe	$325
1-Bass clarinet	500
1-Tenor saxophone	280
1-Baritone	280
1-Sousaphone	500
2-Parade drums (12"x15")	
$75 each	150
1-Scotch bass drum	
(10"x28")	80
1-Pr. of cymbals (14")	45
5-Additional music stands	45
Music and marching folios	250
10-Additional uniforms	
$65 each	650

THIRD YEAR	Budget of $2420
1-French horn	$270
1-Baritone	200
1-Bassoon	500
1-Set of tympani	450
1-Piccolo (C)	95
1-Set of bells	90
Music	250
Repairs	150
5-Additional uniforms	
$65 each	325

FOURTH YEAR	Budget of $2420
1-French horn	$270
1-Sousaphone	500
1-Oboe	325
1-Bass clarinet	500
Music	250
Repairs	250
5-Additional uniforms	325

FIFTH YEAR	Budget of $2415
1-Piccolo (C)	95
1-Sousaphone	500
1-Bassoon	500
1-Alto clarinet	350
5-Additional music stands	
$9 each	45
Music	300
Repairs	300
5-Additional uniforms	325

(Prices are relative and rapidly changing.)

This would give the following school-owned instruments and equipment at the end of the five-year period:

40-Pre-band instruments	3-Baritones
2-Piccolos	4-Sousaphones
2-Oboes	1-Set concert drums
2-Bassoons	1-Set marching drums
1-Alto clarinet	1-Set tympani
2-Bass clarinets	1-Set bells
1-Tenor saxophone	2-Pair cymbals
1 Baritone saxophone	30-Music stands
4-French horns	60-Uniforms

Although most large district music supervisors and directors of music education have budget responsibility, the state music consultant or a county music consultant is often called upon to advise in a program of budget preparation. He is in a position to suggest and provide for the inclusion of *curriculum-centered budgeting* and *long-range planning*. With mobility of teaching personnel, many school districts can fall prey to the fancies of the new music teacher. A new and costly system may be introduced into a school district and then the teacher leaves the following year. A *long-range plan* can become an economical guide to guarantee *continuity* and *consistency* in the music curriculum.

Budget, building programs, inventory are all part of what makes music flow from symbol to sound, from the printed page to the learner.

The music supervisor had better be concerned and be ready to advise with school districts on building. This volume does not presume to be an authority on music buildings; it merely hopes to make the music supervisor aware of the need to be prepared also in this area. MENC handbook *Music Buildings, Rooms, Equipment*[9] ought to be readily available to all music supervisors. It is helpful to be conversant with certain architectural terms, also to know some architect personally who can be of assistance in interpreting blueprints.

Why should the music supervisor be concerned about inventory?

1. A good inventory is basic to good housekeeping. It promotes efficient and economical learning.
2. A good inventory is part of the budget. *We need to know what we have* in order to determine what we need.

The total music department inventory should be examined each year to determine what ought to be eliminated and what needs to be added. There also ought to be separate classifications for each segment of the music program such as (1) elementary general music, (2) elementary instrumental music, (3) elementary vocal music, (4) secondary general music, (5) secondary instrumental music, (6) secondary vocal music. Each building should also maintain separate inventories which are an accurate part of the total district music inventory. The music supervisor ought to have access to the inventory and should be in a position to discuss it with special music teachers, classroom teachers, and administrators in order to guide purchases that keep in mind curricular considerations.

An inventory is a tangible basis for evaluation of the total program.

An inventory is a legal protection for the music teacher, department head, or music supervisor.

An inventory is a basis for providing insurance on costly musical equipment and materials.

For obvious reasons all items on the inventory list ought to have the purchase date and cost.

Planning the Music Curriculum

It Takes Plans and Continuous Evaluation to Make the Music Curriculum Work

This chapter concerns itself chiefly with the "nuts and bolts" of carrying out a music curriculum. Up to this point we have discussed the evolution of the music curriculum itself, the people that it takes to implement the curriculum, the money that it takes to support the program, and the space, materials, and equipment that it takes to get the job done. Course content for the special music programs is limited only by the ability of the instructor plus his initiative and ambition, coupled with the interrelationship of his students and the particular school community.

There is need to evaluate the music program to determine whether the processes are compatible with the product; whether boys and girls are learning music and at the same time experiencing its values. Many devices can be used. Each, however, tells its own story.

These kinds of evaluation have been described earlier in this chapter:

1. Preservice personnel evaluation
2. Personnel self-evaluation
3. Materials, equipment, and other needs evaluation
4. Inventory and replacement or depreciation

We ought also be concerned with evaluation of students' progress. It is not as simple as grading a series of performed arithmetic problems, or sets of spelling papers. *A music student performance file* can give important clues to the instructor on how to arrive at a fair estimate of a student's progress in the designated area:

1. Organization
2. Rehearsal attendance
3. Practice report
4. Improvement in performance
5. Public appearances
6. Music tests
7. Data from interviews

Outside of hearing the student perform and comparing it with previous performances, this sort of evaluation will give teacher, student, and parent a fairly clear picture of progress; and will point out what areas of weakness need be emphasized.

Musical content with all its ramifications is probably a paramount concern. Firstly, if the content does not have musical significance then, frankly, we have wasted our time with all of our elaborate preparations. By significance we mean (a) that it must be great music—no irrelevant stuff that has been inserted in so many of our music books for years just to reemphasize a so-called educational point. And we do not need to argue here what is great music. It's there with all of its grandeur, magnificence, tenderness, dignity, might, and humility. It doesn't need to speak for itself either. At least, just as little as does the deity have to argue its existence.

We also mean (b) that it must have relevance, or appropriateness to the situation at hand. The funeral of a president of our country, the death of a U.N. Secretary General, the marriage and coronation of a queen, the opening of the Lincoln Center, the opening of the new opera house to replace the famed Metropolitan, these have relevance even when studied in retrospect or at the occasion. The great American rodeo, the bullfight, the football game suggest great appropriate music. Thanksgiving, the Reformation, the Pontifical Mass, Easter, Veteran's Day, each suggests its own relevant music, as does nightfall, prayertime, the joy of spring, the clouds, etc.

Secondly, there must be concern and deliberate provision made for the use of contemporary music materials. "It is a pity that in his truly artistic and beautiful compositions Mozart should carry his originality too far, to the detriment of the sentiment and heart of his works. His new quartette . . . are much too highly spiced to be palatable for any length of time."[10] Thus it was always. It need not be now. Mass literacy should have changed people's willingness to accept the new. Music educators are still spending too much time *avoiding* the new and find solace in the ancient.

The *basic structure of music* remains inactive until it is energized or put into action by the *human factor.* The visual, aural and kinesthetic *senses* become the receptors of musical impulses. They give meaning to the structure through the processes of (1) hearing and listening, (2) seeing and reading, and (3) performing (playing, singing, dancing) a varied *repertoire* of music.

The concept inherent in the "spiral curriculum" ought to have much relevance for music education consideration. Basic concepts can be presented at the earliest school age. Melodic, rhythmic, harmonic, notational, form and interpretational concepts are inherent even in the simplest music and can be pointed out and learned in the primary grades through music of significance and using real musical instruments and voices. As the child grows skeletally, intellectually, and in increased musical understanding, he can see the basic concepts present in more complex music. These basic concepts then become beacon lights—generalizations that can guide him to greater understanding throughout his entire school life and into his involvement into the adult world.[11]

The strands (melodic, rhythmic, harmonic, notational, form, and interpretative) or basic concepts will be ever present, constantly reinforcing themselves, giving substance to music and guiding the participant through the wonderland of the world's greatest music. The form, is as it were, a tight band moving upward, supporting increasingly larger spirals carrying the learner through great varieties of music learning complexities, modes, and media, through a most significant repertoire of music. Each strand, held together by the other, proceeds upwards giving stability to the enlarging spirals. Melodic, rhythmic, harmonic, notational, form and interpretative strands form the guiding cable, representing *concepts, skills,* and *objectives* (p. 174).

There is a need to devise workable evaluation criteria for the general music program in the elementary grades. Such criteria must be in terms of real outcomes (see final chapter).

Very recently an elementary school principal expressed this concern: "I would like to have you set up a way for us to grade our children in their classroom music performance. Right now, the kids

THE SPIRALLING MUSIC CURRICULUM
(With music reflecting each learning level and area on the spiral)

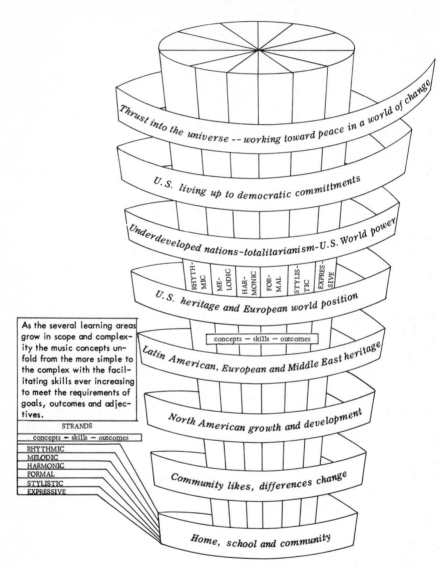

Thrust into the universe -- working toward peace in a world of change

U. S. living up to democratic committments

Underdeveloped nations-totalitarianism-U.S. World power

U. S. heritage and European world position

RHYTH-MIC ME-LODIC HAR-MONIC FOR-MAL STYLIS-TIC EXPRES-SIVE

concepts -- skills -- outcomes

Latin American, European and Middle East heritage

As the several learning areas grow in scope and complexity the music concepts unfold from the more simple to the complex with the facilitating skills ever increasing to meet the requirements of goals, outcomes and adjectives.

STRANDS

concepts -- skills -- outcomes

RHYTHMIC
MELODIC
HARMONIC
FORMAL
STYLISTIC
EXPRESSIVE

North American growth and development

Community likes, differences change

Home, school and community

who are in band and glee club get the *A*'s and *B*'s and the rest are not graded at all except those who are taught by our music teacher, and he gives them *C*'s or below. I don't like this, because it gives an advantage to those students who can afford to blow a horn, or who have special ability to sing in a chorus or blow a horn; and it seems to tell the rest that what they are doing in music really has no value."

Program evaluation is another concern that ought to occupy administrative and supervisory thinking. (See Chapter 15.)

QUESTIONS FOR DISCUSSION, THOUGHT AND STUDY

1. How would you determine content for a course of study in general music for the elementary grades? List the sources you would go to. What other than content bases would you consider?
2. Differentiate between a "course of study" and the curriculum. What does it take to put across a curriculum?
3. List a number of important curriculum considerations.
4. Discuss the validity of
   a. the general music program in the elementary schools.
   b. the general music program in the secondary schools.
   c. the specialized music programs in the elementary schools.
   d. the specialized music programs in the secondary schools.
5. Find the nearest school system with about 1,000 students in the elementary school, and about 500 in the high school. Examine the total music program and make recommendations for what needs to be done.
6. Write to several county school offices in your state and to the state department of education asking for curriculum bulletins on music education. Also obtain music guides published by several city school systems.
7. How do you feel about "music for all" at the secondary level? Suggest how you would accomplish this.
8. How do the different kinds of musical activities listed contribute to musical growth? Do you favor the concomitant values—such as social acceptance, personal adjustment, teamwork? Would you suggest limitations on either "music for music's sake" or "other than musical values"? How do you feel about contemporary music? Relevant music?
9. List the considerations for hiring and retaining special music teachers.
10. Devise a teacher evaluation form for your own music department.
11. How would you spend $5,000 for the total music affairs of an elementary and high school district with about 1,200 students?
12. What budget criteria and principles would you use?
13. List the various considerations for music space as suggested in MENC Music Education Research Council Bulletin No. 17, *Music Buildings, Rooms and Equipment.*
14. Find various kinds of evaluative devices for such concerns as curriculum —personnel—budget—student growth.
15. What is the supervisor's role in each of these aspects of implementing a curriculum?
16. Where is the dividing line between administering a music program and supervision? What does a music supervisor do that a music administrator delegates to others? What does a music administrator do that is not within the realm of activity of the music supervisor?
17. What validity is there for the concept of the "spiral music curriculum" for current program development?

NOTES

[1]Composite Growth Chart, adapted from Follett Publ. Co. and Prentice-Hall, Inc. 1965.

[2]Thelen, *Dynamics of Groups at Work, op. cit.,* Chap. 3.

[3]Karl Ernst and others, *Music in General Education,* (Washington, D. C.: MENC, 1964).

[4]National Education Association Research Division, *Administrative Practises Affecting Classroom Teachers,* Research Bulletin, p. 26.

[5]Adapted from NEA Research Bul., *op. cit.*

[6]Adaptation of scale prepared by E. Jackson.

[7]ESEA Title I List of Recommended Materials (see pp. 284 and 285).

[8]Clarence Sawhill, *5-Year Plan* (LeBlanc Music Instruments Mfg.), pp. 174-178.

[9]MENC, *Music Buildings, Rooms and Equipment,* (Washington, D. C.: MENC).

[10]John Tasker Howard and Jas. Lyons, *Modern Music.*

[11]Jerome Bruner, *The Process of Education, op. cit.,* pp. 52 and 53.

La Sierra Creative Arts School Photo

Chapter 9

Affecting Learning
Situations

Critique of In-Service Programs

The effectiveness of good teaching ought to be measured in terms of product. The music supervisor not only is concerned with content and process, but should be concerned with how such teaching affects the learner in the long run. If music is worth anything at all, the effects of its teaching should be much more than transitory.

The music learning situation is not only the classroom; it goes beyond these confines into segments of the community that may affect the musical life of the learner. Therefore it is important for the learner to have gained something musically significant not only for current utilitarian purposes but also for the ability to utilize his musical learnings in the "out-of-school" world.

How to help teachers create such a good learning situation is the constant concern of the music supervisor. He cannot improve the learning situation without taking into account the teacher, who is responsible for the transmission of knowledge and values. It is important to know in what ways the teacher is disposed to accept supervisory services.

"What is good supervision in one setting may actually be bad in another. Supervision is conditioned in each case by the factors of the local setting."[1] Perhaps the values of a supervisory program can best be measured by the respect and affection shown for it by the teachers. It may meet all the theoretical requirements of a good program; but if it is not accepted by those whom it is to serve, there is something wrong with it.

Much ado has been made about paving the way for supervision. However, sometimes progress does not always ensue because of concern for the feelings of others. So a program is often sacrificed because intelligent people have refused to understand. The music supervisor is in an unenviable position when he must counteract educational forces that actually obstruct progress of a program of music education. Music supervisors must be men and women of valor. They must possess the wisdom of the ages in order to carry out their mission. They must be cognizant of, and able to cope with, ignorance about music education and still move forward.

Some supervisory techniques are more acceptable to teachers than others. The wise music supervisor utilizes the tested knowledge of past experience, and builds his program on the basis of known successes. There is no sense in using techniques that are destined to fail.

Reactions of two hundred teachers in New York to common supervisory practices give good clues to reasonably effective modes of in-service program. This study made by Antell in 1947 is still worth noting.[2]

	Very helpful	Of little help	No help	Detrimental	No contact
1. Demonstration lessons 67%		12%	1%	0%	13%
2. Supervisor discusses routines at teachers' meetings 39		46	11	0	3
3. Individual conference with supervisor 67		22	3	0	8
4. Grade conference to discuss common problems 73		19	5	0	3
5. Professional library in school 86		10	0	0	4
6. Daily 2-second visit by supervisor 11		31	31	10	17
7. In-service courses or workshops 63		25	4	0	8
8. Commendation for outstanding service to Board 32		25	20	10	13
9. Intervisitation of teachers 67		24	5	0	4
10. Educational lecture at school by outside speaker 49		25	4	1	21
11. Teacher's panel discussion 42		38	11	0	9
12. Directed reading 42		36	13	1	8

13. Teacher-conducted con- ference after school 30	39	12	3	16
14. Visiting an outstanding school 73	16	4	0	7
15. Daily morning bulletin 25	31	16	2	26
16. Impromptu formal class- room supervision 8	39	29	20	4
17. Formal classroom visitation upon call 24	37	20	7	12
18. Participation in course- of-study-making 56	20	6	0	18
19. Participation in formu- lating school policy 70	14	3	0	13
20. Teachers' interest committee in school 51	20	4	1	24
21. Comprehensive testing program with analysis 39	33	13	6	9
22. After school open discus- sion of topic of interest 65	19	7	1	8

23. Supervisor acts as con-
   sultant or technical
   adviser 81
	11	3	0	5

24. Supervisor stays away
   from classroom as
   much as possible 30
	15	24	15	16

25. Rigid adherence of
   teacher to fixed daily
   program 3
	4	18	65	10

These clues evolved from the study (60 per cent of the teachers interviewed preferred these techniques over others):

1. A professional library—self-help
2. A supervisor who acts as a consultant or technical adviser
3. Demonstration lessons
4. Grade conferences to discuss common problems
5. Visits to outstanding schools
6. Participation in the formulation of school policy
7. Individual conference with the supervisor
8. Intervisitation of teachers
9. After-school conferences for open discussion of problems
10. In-service courses and workshops

Since this study was made, teachers may have changed their tastes in keeping with significant advances in educational thinking. The clues listed are not the only devices that could be used effectively. But they are an important key to "what goes with teachers." Accordingly, it would be hazardous to overplay the idea of formal classroom visitation, especially the unannounced kind, since this device is in disfavor with many teachers. Had some of the consultants referred to in Chapter 4 availed themselves of this study, they could have avoided a whole lot of trouble for themselves and for those who came within the scope of their influence.

In a study by Bail[3] the most frequently mentioned types of supervision desired were these:

1. Constructive criticism
2. Recommend new techniques and methods
3. Demonstration teaching
4. Recommend materials and equipment
5. Recommend professional books, articles
6. Assistance with special problems
7. Assistance with classroom control
8. Inspirational supervision
9. Interview following supervision

Of these nine only the first four listed were mentioned by 23 per cent or more of those interviewed.

In another study, made by Replogle,[4] in which he interviewed 300 classroom teachers he received these suggestions:

1. Supervisors should respect human personality, be sympathetic, and place people before things.
2. They should place pupil behavior before teacher performance.
3. They should be able to take suggestions as well as give them.
4. They should be able to provide group leadership—to bring a faculty together on a problem.
5. They should be able to express ideas in concrete terms.
6. They should be idealistic but at the same time realistic.
7. Supervisors should know that many paths lead to teacher acceptance. Teachers do not care for a supervisor with a one-track mind.

"Supervisors fall slightly below students as a source of suggestions."[5] Despite all we know about the efficacy of various kinds of in-service programs, it is evident that supervision, at best, is not popular. Clues to the breakdown in supervisory programs can be found in the individual himself. Two people, at least, are involved in in-service education, the giver and the receiver. An answer to the breakdown can be found by observing the way these two people work together on a problem of mutual concern. Have you ever asked yourself, "Do I

___ Let teachers know that I respect creativity and creative teaching?

___ Use some regular system for obtaining teachers' ideas?

___ Tolerate disagreement with my own ideas?

___ Encourage experimentation?

___ Avoid loading teachers with too many extra duties?

___ Make it possible to try out new ideas without failure being "fatal"?

___ Make school atmosphere an exciting, adventurous one?

___ Avoid *overemphasis* on teamwork?

___ Hold meetings in which ideas are evaluated honestly?

___ Help develop sound but exciting ideas from failure experiences?

___ Expose teachers to the creative work of other teachers?

___ Make it easy for new teachers to generate new ideas and stimulate the staff?

___ Facilitate communication between teachers in my school and teachers elsewhere working on related problems?

___ Occasionally question established concepts and practices?

___ Carry on a continuous program of long-range planning?

___ Recognize and try to relieve tension when frustration becomes too severe?

___ Maintain frequent communication with individual teachers but let them make most decisions alone?

Learning is involved in in-service education, therefore, it is necessary to take into account how people learn. According to Kilpatrick, "the problem-solving activities resulting in modification of behavior are called learning."[6] Snygg and Combs say, "All behavior, without exception, is completely determined by and pertinent to the phenomenal field of the behaving organism. . . ."[7] This implies that in order to change the music teaching behavior of a classroom teacher, it is necessary to change her perspective and viewpoint. Also "it is impractical to think of the learner except in terms of his own need, his own desires, and his own point of view." One must find ways by which the classroom teacher can see himself as others do, and also ways through which he can modify his music teaching behavior and still retain his individuality.

The purpose of in-service education is to effect a change so that needs can be met. Dewey said: "It thus becomes the office of the educator to select those things within the range of existing experience that have promise and potentiality of presenting new problems which by way of stimulating new ways of observation and judgment will expand the areas of further experience."[8] All teachers have had some contact with music which was in essence a musical experience. The supervisor needs to assist in recalling this musical experience and help the teacher to utilize it for expanding his own musical horizons. Supervisors must provide a climate whereby teachers can be free from fear of criticism. "If we desire freedom, then we must move in the direction of freedom-giving experiences."

The Professional Library

Eighty-six per cent of the teachers polled strongly indicate that people like to help themselves. A professional library can provide many self-help items that can become important clues to a teacher's musical growth and to her growth in the ability to teach music.

A professional library should contain many kinds of self-helps:

1. Self-teaching books on how to play the piano
2. Simplified systems of keyboard chording
3. Books on playing the autoharp
4. Books that present easy-to-read background information about music
5. Materials on rhythmic activities
6. Holiday music
7. Units for upper grade music appreciation—development of popular music—its relationship to other music
8. Brief musical "how to do its"
9. Lists of music correlated with various learning areas (not thousands of choices—just several good ones in each category)
10. Lists of available musical recordings
11. One or two fairly complete books on music appreciation written at a child's level
12. Stories on the lives of composers and musicians
13. A little musical dictionary
14. Grade expectations for teaching music at a certain level—city, county, or state music guide (teachers really only look at the grade level they are teaching and in which they are interested)

The supervisor also should have such materials available for teachers to look at "which by way of stimulating new ways of observation and judgment will expand the areas of further experience" (Dewey[9]) such as

1. Books on music teaching techniques written in laymen's language— a variety so that teachers can choose the one which appeals to them most
2. Several books on philosophy and psychology of music education
3. Musical periodicals
4. Research journals with pertinent music education research; these materials should be attractive, arresting, and stimulating

Supervision by Technical Assistance

Eighty-one per cent of the teachers polled asked for specific aid that requires certain technical know-how. The supervisor ought to be fully equipped to provide such help. He must possess much exact knowledge. He may not answer in generalities. His expert counsel ought to be seasoned with varied experience. Such experience makes for better empathy.

Miss K was such a supervisor. She was an excellent musician and a good teacher. She had taught school for only four years when she accepted a full-time consultancy; this included teaching junior high music. Whenever she attempted to work with teachers in the schools the principals seemed disinterested. The teachers kept their distance no matter how friendly she tried to be. There was no reaction when she announced that she was available to help anyone who desired her to help.

After a few weeks, she received a call from a beginning fourth grade teacher, who was concerned with how she could get music reading concepts across to the children. She assured the supervisor that she could teach it if Miss K would only tell her how it's done. They arranged a meeting for right after school, at which time approaches to music reading were thoroughly explored. This was all the teacher wanted at this time. But it did not end here. She told other teachers. They finally became interested enough to approach the supervisor for specific help. None of the ensuing meetings were organized around the music supervisor's interest or needs, but around teachers'. The supervisor's technical ability was being utilized.

Demonstration Lessons

Seventy-four per cent of the teachers polled were in favor of demonstration lessons. This is a device that at times is resisted by super visors for these reasons:

1. When demonstration teaching merely serves to relieve the regular classroom teacher from teaching
2. When there is no reasonable assurance that the teacher will follow up with attempts at improvement
3. If this device is initiated by the supervisor merely to enhance the supervisor's prestige
4. If the teacher sees unattainable perfection, and as a result feels that the demonstration is not within her ability

A demonstration lesson can improve the learning situation and the teacher also can lose face as a result. The lesson is doing a service when it improves the teacher-learner relationship at the same time it improves the learning situation. It depends upon who demonstrates; under what circumstances; what the particular purpose; and how the demonstration was conducted.

A supervisor avoids this type of in-service device unless he can be assured that he has the same advantage as the teacher has. He needs to know the children and the particular situation.

Grade Level Meetings

Seventy-three per cent of the teachers polled preferred grade level conferences. This medium automatically "takes the heat off" the teacher, since it prevents an undesirable music supervisor from coming into the room.

Grade level meetings are useful when they are concerned with the teacher's real teaching problems. If they exist merely to pass down the "good word," this can be done through the otherwise ineffective bulletin. Teachers do not resent meeting when there is an underlying purpose. *They are very busy people,* and they resist attending meetings unless there's a real need. When this occurs the supervisor's efforts will not fall on deaf ears.

One music supervisor received requests from upper grade teachers to set up a meeting to help them develop projects on jazz in the general music program. He really preferred giving them a session in teaching beginning part singing, but they placed their need priority in the area of general music. The in-service meeting that resulted was exceedingly well attended by eager and enthusiastic teachers.

A group of primary teachers requested an in-service meeting on the subject of "rhythms." They provided the crowd and the refreshments. The supervisor merely provided them with the technical help they requested. The session involved demonstrations with teachers participating in bringing out various aspects of "rhythms," such as (a) how rhythm is expressed in art, (b) how rhythms manifest themselves musically, (c) and how rhythm and movement are a part of a child's proper physical development. The meetings were well received because they were requested—not superimposed.

When a supervisor can accept as valid that meetings of in-service caliber are destined to be successful if they take into account what the teacher is seeking, he can stop worrying about ways of involving teachers in scheduled activities.

Supervisor Arranging Teacher Visits to Other Schools

All teachers need a change from time to time. There is nothing as therapeutic as a day off during the thick of the school year, especially if it is not on an ordinary holiday. Many schools have been making it possible for their teachers to visit other schools during the school year. The supervisor might suggest that there are usually one or two teachers in each school who do an exemplary job of teaching classroom music. He could suggest to Miss G in the fifth grade, that, since she is visiting school _____ , she ought to drop in on Mrs. R, who has developed a fine method of teaching music reading. Or, he could suggest to Mr. B that he visit Mr. S's room and observe them working on the xylophones which they made in shop. Before the visit, the supervisor could talk to the hosts about the impending visits, suggesting that they bring out certain desirable teaching ideas.

Teachers are more willing to accept change and new teaching ideas from fellow teachers than from supervisors. Among the wonderful effects of such visitations are these: (1) seeing other teachers succeed in what we are trying; or (2) even seeing another teacher not quite succeed where you have tried. This can give one a mighty fine feeling.

A visit is good for both parties involved. It is good for the children, when Mrs. R can tell her children, "Boys and girls, today Miss G from _____ is visiting us. She heard about what a wonderful time we have in music class when we learn to read notes; now she is here to see how we do it." On Miss G's return, she can tell her boys and girls, "Yesterday I visited Mrs. R's fifth grade in the _____ school. You should have seen how those boys and girls enjoy their music lesson. They showed me how they learn to read music. I liked what I saw so well that I thought we could try it here."

The supervisor need not accompany the teacher on such visits. This is done all too often. His presence could easily prevent the teachers from getting maximum benefits out of the visit. All that is necessary is that the supervisor was in some way instrumental in arranging such a visit. Some supervisors create situations whereby they receive all of the credit while the teacher is pictured as a grateful recipient of favors.

Teachers Help Formulate School Policy

Teachers ought to have the opportunity to express themselves in curriculum matters. It is a legitimate activity of teachers as a group to review how they can implement a music program. By working together they can discover the varied musical talents available on the staff, and thus be able to help each other. Special music teachers can also work out their mutual problems in groups. All can be part of a team formulating policies that assure a good program of music education. Teacher-determined policies carry greater assurance of being carried out.

Constructive Criticism

Teachers want constructive criticism from their supervisor. They complain that he displays too little concern for the feelings of the teacher, or that he constantly speaks in generalities. When the teacher is observed by the supervisor, she has the right to honest criticism. Such criticism may have to be tempered with friendly words, but nonetheless it must be honest. It must provide definite clues for improvement and must help the teacher to grow professionally.

The supervisor is wasting the teacher's time if all he can say is that the teacher is doing all right and, "Were I in your situation I couldn't do any better." Both teacher and supervisor know there is something wrong. Supervision has often gone by the board in its avoidance of meeting issues squarely. Professional teachers can take criticism, especially when they ask for it.

Music Supervisor Recommends New Methods and Techniques

Methods, techniques, materials, books, periodicals, and equipment are all a part of in-service education. How these are laid out, when they are presented, and under what circumstances they are presented are guideposts to success of an in-service program.

So many demands have been made on the time and energy of the teacher that she has very little time left to use the many opportunities presented her whereby she can grow in her ability to teach music. The music supervisor must search for new ways to get ideas across, because schools have become a complex business. Today there are more demands on the supervisor's time than heretofore. He is less in the classroom; and because of time limitations, he institutes area-wide meetings, workshops, use of master teachers, employment of outside consultants, preparation of functional teaching aids, working with teacher training institutions, providing growth opportunities for potential leaders, and in-service training via radio or TV.

Area Meetings in Music

In setting up area meetings the music supervisor ought to consider that the classroom teacher's needs are many and cannot be met entirely and effectively. The following is one example of a reasonably effective series of area meetings.

This program is set up through a county school department serving an area of about 25,000 square miles. There are approximately one-hundred elementary schools in this area. Because of distance the music supervisor was restricted to one visit to each school each year. He tried dividing the jurisdiction into six areas, each one of these containing one large school district. Arrangements were made to set up an area meeting center in each of the six districts. Twice each year in-service meetings on different music education topics were announced for each area. During the first semester a series of meetings entitled Developing Music Reading Skills Through Songs were announced. These meetings were held in two sections. On Tuesdays the kindergarten teachers and teachers of grades one through three met for two hours, and on Thursdays the teachers of four through eight grades met. Teachers from each of the schools in the area attended the meeting of her grade level. Each week the meetings were held in a different place. After this series of meetings was completed, the music supervisor spent about six weeks in follow-up in the various schools where he was needed.

Wherever possible, a local teacher was used to demonstrate to the visiting teachers. These demonstrations were among the most significant features of the meetings. Teachers reported that they got most help out of seeing the host teacher demonstrate.

The host schools were flattered to be asked to set up such a meeting and were proud that one of the teachers was to demonstrate before other teachers. The teacher, herself, had an opportunity to re-evaluate herself, and, consequently, grow professionally.

In-Service Program Agendas and Check-Lists

Because school districts plan their total programs and in-service programs a long time in advance, it is important for music supervisors to plan meetings carefully. The following check-lists can be helpful:

MUSIC SUPERVISOR'S CHECK-SHEET
STEPS IN SETTING UP IN-SERVICE MEETINGS

Check or
Answer Here
Yes   No

Have you
A. Determined the specific needs for such a meeting by having
   1. Personally observed schools and teachers?
   2. Interviewed teachers and administrators?
   3. Obtained information through question-naires?
   4. Ascertained area-wide and state-wide needs?
   5. Received requests from administrators or teachers?

Yes   No

6. Noted lack of new and good instructional
   materials such as:
   new books _____
   new course of study _____
   new plan of operation _____
   new philosophy _____
   new pertinent research? _____

B. Determined the scope of the meeting with
   special regard to
   1. Who should be there?
   2. Should this be broken up into grade level
      meetings?
   3. Should this be broken into area level
      meetings?
   4. Do materials or ideas to be presented
      cut across grade lines?
   5. Will the size of the crowd influence the
      effectiveness of the meeting?

C. Determined what 'arrangements' or technical-
   ities must be cared for?
   1. Will it be an after school meeting?
   2. Will it be an evening meeting?
   3. Will it be a released time meeting?
   4. Will it be a Saturday meeting?
   5. What are the outer time limits of the
      meeting?
   6. Have you announced the time limits of
      the meeting?
   7. Do you consider these in setting the
      meeting place, time, and date?
      a. the work load of the teachers?
      b. the individualistic school setups?
      c. the traveling distance of teachers to
         meeting center?
      d. the after-school duties of the teachers?
      e. conflicts with other regularly sched-
         uled meetings teachers are to attend?
      f. other conflicts, events or holidays tak-
         ing place near the time and place of
         the scheduled meeting?
      g. is the subject of the meeting compat-
         ible with the time of the school year?
      h. is the meeting scheduled far enough
         away from Saturdays or holidays?

8. Cleared with:
  a. the various schools' principles involved?
  b. your own departmental calendar?
  c. the head of your own division to avoid conflict with other meetings in the area set by your central office?
  d. do you have definite confirmations in writing or otherwise clear understanding from the administrators and from your department head?

D. Determined the meeting place?
  1. Is it geographically feasible for teachers to get there with a minimum of time and directions?
  2. Are the local teachers and responsible personnel sympathetic toward the meeting? (If not, this can be most embarrassing.)

E. Determined the kind of space arrangements (room) that are needed to best carry out the proposed meeting plan and also accommodate the teachers?
  1. Will it be a one-way presentation by the supervisor?
  2. Will it be a discussion group?
  3. Will space be used for
     singing ———— playing instruments
     ———— listening to music ————
     using projectors and other equipment requiring darkened room ————
     participants taking notes? ————

F. Determined what materials you will need to carry out the meeting successfully such as
  1. Long tables ————, desks ————, folding chairs ———— chairs with writing arms?
     ————
  2. Black boards ————, bulletin boards? ————
  3. Chalk ————, music liner ————, charts ————, music flannelboard ————, flannel figures? ————
  4. Books ————, papers ———— ,pencils? ————
  5. Musical instruments? ————
  6. How much of each of the above?

Yes   No

    7. How much will you bring to the meeting?
    8. How much will the host district supply?
    9. How much will your assistants bring along?
   10. What materials will the participating teachers furnish?

G. Determined the best ways to advertise the meeting
    1. Through an in-service calendar?
    2. Central office general bulletin?
    3. A special announcement bulletin?
    4. School papers in individual districts?
    5. Local newspapers, radio, or television?
    6. A letter of invitation to each school to participate?
    7. A reply, through the principal, confirming the invitation, date, time and place, and listing number of teachers who plan to attend?

H. Determined in advance any teacher or administrative help you may need to set up or conduct the meeting or workshop successfully?
    1. Ask for help from local district to:
      a. set up facilities
      b. provide materials
      c. supply a demonstration group of students
      d. provide hosts and guides
      e. provide hospitality (refreshments)
      f. have local administrator open meeting
      g. use local music teacher as assistant
    2. Give teacher assistants a significant part of program
    3. Call on other talented music teachers, or classroom teachers, who teach music well to help.

I. Determined the need for an outside expert?
    1. Who shall it be _____ and why? _____
    2. How much will this service cost? _____
    3. Will the result be worth the cost? _____
    4. What particular arrangements are necessary _____
    5. What legal restrictions are there to employing _____ an outside expert?

Yes   No

    a. does he or she need to be a certified teacher? _____
    b. does he or she need to sign a loyalty oath in order to draw a stipend or gratuity? _____
  6. Do you subscribe to this expert's philosophy? _____
  7. Will he come by car _____, train _____, plane? _____
  8. Who picks him up and delivers him to meeting place?
  9. Who introduces him? _____
 10. Does he pay for his own meals and lodging (does the gratuity take care of this) what is the prearranged policy or understanding? _____

J. Determined the function of written materials for this meeting
  1. What is the topic?
  2. Do you need a supervisor prepared outline _____, bulletin _____, throw away sheet _____, meeting agenda _____, check sheet for teachers to follow procedures _____, evaluation sheet? _____

K. Determined the exact procedures for the meeting by
  1. Observing outer time limitations (starting and closing time)
  2. When refreshments are to be served so they do not interfere with valuable meeting time.
  3. The detailed plan for each minute during the workshop session or meeting, like:

MEETING AGENDA:
TEACHING BEGINNING PART-SINGING

min.

1. Session called to order by local administrator   1
2. Welcome to visiting teachers by administrator   2
3. Statement of purpose of meeting by administrator   2

	min.
4. Introduction of music supervisor	1
5. Supervisor introduces helpers and acknowledges other local assistance	1
6. Local chairman presents demonstration group of children (if this is part of plan) children will have filed in quietly and are at prearranged places	1
7. Actual demonstration with students	20
8. Supervisor acknowledges demonstrating children	1
9. While children leave quietly supervisor summarizes points in demonstration that lead into topic meeting (if there is no demonstration with children add this time to the presentation which follows or to reaction and question time—and time to clarify points)	3
10. If there is a guest expert, music supervisor introduces same	1
11. Expert or others, or music supervisor: a. demonstrates with participating teachers various steps in beginning part singing (more time if no student demonstration) b. reviews techniques needed c. demonstrates special helpful devices d. uses materials that teachers can readily apply	45
12. Allows for questions and special problems	5
13. Supervisor summarizes meeting	3
14. Supervisor thanks participants and helpers, acknowledges all who require it	2
15. Supervisor returns meeting to local administrator or chairman	1
16. Meeting is closed . . people are dismissed	1

90 Min.

	Yes	No
L. Determined what kind of evaluation should take place (if any)?		
1. Will the participants be asked to evaluate?		
2. Will the administrators involved evaluate?		

Yes   No

3. Will it be a written evaluation?
4. Will a good purpose be served through this evaluation?
5. Can whatever was accomplished in the meeting be measured in terms of the original objective of this meeting?
6. Was the objective of this particular meeting part of the music supervisory program for the year?
7. Was there a real, felt and expressed need for this meeting? and
8. Was this need met?

M. Determined necessary mopping-up operations?
1. Have certain people been vested with the responsibility of putting things away?
2. Has the turning out of lights and locking of doors been designated?
3. Have you provided the outside expert necessary transportation and hospitality?
4. Have you listed who is to receive letters of acknowledgment, such as
   local music teacher
   local administrator
   local students and
   their teacher
   in-service committee
   guest speaker
5. Does your business office have the machinery in motion to send the honorarium or gratuity to the guest speaker?

N. Determined follow-up assistance to individual teachers and schools?
1. Have you listed who needs special help?
2. Will your presence be necessary in giving this help?
3. Will instructional materials suffice?
4. Is this something the local music teacher, administrator, or in-service committee can do upon your suggestion?

Some of these points listed may seem redundant, but neglect of any of these can spell failure for an in-service meeting. Specificity is important in the smooth functioning of as sensitive an operation as a music in-service program.

Current Types of In-Service Program

Indirect In-Service Aid to Teachers

"Live" musical experiences can become a more potent force in teacher growth than many planned in-service programs wherein teachers are taught certain things. Unless there are such events already set up, it is part of the music supervisor's responsibility to help create and set up such events. They should be of such magnitude and caliber that by mere participating in them or attending them the teacher becomes enthused to the point that she wants to do a more effective job in bringing musical values to her students.

Among such events are these:

1. Civic music organizations (civic symphonic or choral groups)
2. Teacher conventions or "institutes" featuring outstanding professional or student musical aggregations
3. Local or regional festivals featuring the finest student talent
4. Symphony and opera performances for students and teachers

Many regions have set up large festivals involving the use of massed groups of instrumentalists and choral students. The effects of such performances have been of inspirational value to students, special music teachers, schools, and to entire communities. They are an outgrowth of a fine program of music education.

To effect such inspirational in-service devices takes much detailed planning. This responsibility to initiate, plan and carry out falls quite squarely on the shoulders of the music supervisor.

The following is a schedule of events that went into the planning of the elementary music festivals held annually in Stanislaus County, California. Each year in this county system two music festivals are set up under the leadership of the County Superintendent of Schools and the music supervisors on his staff: one in the elementary schools, and one for the high schools. The Elementary Festival Guidelines are a brief sketch of the highlights that go into planning an event of this magnitude:[10]

(Guide lines in setting up festivals)
ELEMENTARY MUSIC FESTIVAL
Calendar of Events

September—
1. Meeting to get acquainted and to review Festival plans made in the previous spring
2. Demonstration of playing Latin American Instruments; committee meetings to select Festival music.

October—
1. Instrumental committee supervisor in charge selects music for band and orchestra; start lists of students the teachers think are qualified to participate
2. Choral committee in charge of vocal supervisor.

November—
1. Meeting to get progress report of Festival plans
2. Guest speaker on "Music in the Space Age Schools."

December—
1. Organize final plans for instrumental tryouts
2. Send out sign-up sheets for band and orchestra
3. Send out return postcards to learn which schools plan to participate in choral activities
4. Send out teaching suggestions to choral conductors.

January—
1. Send out follow-up invitations, acceptances and information to all groups participating
2. Begin band tryouts
3. Meet to learn more about audio-visual materials available and how they may be used; progress report of Festival.

February—
Saturday rehearsals begin; band and orchestra weekly; chorus once; arrange for chairs for all groups.
Meet to work on use of social-recreational instruments; progress report of Festival.

March—
1. Rehearsals of band and orchestra continue weekly; chorus once
2. Check all final plans for Festival
3. Get names of participants and prepare certificates for them
4. Begin programs
5. Arrange for photographer for final rehearsal.

April—
1. Weekly rehearsals for band and orchestra
2. Prepare Festival publicity for radio and newspapers
3. Check on programs
4. Check on room and building arrangements; get piano, conductor's stands and podiums in place; borrow risers from M.J.C.; get schedule of activities for final rehearsal and concert to building custodians
5. All groups rehearse individually and in a preview concert at the site of the Festival on the Saturday prior to the concert date.

May—
1. Meet to evaluate Festival, elect officers and make plans for following year

2. Reserve auditorium and curriculum room for all Saturdays next February, March and April
3. Reserve a high school auditorium and other space necessary for the final rehearsal and the concert.

Music Supervisor Utilizing Outside Expert

When the music supervisor is aware of the teacher needs, he may wish to call in an outside expert to work with teachers and students. Such meetings are often part of the program of music educators' sponsored clinics. Noted specialists are usually employed who demonstrate materials and ideas to the teachers and also give them opportunity to participate in the application of new ideas.

A variation of the idea of the outside expert coming in to instruct is when the United States Navy Band was scheduled to play a concert in a nearby town. The local band director made arrangements for a special student concert to be held during the day for the neighboring high schools and elementary schools. Local music dealers and instrument manufacturers cooperatively financed a student clinic conducted by several artist members of the band. This clinic took place between concerts. The music supervisor assisted the outlying schools make necessary arrangements to come in. The special music teachers and their students were given the opportunity to observe artists at work.

The outsider can do much toward exciting teachers to do a better job, and thereby substantiate what the supervisor is attempting. He can also bring a new perspective to both teachers and music supervisor. The supervisor should be well acquainted with what the outside "expert" has to offer. Such a person may see the situation rather ideally and is not able to enter the frame of reference or see the real problems of the specialist or the teacher. The demonstration may be most exciting and bizarre, but if it does no more than leave the teacher excited, and still unable to follow up in her classroom, the cost for such service may have been used to better advantage.

We remember the "expert" who approached teachers like an old friend eliciting classroom trivialities from them. From these trivialities flowed ideas which he used to demonstrate to them. Years later teachers were still asking when he would be brought back. The strength of his presentation lay not in the eruditeness of his message but in the sheer simplicity of ideas expounded and in the manner they were presented. This person had the power to reach into human nature and let it tell him what it wants and needs. The teachers enjoyed this approach. Many of the ideas presented were carried on by the teachers long after he left. The teachers spoke of him, not with reverence, but as of an old friend.

If the music supervisor arranges for the service of an outside expert, he needs to decide whether the inspirational leader, the scholarly leader or the practical leader will do the required job. A well-known team of demonstrators has been fondly acclaimed as one-shot artists, because they have the facility of arousing the enthusiasm of masses of teachers, but after the demonstration is finished, the point of contact between what had been demonstrated and practicality vanishes. Teachers and supervisors love them for their enthusiasm and for the contributions they have made to important aspects of music education . . . but many recognize that they could be of greater inspiration to specialists who possess some necessary musical background.

The Music Supervisor Provides Growth Opportunities for Future Leaders[11]

The secure music supervisor is not afraid of helping a talented teacher on the road to success. He ought to help good teachers to leadership roles in their own schools by cultivating their potential. Many years ago the writer asked each school in his supervisory area to appoint a musically talented teacher from its staff to serve on a regional music education study group. The selected teachers met several times each year to plan the year's program and to receive help in implementing the music program in each of their schools.

These teachers were encouraged to go back to their schools and assume leadership in developing a music program. The principals began to rely on them for ideas, and would help them set up faculty meetings to discuss items pertinent to the music program. Ideas may move more slowly when this procedure is used; but they also may move more surely.

In another community the music supervisor called in the eight consultants serving the area, and with them set up in-service meetings for the classroom teachers. He coordinated meetings where the consultants worked in teams in various areas demonstrating to the teachers. Such an experience gave them valuable growth opportunity. Over and above this, the same supervisor called on the services of an outside expert to observe the consultants in their demonstrations. He met with them before and after the meetings in order to help them clarify what they were trying to do in relation to their effectiveness. None of these consultants were concerned about relinquishing their personal prerogatives. They were concerned about finding better ways of reaching more teachers.

An in-service program is commendable when it promotes leadership in others.

County or regional institutes, still flourishing in many areas of the country, provide professional in-service education in music for the classroom teacher and the specialist. Thus many teachers are afforded formal and informal opportunities to meet outstanding personalities.

Supervisor Working with Teacher Training Institutions

In many states teacher training institutions are located at best just a few hours drive from the most distant educational outpost. Most of these institutions, both private and state supported, are eager to extend their influence into each of the small communities. They want to be known as service centers and as being in the vanguard of educational thinking. These colleges have rather complete music departments with staffs of highly trained artist teachers in most phases of music. They want to work with the music departments of the surrounding schools because they are training the choral and instrumental directors who go directly into these schools. They also know that they will be judged by the caliber of their music educational product, whether they are (1) sending out top flight musicians but poor teachers; (2) good teachers, but inferior musicians; (3) or good musicians who are also good teachers.

The colleges need to know what kind of teaching product is needed in the schools to occupy the many positions of "specialist"; and what type music training is needed to provide also for the regular classroom teacher.

The local music supervisor can be of great service to his own territory when he works closely with the colleges. He can confer with them about their musical offerings and the kind of course content that will do the job best.

In many states there is only a limited amount of music credit required for future classroom teachers as part of their certification. Since it is altogether possible that not more than a median of six semester units in music skills useful in classrom music teaching and in music teaching methods will be required in the preservice training of future classroom teachers, it will be up to the colleges to set up courses within a kind of framework that will give classroom teachers a good start. Here is where the colleges need to confer with the supervisor to receive suggestions as to course content. They should be in the position to observe what really works in the classroom.

Music supervisors ought to draw upon experts from the nearby colleges for in-service meetings for both specialist and the regular teacher. Only by working with the schools of higher learning in the same area on a continuing basis can such institutions feel what is needed and then provide appropriate music leadership to the communities.

Many area teachers' colleges establish music education courses which are taught through extension programs. Such classes can be held in communities far away from the college and be patronized by teachers who have neither the time nor the energy to travel fifty to a hundred miles to the nearest college. Such an in-service device often arranged for and even taught by the supervisor places the supervisor in position of liaison between the college and the supervisory jurisdiction.

Workshop Type In-Service Programs in Music Education

Workshop has become a name for any chance meeting with a teacher. Oftentimes, any two or three teachers gathered together in one room, and listening to the same speaker, are considered either attending a workshop or in the process of being workshopped. Nevertheless, the term exists. It has gained educational respectability. It, as a term, has been used to explain a process whereby teachers learn together the things they need to know in order to do a better job of teaching. It also takes into account that learning is a growth process and does not necessarily eventuate during one brief meeting.

Principles involved in workshops are (a) a person's attitude toward other people; (b) the worth of the individual; (c) the need to build better human relations; (d) the human organism's infinite curiosity; (e) the importance of the individual's current problems; and, (f) the recognition of cooperation as a way of life. From these principles there evolved such workshop purposes as these: (a) breaking down barriers between teachers to promote communication, (b) helping teachers accept and work toward common goals, (c) giving teachers the opportunity to work on problems of current concern, (d) making teachers responsible for their own learning, (e) giving teachers experience in cooperative undertakings, (f) learning methods and techniques that the teachers can use in their own classroom, (g) giving teachers the opportunity to collaborate with others in producing useful teaching materials, (h) putting teachers in a situation where they will evaluate their own efforts, and (i) giving teachers an opportunity to improve their own morale.

A music workshop was conducted in Erie, Pennsylvania, in which one hundred sixteen teachers voluntarily participated once a week over a period of seven weeks. This workshop was set up with provisions for teachers to try out new ideas in their own classrooms. Problems considered were sight singing for teachers, methods of teaching sight singing, conducting, creative activities, voice production, and intonation. This in-service program was successful because teachers were involved in the planning and all of the problems worked at were problems teachers suggested.

Hjelmervik[12] reported a class-piano workshop for elementary teachers. The teachers involved evaluated this workshop in terms of these three apparent outcomes:

1. It was more valuable than any other instruction in music they had previously.
2. The teachers who were already skilled musically gained considerably in teaching confidence.
3. All of the teachers developed resourcefulness and self-confidence in teaching classroom music.

Paul Wentworth Mathews[13] reported on a Missouri workshop on elementary music education, indicating that through actual participation the classroom teacher learned to assume a greater responsibility for the music education program. Morehead State College in Kentucky[14] held a workshop in music education using this theme, "The Basic Musical Needs of the Elementary Teacher." These were the subtopics worked on by the teachers:

1. Development of keyboard skills (two thirds of the participants had no previous keyboard experience)
2. Development of a repertoire of singing games
3. Making simple instruments
4. Much directed listening
5. Finger-painting to develop creativity
6. Develop ways of combining and presenting music with other subjects
7. Help teachers overcome their feeling of inadequacy in trying to present music

Ideally, workshops refer to a series of sessions around a central theme, preferably such sessions extending over a fairly long period of time. A workshop extending over a period of time is problem-centered and job-related. It makes provision for teacher participation and for continuous evaluation. It rests much of its case on taking into account before, during, and after data relative to the problem.

Evaluation is indispensable to any in-service program. It helps focusing effort on the problem. It presupposes a recognition of objectives; and it relies on quantitative and qualitative evidence in determining the extent to which goals have been reached. A device that will tell what goes on in the classroom as a result of teacher's workshop participation is a valid way of evaluating an in-service program.

The Tulare County, California, Workshop in Elementary Music Education[15]

This workshop involved fourth grade teachers who came together once a week to find more effective ways of teaching music reading. The workshop extended over a period of the first semester in fifteen weekly meetings each of three-hour duration. Criteria for successful workshops were subscribed to by the participating teachers.

Each participant joined the workshop group because she felt a need to learn more about teaching music reading. The participating teachers were observed in action before the first workshop meeting. They also took certain tests to determine their status in relation to the workshop problem. From the first meeting on they were provided with many kinds of materials designed to increase their music-reading skills. They were given opportunity to practice using their learned skills right in the workshop sessions. Beyond this they were encouraged to use these skills in their own teaching situations. At each session time was spent in evaluating the success or failure of their classroom teaching efforts. The teachers evaluated their improvement through self-evaluation, testing, and observation, and they were provided with much extra help in presenting song material to children.

The students of these teachers were also tested and observed before, during, and after the workshop to determine the growth they registered in music reading that could be attributable to their teachers' workshop attendance and participation.

Workshop criteria were drawn from the writings of recognized curriculum experts such as Kelly, Corey, Caswell, Krug, and Parker.

Evidence of growth in music-reading skills was obtained through a standardized test of achievement in music. Various interim check tests were administered to determine interim growth. The teachers were observed by the supervisor and other observers periodically during the course of the several months of the meetings. Also, the teachers were provided with self-evaluation forms on which they could periodically record their own progress in the light of their own viewpoint.

SELF-EVALUATION
OF PAST MUSICAL TRAINING AND EXPERIENCES

NAME_____ AGE_____ YRS. EXPERIENCE _____

SCHOOL_____ YRS. IN GRADE 4

KEY: I-check YES or NO with X
II-check yrs., mos., or units viz.:   6 y (for yrs.)
        5 m (for mos.)
        12 u (for units)
III-grade yourself with X in col. A, B, C, D, or E,
        on How well you did or are doing.
IV-check X How much you use knowledge in teaching.

			No. Coll. Units			No. Ed. Units								
			I	II			III					IV			
			YES / NO	no.	y, m, u.	A	B	C	D	E	V-much	Much	Same	Little
1.	Did you take piano lessons?	yrs.												
2.	Other instruments? ( )	yrs.												
3.	Did you have classroom music in grade school?	yrs.												
4.	Did you participate in elementary school band?	yrs.												
5.	Did you participate in elementary school orchestra?	yrs.												
6	Did you participate in elementary school chorus?	yrs.												
7.	Did you participate in high school band?	yrs.												
8.	Did you participate in high school orchestra?	yrs.												
9.	Did you participate in high school chorus?	yrs.												
10.	Did you participate in high school general music?	yrs.												
11.	Did you participate in high school ensembles?	yrs.												
12.	Did you participate in college band?	yrs.												
13.	Did you participate in college chorus?	yrs.												
14.	Did you participate in college orchestra?	yrs.												
15.	Did you participate in college ensembles?	yrs.												
16.	Did you take college music courses (not mus. ed.)?	units												
17.	Did you take college music education courses?	units												
18.	Did you participate in community band?	yrs.												
19.	Did you participate in commity chorus?	yrs.												
20.	Did you participate in commity orchestra?	yrs.												
21.	Do you go to civic music concerts regularly?	yrs.												
22.	Do you listen to Radio or T-V music (once a week)	yrs.												
23.	Can you read music?	yrs.												
24.	Can you play a band or orchestra instrument?	yrs.												
25.	Can you sing a simple song in tune?	yrs.												
26.	Can you sight sing a simple song?	yrs.												
27.	Can you read music with tone numbers?	yrs.												
28.	Can you read music with tone syllable?	yrs.												
29.	Can you read music with letter names?	yrs.												
30.	Can you make up simple melodies?	yrs.												
31.	Can you read rhythm notation?	yrs.												
32.	Can you lead a song? (incl. start and stop)	yrs.												
33.	Can you use a pitch pipe?	yrs.												
34.	Can you play simple chord accompaniments? (piano)	yrs.												
35.	Can you play the autoharp?	yrs.												
36.	Can you play the psaltery?	yrs.												
37.	Can you play melody bells, chimes, tone blocks?	yrs.												
38.	Can you play song flutes?	yrs.												
39.	Can you play rhythm instruments?	yrs.												
40.	Can you improvise simple chord accompaniments?	yrs.												
41.	Can you teach songs by rote?	yrs.												
42.	Can you teach songs by note?	yrs.												
43.	Can you teach songs by tone syllables?	yrs.												
44.	Can you teach songs by tone numbers?	yrs.												
45.														
	Your opinion of student reaction to your music teaching.													

Qualitative evidence through analysis of case studies of each of the fourth grade teachers involved in this workshop indicated favorable progress.

The results of this workshop when measured in numerical advances during a period of fifteen weeks were astounding. These results were

OBSERVATION SHEET FOR CLASSROOM MUSIC ACTIVITIES

TEACHER_____ SCHOOL_____DATE_____

KEY: mark X in proper column. "T"-teacher only; "A"-all; "M"-most; "L"-less than half; "S"-six or less.

MUSIC ACTIVITIES	T	A	M	L	S	MUSIC RESOURCES	T	A	M	L	S
	USED						USED				
1. Discussion about song						1. Piano					
2. Discussion about notes						2. 4th grade state text					
3. Discussion about singing						3. "Sing and Learn" book					
4. Discussion about rhythm						4. "Sight Singing Fun" book					
5. Rhythm reading						5. Melody instruments/flutes					
6. Naming key						6. bells					
7. Naming time						7. strings					
8. Reading words						8. Percussive instruments					
9. Naming notes						9. Autoharp					
10. Naming numbers						10. Pitch pipe					
11. Naming syllables						11. Keyboard chart					
12. Discussion of phrases						12. Blackboard staff					
13. Sight singing numbers						13. Note games					
14. Sight singing syllables						14. Charts					
15. Sight singing words						15. Pictures					
16. Rote singing						16. State text recordings					
17. Whole song method						17. Young Am. Sings flm. & record					
18. Phrase by phrase method						18. Audio-visual aids					
19. Note writing						19. Flash cards					
20. Rhythmic activity						20. Articles & books about --					
21. Listening activity						21. Teachers manual					
22. Instrumental activity						22.					
23. Accompaniment						23.					
24.						24.					
25.						25.					

CLASSROOM CLIMATE						
1. Teacher dominated						1. List the titles of songs used
2. Student interest						a.
3. Teacher interest						b.
4. Cooperative student-teacher situation						c.
						d.
5. Student initiative						2. List strong points you observed in this lesson.
6. Friendliness						
7. Disturbance						
8.						

3. List weak points you observed in this lesson.

General statement about lesson observed

Signature of observer_____

Position_____

calculated from four bases. The first was the teachers' own self-evaluation. This included their own estimates of growth in music reading skills, and the use they made of this skill in their classrooms. The second included observation sheets kept by the supervisor and other observers. These took into account the teacher's use of music reading skills. The third basis of calculating music-reading growth was the evaluation of a series of tape-recorded lessons taken while teachers taught their children. These were analyzed and judged by a panel of music teachers.

FORM 6

JUDGES' RATING SHEET FOR TAPE RECORDED LESSONS
BY EXPERIMENTAL AND CONTROL TEACHERS

INSTRUCTIONS: Please judge only on the basis of actual heard evidences of music reading activities in the following lessons. If you hear a good rote lesson please do not check it unless it contains any of the agreed upon elements of music reading.

Check your estimate of the amount of each element of music reading you may hear. Use a separate sheet for each lesson

IS THERE EVIDENCE OF?	VERY MUCH	MUCH	SOME	LITTLE	NONE
1. Teaching sight singing					
2. Note and syllable reading . . .					
3. Rhythm reading					
4. Reading of musical symbols .					
5. Tonal number reading					
6. Use of neutral syllable					
7. Teacher confidence in teaching music reading skills					
8. Students understanding of music reading skills					
SCORE					

TOTAL_____

Use reverse side for additional comments or criticisms of the lesson.

JUDGES'S SIGNATURE_____

This provided both qualitative and quantitative evidence.

Workshop Results	September (Based on hypothetical 100%)	February
I. Teacher Self-evaluation		
Teacher growth in skill	38%	70%
Teacher use of skill in classroom	6%	66%
II. Observations by supervisor and by other qualified persons		
Teacher's use of skill	3%	57%

III. Tape recorded music reading lessons
presented to students; tapes judged
by panel of special music teachers;
recording made at end of workshop
    Participants rated 49% of pos-
sible; other fourth grade teachers
rated only 9% of hypothetically
perfect lesson

IV. Kotick Torgerson Test of Music
Achievement
    Teachers growth in skills listed
in test items   68%   90%
Students registered a numerical
growth of 38 points on the scale
during this time. The assumption
was that they merely received
some training in relation to that
received by the workshop participants

The progress of the students was an indication of workshop success.
The advances made by the students were not at all outstanding. They
did, however, indicate that something was happening that was attributable to the workshop. The teachers first had to acquire skill and become comfortable in it before they could teach it to their students.
Whatever the students scored was observed learning over but a short
period of time.

The participating teachers had many opportunities to evaluate themselves. This was in keeping with a principle made by Kelley: "When
an individual assumes the responsibility for a course of action, he automatically judges how well his decision worked out . . . what the teacher
thinks of the learner is of passing moment, but what the learner thinks
of himself is of lasting import, because it is built into experience and
modifies the organism from there on."[16]

The semester-long workshop was a workshop with consecutive meetings. One ought not assemble a group of teachers for a common purpose
for just one session and expect group participation, agreement on problems, approaches or solutions, and formulate definite plans for action.
Newly learned ideas must be assimilated by the individual; and the
human organism does not assimilate ideas at the crack of the whip or
at the sound of a bell.

Workshops, consecutive workshops, and *action research* are really
synonymous. It means no more than applying what was learned, testing
the new learnings in actual situations, returning with results, and con-

tinually readjusting these learnings so that they can be transmitted to the student more effectively and economically. It is a practical means of improving teaching and learning. It ties teaching into the learning process.

The Music Supervisor's Preferences

Curriculum planners have always been persistent in considering the likes, desires, wishes, and preferences of the teachers who are the recipients of their planning. As important as this is, it is equally important to consider the particular talents, likes, and preferences of music supervisors in in-service affairs. If a supervisor is to be enthusiastic at all times, he should have some choice in mode of operation. Effectiveness is a two-way operation—it depends on the preferences of both giver and receiver. Because of the complexity of present-day school organizations it is becoming more difficult to set up in-service programs whereby teachers can always be reached effectively and consistently.

A number of music supervisors have listed some of the following among their preferences:

1. Regular grade level meetings as part of a program allowing teachers in-service credit for salary increment
2. In-service courses for college credit to care for local teacher needs
3. City-wide and county-wide general music workshops
4. Building meetings to care for individual school needs
5. Meetings with administrators to explain aims and objectives and to solicit their aid in implementing the program
6. Extension courses and summer courses for teachers
7. Regular monthly meetings with special music teachers

The supervisor of music needs to be alert to all avenues of communication between himself, the teachers and the learning situation.

QUESTIONS FOR DISCUSSION, THOUGHT AND STUDY

1. What is the measure of a good music learning situation?
2. A music supervision program in one school district can be a success. Why can the same program carried out in another community be doomed to failure?
3. What changes in in-service programs have taken place over the past year that may make Antell's findings somewhat obsolete?
4. How do adults learn most effectively? What clues are contained in this for music supervisors?
5. If people prefer to help themselves, is this a good reason for the availability of a professional library?
6. How would you interpret technical assistance? What kind of mandate does this thrust upon a music supervisor?

7. Why do so many teachers prefer demonstration lessons?
8. Why is teacher-requested in-service help especially helpful?
9. How can interschool visitation be a good supervisory device?
10. Mention some ways by which teachers can affect school policy.
11. What is constructive criticism?
12. How can a music supervisor recommend new methods and techniques and have teachers accept these ideas, and do something about them?
13. Outline the mechanics of setting up an area meeting in intermediate grade music principally in the teaching of part-singing.
14. Why the outside expert? What can such a person contribute to a learning situation?
15. How can music supervisors find potential leaders? What can the supervisor do to help such a person grow professionally?
16. What is the role of supervisor and teacher training institutions? What is the difference between preservice and in-service training? What are some of the current criticisms of preservice courses in elementary music education?
17. What is the professional definition of *workshop*? What are its identifying critera?
18. Define action research. Why is it recognized as a powerful in-service device?
19. List the best ways you know to reach teachers musically.
20. Question a group of teachers about their feeling about music supervision. Find out why they feel the way they do. Recommend something to remedy the situation if it is unfavorable.

NOTES

[1]Harold Spears, *Improving the Supervision of Instruction, op. cit.,* p. 443.
[2]Antell, *op. cit.,* p. 606.
[3]P. M. Bail. "Do Teachers Receive the Kind of Supervision They Desire?" *Journal of Educational Research,* 40:9, (May, 1947), p. 713.
[4]Vernon Replogle, "What Help Do Teachers Want?" *The Education Digest* 16:2, (Oct. 1950), p. 9.
[5]Paul Mort and F. Cornell, *American Schools in Transition,* (New York Bureau of Publication, Teachers College, Columbia University, 1941), p. 106.
[6]E. Paul Torrance, *Guiding Creative Talent,* p. 206 adaptation.
[7]Snygg and Combs, *Individual Behaviour, op. cit.*
[8]John Dewey, *Education and Experience,* (New York: The Macmillan Co., 1939).
[9]Dewey, *op. cit.*
[10]Courtesy, Stanislaus County Schools.
[11]ASCD, *Role of the Supervisor and Curriculum Director in a Climate of Change,* (Washington, D.C.: NEA, ASCD 1965 Yearbook).
[12]Kenneth Hjelmervick, "Class Piano for Beginners," (Washington, D.C.: *MENC Journal,* XXXVI, Feb., 1950), pp. 30-34.
[13]Paul Mathews, "Missouri Workshop for Elementary Teachers," (Washington, D.C.: *MENC Journal,* XXXVII, Jan. 1951), p. 49.
[14]Lureate Martin, "Basic Musical Needs of the Classroom Teacher," (Menc *Journal,* XXXVIII, Jan. 1952), p. 52.
[15]Rudolph Weyland, "The Effect of a Workshop on Certain Fourth-Grade Teachers' Skills in Teaching Music Reading," (unpub. doctoral dissertation), Univ. of California, Berkeley, 1955.
[16]Earl Kelley, *The Workshop Way of Learning,* (New York: Harper and Brothers, 1951).

Chapter 10

Facilitating the Flow of Materials

Informing Schools as to Musical Needs

Promote Materials

A skilled teacher can teach without a great abundance of materials. But not all teachers are equipped by training and talent to do a creative job of music teaching. Most teachers need special aids in the form of music materials and equipment. The supervisor has an obligation to call school administrators' attention to material and equipment needs.

The list presented in Chapter 12 (pages 254-255) was designed to call attention to needs. It was intended as a guide to the school administrator, who with assistance of his teachers and music specialists, works out a plan whereby these kinds of musical needs will be met. A list of priorities to meet music instructional needs ought to include an item description, purpose, cost, and local inventory.

Many schools that have no music consultant encourage the use of materials thus:

1. Designate one teacher to be the musical aid representative for the school
   a. to coordinate special music activities
   b. to order special music aids
   c. to see to it that needed materials are available in one central place
2. Set up a central place for music supplies and equipment—available on a scheduled basis to all teachers
   a. Provide a check-out system for infrequently used materials, or materials that pertain only to a limited number of grades

    b. Arrange a schedule for use of items like autoharp, song bells, phonograph, tape recorder, projectors, special aids
3. Provide music carts so that special aids can be pushed from room to room in a safe manner (to be kept in a special music depository, except when in use—one for each six or eight elementary classrooms; or one per building unit or wing)
4. Encourage teachers to provide a special *music corner* or *atmosphere* or *center* from time to time during the school year

The listing itself is the result of a study by music specialists, teachers, and the county music supervisor working together. It was designed originally as a guide to schools planning special music purchases through E.S.E.A. Title I funds (p. 254-255).

Use Materials

Many teachers need help in the proper use of phonographs, recorders, filmstrip projectors, slide projectors, or movie projectors, despite courses they took dealing in the proper utilization and operation of audio-visual equipment. Consultants ought to be willing to help teachers in the proper selection of materials and in the proper operation of equipment.

Display Materials

In-service meetings provide a good time and place to display good materials and equipment. Supervisors frequently bring a carful of music materials, which are then displayed on several tables near the entrance of the room in which in-service meetings are held. This gives visiting teachers the opportunity to see and manipulate materials both before and after the meeting.

Try Out Materials

A list, such as the one in Chapter 12, is not the only answer in facilitating materials. The supervisor has the prior responsibility to interest the school, the teacher, and the administrators in necessary equipment and materials. The supervisor may have to demonstrate or provide for a demonstration of these materials. It is not the best procedure to expect a school to purchase materials just on the recommendation of the supervisor. So often materials, purchased for that reason, are not used. It would be far better if a need is created and the teachers' appetites are whetted for certain things.

One music supervisor was told by his instructional director never to demonstrate to teachers materials that they do not have on hand. This may be a realistic approach to some, but by so doing the supervisor really relinquishes one of his responsibilities of exerting his educational leadership in broadening the musical horizons of the teacher.

The music supervisor should become thoroughly acquainted with the many instruments, devices, and materials that can aid teachers in teaching classroom music. Since teachers have so few opportunities to see materials they cannot always judge quality and usability. The supervisor ought to select from the best of these devices and show them to teachers and let them use them in their daily work.

Some supervisors prepare music teaching kits containing new materials for circulation to various schools. This is in lieu of having them on display, and it gives teachers an opportunity to use these materials, or just to try them out.

Lending Materials to Teachers

Many large districts, city school systems, county school offices, and other intermediate school offices maintain audiovisual centers that lend music teaching aids and equipment to schools.

Such service centers also maintain libraries of professional books which are available to the classroom teacher. The supervisor should make teachers aware of such help and facilitate their getting such materials.

Song bells, autoharps, certain kinds of rhythm instruments, and other kinds of musical devices that can facilitate music programs should be the property of the school and available to any teacher. (See Recommended Materials, Chapter 12.)

One consultant demonstrated the use of a certain kind of chromatic song bells in teaching songs and developing music-reading concepts at a regional teachers meeting. He brought ten sets of these song bells along to the demonstration. After the meeting he lent one set to each of ten schools represented, suggesting that all teachers in each of the schools be given an opportunity to use these. An instruction sheet was provided with each set so that teachers could instruct themselves on how to play tunes on the instruments. Some weeks later a local music dealer called the consultant indicating that he was swamped with orders for this kind of song bells—"and please can you tell us in advance when you are going to push an item so we can have the material on hand?"

Supervising the Use of Required Materials

Many states adopt one or more series of school music books for required use in the schools. County education departments and large city districts often make independent or supplementary adoptions. A state adoption of a single series can tend to (1) assure a minimum program for each school, (2) assure a consistent philosophy, and (3) avoid the purchase of a new series each time a music teacher or supervisor moves in from another state. These are the current series of classroom music textbooks:

Birchard Music Series ....Summy-Birchard Company
Discovering Music Together ....Follett Publishing Company
Exploring Music ....Holt, Rinehart and Winston, Inc.
Growing With Music ....Prentice-Hall, Inc.
The Magic of Music ....Ginn and Company
Making Music Your Own ....Silver Burdett Company
Music for Young Americans ....American Book Company
This Is Music ....Allyn and Bacon, Inc.

There are hosts of other instructional materials published that supplement these series or specialize in a particular aspect of a music.

A major task of the supervisor is assisting in the evaluation of textbooks (see Evaluation, pp. 302-308) and the implementation of the series.

Supervisor Helps Implement the Series

Music books, unfortunately, are known to be the most unused books. Bookshelves are beautifully decorated with long rows of unsoiled music books. Each series, used or not, contains music of intrinsic and significant worth which was most carefully selected. But often the teacher has not the time, the inclination, or the talent to search out song material and musical ideas for teaching.

Thus it remains someone's job to implement the books so they are used. It is of prime importance to ask oneself in implementing books, "What are we trying to achieve musically; and how are we going to do it?" This means determining the end-product and then searching out a program in the books that will lead there. All series claim a program but the arrangement of materials too frequently leads to no goal. In some, the program is laid out quite specifically so that the teacher can see for himself the scope and the sequence of musical experiences and learnings he ought to be getting across to the children during a year. Even though a program may be apparent in some series, it is not used optimally. The job of the supervisor is to help the teacher to make good use of music textbooks.

Supervisors Help Teachers Use the Teachers' Manuals

Teacher manuals also adorn the shelves of curriculum libraries. They can be an excellent source of guidance to the teacher. The supervisor does well placing them in the hands of the teachers. Even a bookmark to draw attention to certain items may aid the teacher in availing herself of this aid.

Supervisors Help Teachers Find the Program of Musical Learning

All series of elementary grade textbooks in music claim to have a design, a program, or a central idea which the authors are trying to get across. This program may or may not be what is wanted in a particular region. Often it is not clearly spelled out. The supervisor must show teachers how they can discover a program. In the absence of a clearly defined goal, or end-product, a program is anticlimactic.

In searching for a program the writer examined each song in several series for its use for many of these purposes:

1. Can it be chorded on the autoharp, using just the simplest chords, I, IV, V in keys of C, G, and F?
2. Is it within the easy keys and the range of the song-flute type instrument?
3. Can the tune be played on chromatic song bells?
4. What are the recurring melodic patterns at each grade level? Are they basically diatonic, or choral?
5. What are the songs at each level that can be enhanced with rhythmic movement?
6. What is the sequence of types of dances presented?
7. What are the big ideas stressed at each grade level?
8. How much material is in each book that will be usable in other learning areas of that particular grade?
9. Are the repeated songs at each grade level of such quality that they can stand to become a cumulative repertoire?
10. Is there enough of a program in the series, that, if taken grade by grade, the children will evolve as music-loving and musically literate people?

Without some criteria one could go through much wasted motion. One can't pay little heed to sequential learning or to the scope of the program and "Just follow the book—and the kids will grow into musical adults!" There is really no statistical evidence that will bear this out. Good teaching and a developmental goal-centered process need to be considered.

The value of a music program should not be gauged by its sporadic experiences. These experiences are frequently considered in isolation instead as part of a total developmental program.

The musical growth of the child is as important as its linguistic growth and proceeds in the same manner as its linguistic growth and as its growth in other learning areas. School experiences designed to promote growth in other learning areas are very deliberate. They are a result of research in how children tend to respond to instruction. A program of elementary music education must never be unrelated musical experiences, but it must have an apparent developmental program. Experiences must be arranged in such sequence that they will promote and help unfold further and deeper musical experiences. It is the task of the supervisor to help the teacher find this program. (See Bruner[1] and Textbook Selection Criteria p. 302-307.)

Music Supervisor's Responsibility in Providing Professional Reading Materials and Other Printed Matter

All teachers need instructional materials. To summarize: such materials include audiovisual equipment and materials; musical equipment, instruments, and proper music; and printed material in either book or pamphlet form. True, we have not exhausted ideas about instructional materials. The ideas already mentioned are merely clues which the supervisor can develop and expand.

They all represent the encroachment of *ideas* into the classroom that would ordinarily find difficulty in presenting themselves. Some of the *ideas* are *issues* which the intelligent music supervisor must clear in his own mind and conscience if he wishes to presume leadership in music education in this period of educational history.

QUESTIONS FOR DISCUSSION, THOUGHT AND STUDY

1. What determines the need for special instructional materials in music?
2. Make a list of musical materials that would enrich a classroom music program.
3. How can schools provide necessary and desirable music instructional materials?
4. How would you solicit the interest and backing of the principal to get materials?
5. Why do we use recordings of songs in the several textbooks?
6. Check your nearest audiovisual center for special films on music. Find out how these films are selected.
7. How would you call teachers' attention to instructional materials?

8. How do you feel about exposing teachers to materials which are good, but not available to them?
9. Find out as much as possible about the school audiovisual center nearest you. How accessible is it to teachers? What do schools have to pay for its service? Can teachers come to such a center and browse around for materials?
10. What do you think ought to be a policy for the temporary loan of instruments, such as autoharps?
11. What should be the supervisor's role in implementing a new series of classroom music books?
12. How would you make supplementary music books available to teachers?
13. How would you as supervisor identify a definite program from music books and get the idea across to teachers?
14. Discuss the effectiveness of various types of teachers' manuals that accompany classroom music books. What do teachers look for in a manual?
15. How do teachers react to short bulletins?
16. How can you keep teachers aware of materials and procedures for obtaining them?
17. Ought the music supervisor maintain a place where pertinent materials are on display?
18. Discuss *product* and *process* in relation to typical arrangement of materials found in current music books for grade schools.
19. How can current theories of learning help in formulating a program?

NOTES

[1]Jerome Bruner, *Toward a Theory of Instruction,* (Cambridge, Mass.: Belknap Press, Harvard University, 1966).

Part IV

The Music Supervisor as a Leader

...he makes decisions
...he utilizes research
...he grows professionally
...he thinks creatively

National Music Camp Photo

Chapter 11

Making Decisions
About Issues and Ideas

A Philosophy of Education and Music Education

The music supervisor is called upon to make decisions that will affect the music program of the schools or area he is serving. He is often expected to make such decisions in conversation with teachers, administrators, specialists, children, or community members or as public pronouncements before groups of people, through the press, or through other community media.

Therefore, it is important that he is armed with learned opinions and ideas about issues that confront him. If his training and experience have given him ideas that have evolved as patterns or predictable trends of thinking about music education, he will be unhesitating in his response. The modern supervisor, who is no longer an inspecting officer, must have a philosophy of education which is a predictable part of his reaction pattern.

Beliefs about which way education should go, or what education should accomplish, are quite involved. There is little agreement in practice. Some would say that great minds elaborate great thoughts which, in turn, are given to the people as a guide to living. Others would have it that great minds have observed man in his multivaried activities, and have recorded his movements as patterns or trends. These trends gradually grew into and became accepted as a philosophy.

A philosophy is a directional guidepost which men observe and go by, and to which they constantly readjust in the light of changing circumstances. In education great men have from time to time observed children learn and teachers teach. They have also observed the varying conditions under which teaching and learning took place and have noted any extraneous influences. These observations have formed a pattern of trends and guides for action.

Music education must also have a philosophy in keeping with educational goals.

The music programs in many of our schools are indeed exemplary from our artistic viewpoint but, have we ever examined them in terms of objectives to determine whether they are the *right* things? What ideals have been trampled upon in the accomplishment of the glamorous end goal?

Issues and philosophies need to be discussed in terms of their spokesmen. Writers about music education are frequently glibly referred to, misquoted, or their sayings misapplied. One supervisor mentioned when asked what she did about music reading in her schools, "We don't believe in music reading because we follow_____'s philosophy." The questioner wanted to ask, "Which page in Dr._____'s book?" but instead, put tongue in cheek.

We need to think about aims, goals, or end-products in music education. What are these? Who thought of them? How do they apply? Are they in agreement with a commonly accepted philosophy of education?

The following ten conditions for effective music learning are paraphrased from an article by Ralph Tyler.[1]

1. The student should have musical experiences that cause him to work at the kind of musical behavior contained in the objectives.
2. These musical learning experiences should be of such a nature that the student finds satisfaction in behaving in a manner implied by the objective.
3. An important condition for learning music must be the motivation of the learner, i.e., the force that causes him to become involved.
4. By recognizing previous unsatisfactory ways of learning music the learner should be stimulated to try new ways.
5. The student should have expert instruction while trying to work at the new music learning behavior.
6. An abundance of complementary and appropriate materials should be available.
7. The student should be allowed sufficient time, not only to apply the new musical behavior, but to practice it until it becomes part of his repertoire.
8. Repetition should be avoided, but much sequential practice in the new musical behavior should be provided.
9. The student should be encouraged to set goals with restraints (standards) that cause him to go beyond his performance level. These standards must be attainable, however.

10. The student must have means by which to judge his own musical behavior (performance) to check how well he is doing in his quest for goals.

What Do Music Supervisors Know About the Aims of Music Education?

Mursell[2,3] indicated five aims of music education. These may not be final. It is for the music educator to think through these and try to add additional ones. The points that Mursell lists are based on his Principle Number II.

The aims of the music program should take the form of specific statements of the tangible, practicable effects that music can and should have on human nature, human living, and human growth.

These are some of the effects that Dr. Mursell spelled out for a program of music education:

Is enjoyment a desirable aim? "Through our music program we will try in every possible way to bring children full, rich, varied experiences of musical enjoyment."

If enjoyment is any and all of these plus all of their shaded over- and undertones, such as *like, relish, be pleased with, derive pleasure from, take pleasure in, delight in, rejoice in, tread on enchanted ground, go into raptures, bask in,* then materials ought to be selected that will do just these things. Is there joy in playing one's first tune? Is there joy in succeeding to sing in harmony? Do you get a lump in your throat when the band goes marching by playing a Sousa March? There was joy that expressed itself in young Ron's entire being when he discovered that the music he was making with the band (even on his battered clarinet) suddenly sounded like symphonic music he had heard years before. In fact, his joy was so profound that this critical incident[4] forced his parents into buying a new expensive wooden clarinet for him. This may also have been a real turning point in his life.

Real enjoyment is not automatic. It needs to be learned. It needs to be broken down into different real things people do musically through which they claim enjoyment. Let us involve our students in these activities; teach them the skills and knowledge to be comfortable in them. "Great art is not sensuous pleasure. If it were, it would appeal —like cake or cocktails—to the untutored as well as to the cultured taste."

Is succeeding a good aim? "We will endeavor to bring to children experiences of successful achievement in and through their dealing with music."

If we accept success as a desirable aim then we must present a system of well ordered musical successes. Before young Ron experienced the "critical incident" he was presented with a series of progressive musical successes. A kindergartener can't hold a big bass horn properly, much less blow it, but he can sound a motive on tone blocks successfully. The need for success is a plea for a sequential program.

What is pertinent about disciplining oneself to learn the arts? "We will constantly seek to bring children disciplinary experiences of devoting their full energy and efforts to attain goals that they desire and that seem significant to them."

Do the slogans "music is fun," "you too can learn music," and "music is easy" hold water? It is not easy for children to blend their voices together for the first time. Neither is it easy for second graders to tap rhythm sticks on uneven beats. It takes putting one's whole mind and being to achieving the goal, that is, if the goal is feasible, attainable, and musically desirable. Does one discipline oneself toward a more desirable goal? We stop trying to climb walls that are too high and too slick. Trees are more attainable because they are not so slick. Discipline makes way for frustration if the goals are not spelled out as feasible, attainable, and desirable. Goals are also the many smaller steps or levels. All of these must be spelled out with clarity; then discipline and effort will yield success and enjoyment. Ron utilized this factor most successfully after the impact of music appeared to him with crystal clarity.

What about social development through music? "In and through our music program we will seek to promote the social development of children by means of constructive social relationships and experiences."

The concept of "other values than music" is being disputed in many places. Let it be remembered that music exists, flourishes and has affectivity value only in the context of social relationships, i.e., composer and performer, conductor and performer, listener and performer. To remove music from the dancing and playing of people, the church, the night club, the parade, or the radio and television's advertising and accompanying and leave it solely in the concert hall would belie the very nature of music.

Many years ago I accompanied my small town high school band to the big city where it marched across the field with seventy-five other bands at a university homecoming game. They just played one tune. I saw Marilyn during the half. She had an ice-cream bar in one hand, a bottle of pop in the other and a bag of popcorn bulging out of her uniform pocket. Her saxophone was attached to her very securely. She just beamed at me and said, "This is the first time I ever was in a city." It was Ron's first time to wear a tie. His family was so proud that they and several cars full of relatives saw him off on the school bus. One tune, and a world of new relationships opened up! This was preceded by discipline, success, and equipment. This was a celestial reward in the form of socialization through the vehicle of music

Does music widen cultural horizons? "In and through music we will try in every way to widen the cultural horizons of children and young people, and to lead them to a growing awareness of the vast range and variety of human experiences."

We widen cultural horizons when we open doors for our students. Ron and Marilyn walked through the open door. Charles, the welfare boy who was placed in eight successive foster homes over four years, somehow found his way into the band room. The new recording bass needed a master and he decided to be it. He stayed in the same foster home for four years, and later worked part of his way through college playing in a dance combo. Beatrice, the oldest of eleven children of a non-English-speaking poor rural family, learned to play the clarinet. This ability opened many doors for her. A few years later she appeared on television playing her clarinet and demonstrating an original cake recipe, for which she was awarded a scholarship to finish her schooling. Music may not have widened her cultural horizons, but through music the door to greater cultural involvement has been opened.

To many the ultimate objective is "appreciation." But this term needs to be spelled out in operational activities that answer[5]: what does a person really do when he appreciates? Does he have knowledge, experience, insight, judgment, and perception about certain aspects of music. An appreciator both knows and does certain things that mark him in no uncertain terms.

MENC statements of guiding principles[6]

1. Music offers an opportunity for self-expression through group activity. This emphasizes the social values of music.
2. Music offers an opportunity to develop moral and spiritual values and to satisfy aesthetic needs.
3. Music provides a medium through which boys and girls can make direct contributions to their community during their school days and thus acquire the consciousness of the responsibility of the individual to the community.
4. Music provides a medium for understanding other people, their culture, and their problems.

5. Through music the student is led to a realization that the arts, of which music is one, have been of indisputable importance in all history.

"I believe I would put education for citizenship as its most important function. *This is music's most important stake in education.*"[7]

Growth and Development Principles
Also Apply to Music Education

Growth is a process of aging and changing to a mature state. Development implies not only aging, but also improving in ability and skill. Maturing is that aspect of growth that takes over when the growing object has become ready to perform its normal function. Maturity is that state where the process of maturation has ceased and growth and development are at their maximum. Learning means changing behavior responses because of new information, new insights, skills, or attitudes. Learning is what happens when growth, development, maturation, maturity, education, and the education process are all at work.

The music supervisor will be able to guide learning experiences more wisely if he recognizes the implications involved in the psychology of learning. The following implications are derived from Otto's *Twenty-four Principles of Learning*:[8,9]

1. Man's musical behavior can be modified by his interaction with a musical environment
2. Music learning and experiences should be geared to his physical, emotional, and social development
3. The student's musical responses become more refined with personal growth and development
4. There is a positive correlation between superior children learning music more readily than others
5. All factors considered, musical growth follows an orderly pattern
6. Musical growth can be continuous, even though the rate of growth may change; each stage of learning unfolds into more mature functioning of processes that have been going on for a long time
7. Fluctuations in rate of musical learning are caused by the kind of musical diet fed to the student
8. Certain kinds of musical diet are more apropos for certain age levels than other ages; there is a time for belonging to the band
9. Individual differences apply also to people involved in musical learning as in other learning
10. Boys and girls may differ in the way they learn music and in their musical preferences

11. Social and personal aspects have a lot to do with how boys and girls grow musically
12. The emotional impact of music can spur learning, especially when it creates an unresolved need; the unresolved drama of music creates a suspenseful situation in the learner to want more
13. Learning is facilitated when there is something constantly new and challenging in music that will demand new ways of meeting needs; learning experiences ought to be presented in context with "live" music
14. Music learning and behavior are caused—they don't just happen
15. The total child reacts to music—and he reacts to all the *strands* of music simultaneously, the melody, the rhythm, the harmony, the form, the style, and the expressive structure
16. The setting in which the child finds itself and the setting in which music is presented has much to do with learning
17. Learning music involves proceeding from one problem-solving situation to another
18. Music learning implies involvement; it implies making music, or working at the process of making music
19. Freeing a student so that he can act creatively in his musical environment (thinking, interpreting, devising new, rearranging, etc.) helps musical learning
20. Worth-while extrinsic and intrinsic motivations must be arranged to facilitate learning of music; this may mean drama, suspense, rewards, etc.
21. The music to be used in the learning situation must have significance and stimulus value
22. Music learning results from the deliberate arranging of significant musical experiences in progressive sequential steps; one good music learning experience ought to lead into a problem-solving situation, which, in turn, opens the door to new experiences and new problems to be solved, so that the entire learning process becomes one of unfolding, and not of adding experiences (Otto, Mursell, Bruner)

Determining the Scope and Sequence of the Music Learning Program

It has become traditional to refer to the twins, scope and sequence, in one breath. This is despite the irrelevancy of the implied validity of this posture. Scope deals with the magnitude of the problem. It deals with the multitudinous facets in breadth, depth, and quantity of music determined for inclusion in a "course of study." Sequence deals with the arrangement of the very many items that go into making music learning feasible. Neither of these carry any relevance by themselves or in partnership unless they deal in terms of *objectives*.[10] And here is where most of us in education have failed. We claim that we have objectives well in mind, but too often what we think are objectives are really *untested prejudices*. The music educator must ask himself these questions:

1. Given a period of time each week—just what is the music content I must teach?
2. How will I know that I have taught it?
3. What aids and processes will best help me teach what I am to teach?

Despite controversies in the field, the arithmetic and the reading people have decided upon goals they intend to reach at the end of their course. They have set up relevant procedures, content, and methods which "cause the student to interact with appropriate subject matter in accordance with laws of learning." Objectives are being worked at more assiduously now than ever before and by people who exert the utmost in scholarly zeal and exactness. In viewing the numerous new elementary school music books and in studying their respective rationales one can see a more discernible concensus about goals. Words like *appreciation, understanding, ultimate concern, desirable outcome*, however, are still standard descriptions of objectives.

We should be interested in the *terminal musical behavior* of the student. This is the operational behavior your students are expected to demonstrate after having been instructed for a specified period of time. And the only way one can discover whether this terminal behavior has been achieved is by applying a *criterion* (a standard, or a test) by which this terminal behavior can be evaluated.

The day is past when the music teacher teaches one content for a specified *terminal behavior*, and actually tests for something else. Limited music teaching time, expanding student clientele, and the need for justification of a program will demand setting up objectives in terminal behavior terms and checking whether this hoped for behavior eventuates. *Objective* really is the *intent* of a program described in terms of proposed change in a learner. What will the learner look like (sound like) musically after the successful completion of the learning experience? Will the tests or guideposts given along the way tell the teacher and the student the degree to which both have been successful in their course objectives? The student *performance must be measured in terms of the goals*.

In order to establish meaningful goals in music education one must spell out the program in "action" words, such as play an octave on the flute starting on middle C; play an octave in the key of G starting on G above middle C; play "The Star Spangled Banner" on the trumpet in the key of B♭; sing the alto for "Home on the Range" as it is written on page____ and in_____ book. These are specific operational instructions. Both student and teacher know whether these objectives have been achieved. Of course, it is difficult even to describe operational activities that go into appreciating music. One must seek out illustrative activities that mark a "music appreciator" from a nonappreciator.

In stating objectives one must indicate *how well* the objectives are to be performed. The teacher owes the student a statement of the minimum acceptable performance desired. The student will then know exactly what is expected and upon which his performance of the objectives will be evaluated. Such a statement must be in words that describe the time limitation, the speed or the quantity plus other measurable *criteria*. Limitations placed on criteria are called restraints.

Aims and Concepts

Aims in music education must be a prime concern to those charged with the administration of programs. One has to know where all of this effort is headed and why.

> The first object of any act of learning, over and beyond the pleasure it may give, is that it should serve us in the future. Learning should not only take us somewhere; it should allow us later to go further more easily.[11]

If music is part of the learning program or of the school's curriculum it has to be reconciled with this concept; and, contrary to much loose thinking for many years,

> We begin with the hypothesis that any subject can be taught effectively in some intellectually honest form to any child at any stage of development. . . . No evidence exists to contradict this. . . .[12]

Education is tending to move in the more positive direction indicated in these statements. Music education can fall in line handily if the profession is willing to place its activities under the impersonal eye of the researcher and say with honesty (cont. 232):

GRADE BY GRADE CONCEPT CHART[13]

	MELODIC	RHYTHMIC	HARMONIC TEXTURE
KINDERGARTEN	Awareness of melody as the tune of a familiar song of recording Distinction between singing a melody and merely talking the words Sensitivity to pitch levels	Awareness of the everyday rhythmic activities in the lives of children and the natural relationship of these activities to rhythm in music Distinction between meter, accent, and the rhythm of the words	Awareness that harmony is most often r̶ to as the combination of musical tone̶ Awareness that chords generally serve a̶ accompaniment to the melody Awareness of accompaniment as well as melody
GRADE I	Realization that melodies are composed of repeated tones, skips, and steps Awareness that a complete melody is composed of like, similar, or contrasting phrases Awareness that melodies are often based upon simple melodic patterns, and sometimes on a pentatonic (five-note) scale	Introduction of the visual concept of rhythm Distinction between meter, accent, and rhythm of words Realization that creative dramatization may be based upon rhythm	Awareness that some songs may be accompanied by one chord and other s̶ may utilize more than one chord Recognition that chords are referred to s̶ letter names Development of aural and visual awarene̶ tonality
GRADE II	Awareness that melody may go up, down, or straight across, and that it moves up and down by steps or skips Tonal relationships in the following melodic patterns: 1-3-5 (do-mi-so), 8-7-8 (do-ti-do), and 3-2-1 (mi-re-do) Relationship of melody and text	Understanding of the meter signatures $\frac{2}{4}, \frac{3}{4}, \frac{4}{4}$ Awareness of $\frac{6}{8}$ meter through rote Awareness that recurring accents form a pattern for the measures of a song Recognition of the difference between walking and running rhythm	Awareness that sound in music is enhanc̶ its harmonic structure Understanding of the symbols for chord accompaniment Desirability of chord change in an accompaniment
GRADE III	Awareness of up, down, straight-across movement Distinguishing between steps and skips Recognizing phrases Distinguishing between like and unlike phrases Understanding tonality	Distinguishing between rhythm of the beat and melodic rhythm Understanding meaning and function of tempo Sensitivity to distinction between these meters: $\frac{2}{4}, \frac{3}{4}, \frac{4}{4}, \frac{6}{8}$ Understanding rhythmic value of dotted and tied notes	Awareness of meaning of harmony in mu̶ Awareness of difference between a harm̶ melody and contrapuntal effect Sensitivity to primary chords (I, IV, V)
GRADE IV	Realization that melody has direction, and that changes in it afford interest and variety Awareness that melodic sequence is a tonal pattern repeated at a higher or lower tone Function of the home tone and how to locate it from a key signature Awareness that a chromatic tone is a nonscale tone that adds color and variety to melody	Realization that the pattern of beats in music is the meter and that the speed of the beats is the tempo Awareness of the relation of notes to the meter signature Understanding dotted rhythms ♩♪ and ♩. ♪ Syncopation in the melody rhythm Importance of changes in tempo, and the way these changes are indicated Understanding $\frac{6}{8}$ meter	Awareness of the significance of harmony̶ an element of music Sensitivity to consonance and dissonance Function of the primary chords (I, IV, V̶ Major and minor tonality Understanding that harmony is produced ̶ chordal and contrapuntal (rounds, des̶ techniques
GRADE V	Awareness that melody is formed from combined tonal patterns: chord outline, scale, skips Understanding that the pentatonic as well as the major and minor scales can be the basis of melody Realization that an interval is the distance between two tones Understanding that tones in a melody have a natural tendency to move to other tones Realization that transposition is the moving of a melody from one pitch level to another Awareness of the chromatic scale	Aural and visual awareness and understanding of dotted rhythms Sensitivity to the effect of changes in meter Understanding of $\frac{2}{2}$ meter Understanding of the triplet as a subdivision of the basic rhythmic pulse	Refinement in understanding harmony as musical element Awareness of chordal and contrapuntal techniques in creating harmony Sensitivity to the effect of harmony in the major, minor, and pentatonic modes Recognition of the significance of the thre̶ primary chords (I, IV, and V7) Realization that chords have a normal progression from one to the other
GRADE VI	Awareness that melodies move by steps, skips, and repeated tones Recognition that melodic skips may be based on chords Awareness of melodic variety possible through the use of major, minor, pentatonic, whole-tone, and other modes, and tone row technique Understanding that melodies may be transposed from one pitch level to another	Understanding that all music is rhythmically organized in accented patterns of regularly recurring beats Realization that a note other than the quarter note may be used to represent a beat Understanding of $\frac{5}{4}$ and $\frac{9}{8}$ meter, and review of simple meters Recognition of subdivided beat patterns	Awareness that harmony may be produce̶ with chords and through various vocal techniques Distinguishing active from restful chords̶ Recognizing rounds, canons, descants, companion songs, and chordal harmon̶ Awareness of contemporary as well as traditional harmony; consonant as we̶ dissonant sounds

NOTATIONAL	FORM AND STRUCTURE	INTERNATIZATION AND INTERPRETATIVE
ual representation of pitch level: high, middle, down, across ual representation of pitch level; high, middle, low ual representation of the meter (basic beat), accent, and simple rhythms of the words ual representation of the musical phrase ual representation of like, unlike, and similar phrases	Sensitivity to the musical phrase Awareness that musical phrases may be alike, different, or similar Musical structure (form) determined by the arrangement of like, different, and/or similar phrases	Identification of mood as an emotional characteristic in music Dynamics as the relative contrast between loud and soft Tempo as the relative contrast between slow, moderate, and fast speeds in music The musical phrase as it corresponds with the literary phrase Sensitivity derived from the text Tone color as it is related to voice quality or type of instrument
areness of melody movement by steps, skips, or repeated notes ual representation of melodic direction: up, down, across ual representation of pitch level: high, middle, low ual representation of the meter (basic beat), accent, and simple rhythm of the words ual representation of the musical phrase ual representation of like, unlike, and similar phrases	Aural recognition of the musical phrase Recognition of the fact that musical phrases may be alike, different, or similar	Identification of mood in music Awareness of effect of tempo, meter, dynamics, harmony, style, phrasing, and tone color on the mood of a selection of music Awareness of variation in dynamics Awareness of variation in tempos Awareness of phrasing and its relation to form Recognition that song text oftentimes determines phrasing, dynamics, tempo, and style Aural and visual recognition of various voices, instruments, and ensembles
alization that notation is the printed symbol for the sound of music, including melody, rhythm, harmony, and interpretation areness of melodic direction and of steps and skips in notation ationship of key and home tone or key center ierstanding of the use of syllable names or numbers for the notes	Awareness that a phrase is a complete music thought Realization that phrases which look alike sound alike Recognition of two-part form (A–B), three-part form (A–B–A), and through-composed form (A–B–C, A–B–C–D) in music Awareness of the march and suite forms of music	Awareness of the relation of tempo and dynamics to the text Understanding of interpretative markings: soft, loud, fast, moderate, slow Awareness of the importance of good phrasing Identification of mood in music
tinguishing between steps and skips on the staff ating the appearance of a tonal pattern with its sound ierstanding the use of repeat signs cognizing the difference in notation between half and whole steps ierstanding the function of sharps and flats areness of notation of the major scale	Awareness that a melody consists of a group of phrases Awareness that both unity and variety are provided by the phrase structure of a melody Awareness of question and answer phrases	Awareness that songs have various moods — gay, sad, humorous, etc. Realization that the words of songs help guide interpretation Recognition that tempo, dynamics, phrasing, and tone color are used to express each song properly
ined association of the printed symbol with the sound as regards melody, rhythm, harmony, form, and interpretation areness that syllable and number names represent relative pitch, and that letter names represent fixed pitch areness of the relationships among key, home tone, and the scale	Recognition of the symphonic poem, ballet, and theme and variations as musical forms Realization of the relation of the principles of repetition, contrast, and variation to musical form Refined awareness of the musical phrase Realization that form may be seen as well as heard	Realization of the effects created by tempo, dynamics, phrasing, and tone color in songs sung and played and in music listened to Awareness that tempo and dynamic levels may be indicated by written symbols Discovery of the relationship between textual and musical phrases in songs Awareness of the implications of tone color in instrumental "families"
ierstanding the relationship between the printed symbol and the sound of melody, rhythm, harmony and the aspects of interpretation areness of the relationship between key, key signature, home tone, and scale ierstanding the visual implications of intervals ociation of syllable and number names with relative pitch and letter names with fixed pitch	Realization of the importance of the musical phrase as a basic structural element Refinement of awareness of repetition and contrast as they relate to and determine form in music Awareness of larger forms of music: fugue, sonata, concerto, and program music	Sensitivity to the effect of phrasing, tempo, dynamics, and tone color as aspects of interpretation Understanding written symbols and markings for tempo and dynamic levels Awareness of text as a factor in determining an appropriate interpretation and style for songs
areness of the value and functional meaning of notation ognition that notation can be read with syllables, numbers, letter names, or some degrees ierstanding that interpretive markings and directions for performance are part of notation	Awareness of the function and importance of the phrase Understanding the importance of unity, variety, and balance in form Insight into basic structure of such large forms as chamber music, sonata, symphony oratorio, and opera	Awareness that interpretation is the means by which a musical composition is brought to life Awareness that symbols of interpretation guide, but do not dictate to, the performer, so that each performer may express a song as he inwardly feels its meaning

1. Since music is an irrefutable part and parcel of everything about us, all the way from praising the deity, bemoaning our lot in life, selling products and singing the praises of our Alma Mater . . . for its various efficacies, it needs nurturing.
2. Since music is part of our past it can give color and style to what we hear and read about others and about ourselves; it can interpret, mythologize, emphasize, or glamourize the past to give meaning to the individual and to the present. If there is efficacy in this, it deserves nurturing.
3. Since man's desires and emotions are reflected in his art there is a vast area of personal identity that man can experience by becoming involved. If there is pertinence to finding kinship with a Bach "Toccata," a Beethoven "Appassionata Sonata," a Brahms "Academic Overture," a Stravinsky "Rite of Spring," a Debussy "Claire de Lune," a mountaineer's lament, a troubador's song, a madrigal, a Beatle, or an Alpert, then, by all means, it needs nurturing.

It stands to reason that not everything can be taught. In music education we can only open doors and provide handles onto which the student can hold fast while he is transported through the wonderland of sound.

In music education we choose to call these *the basic concepts of musical structure*: "The curriculum of a subject should be determined by the most fundamental understanding that can be achieved of the underlying principles that give *structure* to a subject."[14]

"These concepts must form the central core of the music curriculum. Every field of human knowledge possesses such a core of concepts; they are the essence of knowledge in any field since they comprise its essential structure."

Such concepts are found underpinning most music of all ages.[15,16] They are the eternals. The concepts that make up the structure of music are the familiar ones—melodic, rhythmic, and harmonic, grammatical or syntactical, expressive, and stylistic organizations.

These basic concepts can be successfully introduced at an early age in such a meaningful way that they form a basis for transfer of learning. As the child grows in his ability to verbalize, he can easily acquire more precise terminology to help him recognize and rationalize these elements.

Concept System. The Total Structure Encompassing All Music

Rhythm—Melody—Harmony—Composition—Expression—Style. All of these elements operate as a unified whole on the participant. The totality of these makes music.

CONCEPT I. The substructure called *rhythmic structure* is inherent in all music. It is the progression of sounds and absence of sounds that form a recurring pattern controlled by an underlying feeling of movement. These include even and uneven patterns of varying duration, regulated by a steady continuous "beat." Such beat can be heavy or light alternately.

CONCEPT II. The substructure inherent in most music is called the *tune*, or melody. It is a progression of tones moving up or down either stepwise or skipwise, or a repetition of tones. A melody may contain all of these. It receives its moving impetus through the underlying rhythm, but is also controlled by a factor called tonality (the starting point at which the upward or downward originated).

CONCEPT III. The substructure inherent in most Western music where tones are sounded simultaneously, either in chordal form (tones placed vertically), several melodies progressing parallelly (polyphonic)—the *harmonic* structure.

CONCEPT IV. The substructure present in all music that ties all elements together into a meaningful whole (*compositional* structure). This includes a motive (a word in a musical sentence); the phrase (a musical sentence); and the alternate repetition and contrast of such phrases, also variation.

CONCEPT V. The substructure that breathes life and meaning into music, i.e., melody, rhythm, and harmony tempered by *tempo* (fastness, slowness) *dynamics* (loudness and softness) and *tone color* or timbre (produced by the medium, instrument or voice). Both tempo and dynamics contain the properties of gradualism also.

CONCEPT VI. The substructure connoting *style*, such as roccoco, baroque, Victorian, romantic. Each of the elements in the above substructures has its own idiosyncratic way of contributing to style. What is there about music, that, once learned, the listener can tell whether it is classic, or Schumann, or folk? This is the flavor.

The six *concepts* must be a planned part of the curriculum and must be presented through real music so that the learner can acquire the skill of transferring the knowledge inherent in these concepts to musical compositions of all sorts. In other words, the *basic structure* contains the six *concepts*; and these concepts are presented through a repertoire of music literature. The literature (or music) selected must be arranged in such sequential order that *learning* builds on *learning* and *concepts* become firmly embedded.

The *concepts* are reinforced through a foundation of skills with which the individual can partake of, perform, enjoy, and internalize music. These common skills are listening, performing (singing, playing instruments, and moving to music), reacting creatively (in making or interpreting music), and reading the symbols that represent musical sounds.

These *skills* are ideally learned, practiced, and solidified through "real" music, or through a repertoire of music literature arranged in such a progressive order that simpler concepts and skills unfold into the more complex.

This *repertoire* of music literature consists of folk music, art music, pop music, concert music, contemporary music, and music from other ages, and it comes to us through various musical media.

The *musical media* are the instruments that produce the music:

1. The many kinds of voices, individually and in ensemble
2. The many kinds of instruments, individually and in the many available kinds of large and small ensembles

The *basic structure* containing the *six concepts,* the *four skills,* the complementary *repertoire* and the *media* appropriate to each age or developmental level are the important items that should determine the *aims* and *means* to achieving the aims. (See spiral curriculum, page 176.)

QUESTIONS FOR DISCUSSION, THOUGHT AND STUDY

1. What was the purpose of music education in ancient history? Grecian history? Roman history? Middle Ages? Renaissance? Modern times? Early American history? Present day?
2. List the books in music education that have contributed most toward crystallization of a music learning theory.
3. List educational writers (psychology and philosophy) who can make an imprint on school music.
4. What was James Mursell's contribution? To what extent is his concept being changed?
5. How can the thinking of Dewey, Thelen, and Bruner affect the course of music education?
6. What effects do the "Basic Concepts in Music Education" (NSSE Yearbook) have on new thinking about music education?
7. Select objectives for a phase of music education and describe these in behaviorial terms with necessary identifying criteria and restraints.
8. Translate the following words in behaviorial terms:

   a. playing the piano
   b. whistling a tune

   c. learning to whistle
   d. loving music

e. enjoying a passage
f. writing music from dictation
g. recognizing time values

h. play loud!
i. play slowly!
j. enjoy this passage

9. Select objectives from several major school music series and write a critique.
10. Differentiate between *process* and *product* in working with teachers.

NOTES

[1] Adapted from Ralph Tyler's article "New Dimensions in Curriculum Development," *Phi Delta Kappa*, Vol. XLVIII, Sept. 1956, No. 1, p. 27.

[2] James Mursell, *Music Education Principles and Programs*, (Morristown, New Jersey: Silver Burdett Company, 1956), p. 36-39.

[3] James Mursell, *Education for Musical Growth*, (Boston: Ginn and Co., 1948).

[4] R. Corsini and D. Howard, *Critical Incidents in Teaching*, (Englewood Cliffs, N.J., Prentice-Hall, Inc., 1964).

[5] Robert Mager, *Preparing Instructional Objectives*, (Palo Alto: Fearon Publishers, 1962).

[6] *MENC Source Book No. 2*, p. 3.

[7] Benjamin Willis, "Stake of Music in Education," *MENC Journal*, XXXIX, (Feb. 1953), pp. 62-64.

[8] Henry Otto, *Principles of Elementary Education*, (New York: Rinehart and Co., 1948).

[9] Bruner, *Toward a Theory of Instruction, op. cit.*

[10] Mager, *op. cit.*

[11] Bruner, *Process of Education*, p. 17.

[12] Bruner, *Process of Education*, p. 33.

[13] Adapted from scope and sequence chart by American Book Company, 1965.

[14] B. Bergethon and E. Boardman, *Musical Growth in the Elementary School*, (New York: Holt, Rinehart and Winston, 1963), p. 4 ff.

[15] NSSE Yearbook, *Basic Concepts*, Chap. VI, VII and X.

[16] MENC Source Book III, (Washington, D.C.: MENC, 1966).

Chapter 12

Making Functional Decisions

The previous chapter focused attention on ideas that affect the direction of music education and eventually affect the decision-making of the supervisor. This chapter intends to put the spotlight on numerous current practices that need to be re-evaluated in light of clarified approaches to learning music.

Rote or Imitative Singing

Most children come to our schools in the first grade, even in kindergarten, nursery school and in the Headstart programs with very little experience in singing. Their mothers have not sung to them from infancy on. Whatever music there was in the home was obtained quite incidentally through radio or television. It was "out there," not "here and now" for them.

Most children coming to school at age five or six are ready to read linguistically. But this is after five years or so of hearing words and sentences and thoughts, and after four years or so of speaking words, sentences, and thoughts. The school must take time to help the child assimilate these experiences into a meaningful whole before reading begins. Thus the world of the real gradually gives way to the world of the symbolic.

Since music making is a relatively new experience for many children upon entry in school, they will need to establish a repertoire of music containing the multitudinous recurring patterns (rhythmic, melodic, and harmonic) before they can begin to translate what is heard, sung, and played into symbols. Music reading cannot start in a vacuum; it must be based on the child having experienced real and "live" music—by rote.

Closely akin to rote singing is "playing by ear." How often has this been discouraged by the piano teacher of yore. Now it is considered an invaluable skill when one is able to play back what has been heard. One is then playing what is heard in the mind. A next step is improvisation, the ability of which is a mark of musicality. Improvisation is also the mark of a musically creative mind. Out of this skill is born the ability to compose. The steps to musicality then are:

1. singing by rote or imitation
2. playing by ear (playing from memory without notation)
3. harmonizing with others, jam session
4. improvising alone and with others
5. composing music

The music that is not dependent upon notation but is residual in the mind of the performer as part of his experience background—the music that has become internalized—will form a configuration of tonal reactions that will facilitate new musical learning.

Music Reading[1]

Music reading is the act of making musical sense out of representational symbolism. Music reading can be easy or difficult, depending upon the established configuration of musical reactions already present in the mind of the learner. If such a background is lacking or the learner is deficient in it, i.e., if he has no established repertoire of music that he can recall, then the process of teaching music ought to be delayed until the desired frame of reference has been set.

The concept of music reading has been the greatest obstacle to executing a program of elementary music education, especially in the self-contained classroom. If it is taught at all, it is done either by syllable, by shaped note, by number, by note name, or by combinations of several of these. We now know from research that children can learn equally well both the new math and the old math. They learn equally well either of the several reading methods. It has been discovered that the success of any method is the skill and zeal of the teacher. Kodaly and Orff have been equally successful with the syllable method, even to the extent that children upon hearing a complicated instrumental passage can demonstrate the skill of repeating the passage with syllables, unaided and without notation before them.

STAIRS TO MUSICALITY

Identification of key signature
Recognizing I, IV, V, V$_7$ chords
Review of time and key signatures
Read rhythmic notation
Minor, major modes—pentatonic scale
Understanding notation on bass staff

Greater skill in reading music in   GRADE 8
   unison and parts
Becoming familiar with bass staff
Review of time and key signatures

NOTE: means are not confused
   with objectives
   The grade by grade
   sequence is
   cumulative

Understanding minor mode   GRADE 7 - -
Comparing major and minor modes
Pentatonic melody patterns
Syncopation
Form of songs
Signs and terms of musical score

Song structure and organization   GRADE 6 - - - - -
Knowledge of staff, meter and key
   signatures, music symbols
Read, play rhythm—tonal patterns,
   simple melodies, descants
Understanding of compound measure
Recognition of chords

Sight reading from notation   GRADE 5 - - - - - - - - - - -
Bell parts, instrument parts,
   percussion, from notation
Meter and key signatures
Playing tonal-rhythm patterns
Relate duration—tonal patterns
Musical notation

Discovering rhythmic patterns in GRADE 4 - - - - - - - - - - - - -
   familiar and new songs
Awareness of key note on staff
Recognizing tonal patterns
Discovering musical ideas
Singing tone names

Correlation of notes and music   GRADE 3 - - - - - - - - - - - - - - -
Rote singing of tone names
Awareness of notation while singing
   phrases
Identify tonal patterns
Identify duration patterns

Color notation for instruments   GRADE 2 - - - - - - - - - - - - - - - - -
Awareness of high-low, fast-slow
Awareness of melody direction
Singing "favorite" songs from a book

GRADE 1 -

Many of the simple folk in isolated areas of southeastern United States can read music with astounding aplomb by the shaped note method. However, NO method is right because many people can learn by it. One needs to ask, "What are the objectives?" If the objective includes this kind of performance through these means, then—fine. Intellectual honesty would urge the music educator to spell out music-reading objectives in operational terms (in behavior terms), then set up economical and interesting procedures to get there. The following cumulative steps to music reading make no mention of associational crutches, but state reasonable terminal behavior within restraints.

It is no longer an issue whether music reading should be taught. The decision has to be made on *how* it should be taught, *when* it should be taught, and *by whom* it should be taught. Music educators have taken so many circuitous steps toward the goal—but they never reach it. Were we to teach music reading with one-tenth the diligence as we do linguistic reading, but with the best tested modern methods used by reading teachers, our nation would be truly musically literate. Remember, the process starts in kindergarten or before.

Alternatives in Methodology

What questions would you ask upon seeing a class write a test on note reading or an oral recitation of notes from the printed page, without singing? How would you react to children singing a song by piecing together diatonic and chordal patterns, and watching for musical repetitions? Can you justify the efficacy of students drawing in the air the melodic contour of a song? Would you advocate whole learning, or whole-part-whole, or phrase learning? Why would you choose one over the other? What does the preference have to do with how children learn?

If the objective of music reading is to be able to make music out of musical symbols, then let us be frank and honest, and decide which system does the job best, quickest, and with greatest student interest: note spelling, syllable recognition, number designation, keyboard space-frame reading or musical phonics (choral, scalewise and repetitive passage recognition)? Carefully applied systems analysis could perforate some well-guarded haloes. Unfortunately, we have looked at music reading through nine centuries of biases, reinforced by stalwart heroes along the way. What ought to be very simple has turned out to be a proliferation of old, obsolete processes.

Music reading should be taught always in direct context with "live music." The isolated tone is not music. If we are after music reading (interpreting the musical thought process) then we should look at combinations of tones in relationship to the several rhythmic patterns in which they appear, and as these are found in real songs. If music reading is not approached in a positive manner, then we are relegating our responsibility for musical literacy to the untutored private teacher. We ought to develop in students concepts about basic reading skills from which he can generalize and reapply in many music reading situations.

The Other Skills

"Oh, yes, we have rhythms on Tuesday, and on Fridays we have instruments," or "Thursday is listening day, the radio program, you know!" Monday is singing in many places, maybe because it's blue Monday, or maybe the teacher is trying to buy time so she can just get through the week. The supervisor must be able to demonstrate to the school authorities that one or the other of these activities may be just the vehicle by which some children achieve musical growth, or that some children achieve musical success more easily with one activity than with another.

If it is true that music comes to some children differently than it does to others, then is it fair to have "rhythms" just once a week? Now it is possible to present a lesson in which some children play the accompaniment on several instruments (piano, autoharp), while others play the tune on song flutes and resonator bells, and still other children play rhythm instruments and move to the rhythmic beat while the other children sing. At no time should concepts and skills be taught out of context with "real'" music; and whenever real music is being used, a segmented approach would be incongruous to the nature of music and to the integrative learning process.[2]

Listening

Listening (we use the term because most of the major teaching methods and series of books use the word) means more than it says. Teachers need help in devising and presenting listening lessons that will pave the way for increased musical learning. Specific concepts, such as melody, rhythm, harmony, form, notation, and interpretation, also musical texture, composer, the era, the country, and the occasion give added insight into the music. The relationship of composer to performer and to listener are also important considerations. Knowing something about several of these aspects will increase a child's enjoyment of music. The music supervisor should encourage and assist in setting up music listening programs appropriate to the student's age and understanding. All such programs must be *meaningful,* i.e., the student must be able to discern and internalize musical elements he hears. According to Bloom's *Taxonomy*[3] the child should *receive* musical impressions, *respond* to them, place *value judgments* on them, *organize* the impressions into his learning and knowing system, and finally, *characterize* them (give them a special identifying label). Many of the planned programs on the market can assist in this task of making listening an educational venture.

Singing

Singing is often referred to as the most common of all musical activities. The teacher must be concerned about the following aspects:

1. How to develop a beautiful singing voice
2. How to increase the vocal range at various age levels
3. Vocal range for the parts in choral groups
4. Tone development and enunciation
5. The defective singer, the nonsinger, the changing voice
6. What song will insure improvement of singing
7. Use of song materials (folk, art, religious, patriotic, popular) to teach concepts and skills
8. Directing group singing (tempo, rhythm, expression)
9. Sequential methods in developing part-singing (selecting materials)
10. Grade placement for introduction of part-singing
11. Ways of teaching a song (sounding pitch, starting)
12. How to use a phonograph and recordings in song teaching

Rhythms

Rhythms has meant anything from the organized rhythm band, children marching around the room while a record is being played, or folk dancing and square dancing all the way to free creative movement.

A music-learning program utilizing rhythmic activities is based on growth factors and involves fundamental movements which are natural to the child (locomotor and axial movements). Interpreting music through movement is the practical application of the structure and form of music. The supervisor must be concerned how these activities contribute to the musical growth of the child and how they can sensitize the child to music (help the child internalize music). The rhythm the child discovers in the song and in the listening lesson is as valid as the isolated rhythm activity.

Playing Instruments

"Preorchestral" instruments carry a high priority in a program of musical learning. By playing an instrument, (autoharp, tone blocks, rhythm instruments) the child can try out the music and find out to what extent he can handle it. Again, it is another way by which the child can internalize music and make it his very own. There is no greater thrill for a child than taking a musical instrument home and showing that he too can make music. *The Music Man* brought this point home clearly. These preorchestral instruments should be on hand and in such reasonable quantity that the teacher can feel free to utilize them as a continuous aid in learning. Too frequently does one note that the "music consultant" enters the room carrying the autoharp, demonstrates from it, and leaves again. (See list of recommended music materials, pages 254-255 for quantity.)

Social Instruments

Unfortunately, there is no place for the accordianist in most high school ensembles; and preserve us from the strumming guitarist! Tremendous media for reaching young people through music are thus ignored and actively discouraged for the sake of the performing band and orchestra. Perhaps the supervisor should take a stand on the issue of "social instruments." If children ought to have the experience of listening and moving to music, they also ought to be instructed in the most commonly used instruments. We sing folk songs, we dance folk dances in school—why don't we use folk instruments? Wasn't it Thaddeus P. Giddings who carried a sackful of ukuleles from school to school teaching the children to play this instrument? He observed that they could carry this skill with them, and that they could simultaneously play and sing with the aid of a very inexpensive instrument. The following 1964-1965 instrumental sales statistics speak loudly on what the national instruments of America really are:[4]

ANNUAL RETAIL SALES VALUES
BY INSTRUMENT CATEGORIES,
IN MILLIONS OF DOLLARS (ADD 000)

Year	Piano	Console Organ	Guitar[1]	Strings	Woodwind	Brass	Accordion	Drum	Portable Electric Organ
1930	40,000		NA	NA	NA	NA	NA	NA	
1940	95,000		19,000	NA	NA	NA	NA	NA	
1950	125,500	14,000	22,000	NA	NA	NA	25,000	NA	
1955	133,500	78,400	23,000	NA	25,300	16,900	25,000	NA	
1958	144,750	140,000	24,000	4,000	42,000	27,000	19,400	9,000	
1959	149,700	147,000	32,000	3,800	42,600	27,400	19,800	10,000	45,000
1960	148,650	161,000	35,000	5,000	45,300	29,700	18,000	12,000	51,250
1961	148,490	161,000	34,000	6,900	49,100	31,500	16,500	12,750	28,000
1962	161,350	178,200	41,000	7,500	54,100	32,900	16,250	14,280	29,120
1963	167,100	174,000	65,000	7,900	55,600	35,400	15,300	21,000	14,000
1964	$170,500	$175,500	$95,000	$8,700	$59,300	$38,200	$13,000	$27,000	$16,000

[1] Includes amplifiers.

Before World War II and during 1945-46 the musical instrument business was declining; today it is booming. Retail dollar volume is 8.7 times what it was in 1940 and almost 3.2 times what it was in 1950. A billion-dollar volume is forecast for 1970, based on the current growth rate of the industry and the expected increases in population, consumer purchasing power and leisure time.

The 1963 volume of $673,000,000 compared with $1 billion spent on books, $380,000,000 on operas, concerts and the theatre, $608,000,000 on all records and $450,000,000 on cameras, home movie equipment and film.

The music industry's percentage of annual personal consumption expenditures has increased from 0.110 per cent (of $82 billion) in 1941 to 0.186 per cent (of $399.2 billion) in 1964.

Annual unit sales by instrument category:

ANNUAL UNIT SALES BY INSTRUMENT

Year	Piano	Console Organ	Guitar	Strings	Woodwind	Brass	Accordion[6]	Drum[7]	Portable Electric Organ
1909	364,545[1]	None						NA	
1931	51,752[2]	None						NA	
1940	136,332[2]	None	190,000					NA	
1950	172,531[2]	10,000[4]	220,000				123,200	NA	
1955	158,087[2]	56,000	245,000	36,800	209,500	120,700	120,200	NA	None
1958	153,000	100,000	305,000	36,600	234,000	149,000	92,000	NA	123,600
1959	199,600	105,000	400,000	35,000	235,000	151,000	93,000	NA	350,000[8]
1960	198,200	115,000	420,000	40,600	241,000	153,000	100,000	NA	275,000
1961	191,600[3]	115,000	400,000	46,000	249,000	160,000	82,000	NA	210,000
1962	208,200	132,000	435,000	51,300	282,000	172,000	69,000	NA	208,000
1963	215,600	121,500	700,000[5]	55,000	298,000	190,000	70,000	NA	160,000
1964	220,000	121,500	1,065,000	58,200	317,500	201,000	58,000	NA	185,000

[1] U.S. Department of Census — includes 34,516 player pianos. Other totals do not include player pianos.

[2] National Piano Manufacturers Association; others attributed to AMC.

[3] Figures since 1961 include imported pianos, mostly from Japan and the United Kingdom.

[4] Sales of home console organs totaled 8,000 in 1947, the first significant year for this instrument.

[5] Figures for 1963 and 1964 include imports, mostly from Japan.

[6] Includes concertinas and non-piano accordions.

[7] Drums are often purchased in sets, thus making it impractical to determine unit sales.

[8] Figures since 1959 include imports, mostly from Italy.

The Non-Singer and Problem Singer

The monotone is the child who, for the most part, sings on one tone. His range may increase with encouragement and persistent exposure to singing opportunities and meaningful listening opportunities, especially when coupled with maturation. There are as many reasons for the condition as there are reasons for the cure. It is important that the teacher knows how to work with the deficient child to help overcome the handicap. These are some useful guides:[5]

1. Provide the child with listening experiences that will make him more aware of pitch differences, in (*a*) song and instrumental recordings and (*b*) hearing others speak and sing.

2. Provide him with many opportunities to use his voice in these types of musical activities: (*a*) group singing, (*b*) choral verse, (*c*) call response games, and (*d*) conversation songs.

3. Encourage the child to sing short phrases of songs at a pitch level natural for him; then gradually raise or lower the pitch as his vocal range develops.

4. Encourage him to dramatize such differences as high and low; loud and soft.

5. Hold melody bells in the vertical position so that the child can see and hear concepts as (*a*) ascending and descending patterns, (*b*) high and low pitch, (*c*) small and large skips.

6. Illustrate pitch and tonal patterns with such graphic aids as chalk board, charts, flannel board.

Competition Festivals

Competition festivals usually take the spotlight for a part of each school year. The supervisor is frequently called to assist, guide, and give his opinion, especially since schools are more concerned now about the great expenditure of time and money plus the strain which the director and the students undergo.

Competition festivals can have a fine stimulating effect. This depends upon the maturity of the individuals involved. Our concern is, Does it really have educational validity? Does it do what it purports to do? It is certainly not evaluation in depth when a fifteen-minute performance takes place in a strange empty hall with three strange judges making value judgments on a whole process from this brief and minute slice of the program. Fortunately, we are somewhat past the day when board members waited for the rating at the host school office, and from it decided whether they should retain the music man.

What are we testing for at a festival, and are we getting the answers? Will the day arrive when we can set the computer for a certain musical composition, making allowance for the many variables, then have the musical aggregation perform into it? Can we program our learning program better when we know what the machine will test, and when we do not have to depend upon our relationship with the judge? Is competition festival worth the

1. Preparation for the festival, filling out forms, etc.
2. Registration fees for each person and each group.
3. Extra rehearsal time in order to perfect end results.
4. Adjusting the school day so that education can go on for the majority of students left behind.
5. Getting clearance from parents, setting up a system of chaperones.
6. Even hiring substitutes for teachers who need to come along to help with holding papers and keeping order.
7. Setting up and enforcing rigid rules for festival behavior, on bus, off-stage, on-stage, after performance.
8. Waiting in line for the ratings; reading between the lines of the comments by the judges.
9. Shaking hands with colleagues amid encouraging remarks, such as "See you next year, Bill; one more year can do wonders with your gang." "My, they really are a gang, and to think you came 120 miles." "Chalk it up to experience." "Sometimes I wonder about the judges we are getting nowadays."
10. Meeting a grateful community upon your home arrival. Are they really grateful, or are they asking questions, what with a new tax election coming up?
11. Newspaper and radio publicity you receive. "School says it's against policy to divulge ratings." "Well, that's their buisness, however, we know the football scores."
12. Unless you are a persistent winner———.

I have heard it said, "My administration won't let me go to the festival this year. They're against the music program." If they are not music minded, they ought to be interested in what is happening to children under the guise of a very costly activity.

The Big Trip

Many districts have adopted a policy of not allowing overnight trips for their musical groups. The amount of money it took to send two

West Coast school bands to a recent presidential inaugural parade ran into astronomical figures. With the amount spent by district, community, and students, several hundred students could have been furnished with high quality musical instruments. The venture was chalked up to the school's responsibility in teaching human values, our country, etc. A study tour for that purpose would be more profitable. However, tremendous values did evolve from this venture. It depends upon what we feel we have to pawn in order to find musical values. Do we need these devices to make music speak to us? Or are we doing these things for other reasons? Is music the valid excuse to embark on such excursions? *It is better to raise the question before the event.*

The Public Performance

What place does the public performance have in an elementary school music program? Should a concert be a means to raise much needed funds? Should it be a teaching demonstration? Should it be a public display of an end-product, reflecting the process? Or should it be an opportunity for the director to have his own needs met? Is there a difference in objectives between a high school and an elementary school concert? Do school music departments have legitimate responsibilities to bring music into their communities?

The music supervisor has the obligation to help music directors and administrators evaluate their public performance policies in the light of desired objectives of the music curriculum.

Despite current academic pressures, there is a concern that high school graduates who have had four years of concentrated work in performing groups are avoiding this kind of activity in college. These students are saying, "We've had it, marching every other Saturday, practicing after school every night, playing for the games while others are having a good time." Or, "We had to go on extra Saturday trips while we could have been earning money!" Have schools emphasized the public display end of a musical program to the extent that such spectaculars hide the better purposes of the program?

How are school music programs transferring their values over into the community and contributing toward its cultural advancement? Has the quality of the church choir improved noticeably? Have the listening tastes of the American people improved because of———? Or have music industry and the great communications media been a greater educational force in the arts than the schools? Who does the musical *taste making* in your community?

Time for Music

Recommendations of several state departments of education suggest about 100 minutes a week of music teaching at each elementary grade level. This amount of time well spent, working with the best knowledge available, good materials, equipment and space and a good teacher can do miracles toward the attainment of the objectives. Of course, some teachers invariably suggest, "It counts for music when I take the children out for an hour of rhythms." This, too, is too frequently observed; the teacher will show a musical movie or play a stack of records without comment; and while the children are busy listening, she is correcting papers.

Releasing students from general classroom work for ensemble practice or a private lesson constitutes a serious problem to the entire school. Only the music person is really happy. How necessary is it, beyond the daily, biweekly, or triweekly rehearsal period, to draw students out of class for special music help? How far can music crowd a crowded curriculum? A quality music class, where students are busy working toward tangible objectives, and where they become excited and enthusiastic for music, carries more validity than many extra periods of whipping students into shape for the next performance.

The emphasis ought to be on quality and scope, and not on quantity measured in minutes per day. Junior and senior high schools are so heavily scheduled with performance groups that the specialized teaching talent is not available to teach music to the nonperformers. Neither is there time in the schedule.

Music education leadership must work patiently but surely at pointing to better ways of scheduling a larger variety of musical offerings for more students. With not more than 330 minutes in a schoolday a performing elementary student is in rehearsal for sixty minutes. What happens to the seven or eight other subjects? And what happens when the student is expected to come to music for more than a period a day? At one time teacher tempers were assuaged when the music director presented a rotating schedule.

The relatively untried field of modular scheduling and computerized scheduling can be a profitable direction. However, the music teacher dare not expect to remain immobile and adamant when the entire system is moving. He must be reminded of Russel Morgan's statement of philosophy: "As fine as music is, it is only one window, and a good life calls for a broader vista than one single direction."[6] And, "This is the moment for educators to contribute richly, through music, to a renaissance of the powers within the individual."

Music in Other Learning Areas

Music has always been part of the living experiences of man. It has not been artificially injected into situations by man. It has existed in many of man's activities from the dawn of civilization. Let's say that Divine Providence has integrated music into the life stream of civilization, and has done it with greater ease, naturalness, and power than we could ever hope to imitate. Too frequently music supervisors are asked to tie a pretty bow onto a social-studies or a language-arts package. The general consultant asked, "Will you help me find some cute rhythms to go with a new social studies unit I have just written? I think the more of this integration we do the better it is . . ." Yes, music can ennoble, enhance, and enrich many things that are taught in schools. Care must be taken not to utilize it out of context. Fine, if it deepens understanding of the subject at hand! Music is an integral part of everything.

Creativity

"Creative activities refer partially to the creation of original music but more importantly to a quality of teaching and learning which should pervade every educational experience."[7] Creative learning puts meaning into what is learned. It has to do with developing the power of sensing and seeing relationships, and interpreting in the light of the known. Creativity is the spark that ignites the desire for more learning. It is the learned ability to arrange facts or acts into concepts and from these draw generalizations which can be applied to new situations and approaches. The job in music education is to foster an inventive mind, a mind that can dream dreams and find ways to reapply these dreams to reality so that music finds a greater followership. The job of the music supervisor is to identify the creative teacher and to encourage her in inventive approaches to teaching. A mission of the supervisor ought also involve helping the teacher see creativity in children, and help them to foster this ability.

The Musical Environment

The inventive teacher does not have to be encouraged to make her room environment musically exciting. Physical arrangements that produce a musically stimulating environment are merely reminders of the real atmosphere. What goes into the *music corner* is not so important as what is done about it! Music ought to be represented with more than icons; an exciting musical atmosphere ought to pervade the room, and even the school.

Improvement of Special Programs

The supervisor ought to be the catalyst in the process of program improvement. The band instructor may have used the same method of class instruction for many years. This may be all right, provided the method itself presents a sequence of learning situations that noticeably affect students' progress. If not, this may be the time when the supervisor needs to suggest new materials. There are many instructional methods available; they must be evaluated and classified in accordance with well-defined criteria that take into account immediate and long-term aims. The teacher should be assisted in seeing objectives clearly and assisted in selecting materials that will help him in reaching his objectives with greater ease and quality.

Observation-Visitation

Observation and visitation are among the traditional ways of supervision. They are an indispensible part of the in-service program. No improvement can be considered unless the situation has been assessed. Much of this can be done by talking with the teacher informally, at informal occasions, the playground, after school, etc. If the visitation takes place in the teacher's classroom, it is most important how it is done. The supervisor must remember that he is not the judge; he is, however, the catalyst. *He may place a value on the apparent end result, but never on the teacher.*

In some districts the supervisor is able to visit each room regularly and give good inspirational help. Depending upon the size of the district, he may have the time and opportunity to build relationships that make him welcome. There is a danger, however, that the supervisor may appear to replace the teacher, and instead of helping her, he may delay any concern about developing her potential. One of the most wholesome aspects of such a close working relationship is the opportunity to observe children at close range.

A supervisor new on the job ought to visit many classrooms in quick succession in order to gain a good perspective of the problem areas, and as a good exercise in developing working relationships with teachers. He should ask himself:

1. How is my visit helping the teacher improve her technique?
2. How can I tell whether I am welcome in her room?
3. How does my visit affect student-teacher relationship?

The current neglect of the classroom scene is as great as the potential dangers of too frequent visits. Teachers have a right to on-the-spot help. Spears says, "A good supervisory program grows out of the classroom and returns to it."[8] Classroom visitation is a logical follow-up of an in-service program. As such it places major emphasis on program and less on the mistakes of the teacher.

Music supervision ought not begin with the premise that classroom teachers cannot teach music, but ought to present opportunities to be of assistance in interpreting the program. The new supervisor ought to view the whole learning situation, and not just the teacher.

Demonstration Teaching

Classroom demonstrations by music supervisors are often a device to make sure that uniformity of approach is assured, with this typical assumed motive: "Now, you saw how I did this. I'd like to have you follow up next week—but don't start anything new." This does not free a teacher for creative teaching. Emphasis needs to be placed on the improvement of the teaching and learning situation. Ask yourself, "After all, who is the teacher here?" and "What is the program to be implemented?"

When supervisors are taking valuable teacher time, they must have something vital and significant to offer, something that can measurably affect the learning situation. The new supervisor must decide on these issues:

1. Classroom visitations: their proper use, under what circumstances, how often, for what purpose, with what end product in mind?

2. Demonstration lessons: do they truly help teachers grow in ability to teach music more effectively? To what extent are objectives apparent in such a lesson?

Humanities in Music—or Make Music Academic

Music is part of the humanities. There is no special advantage in publicizing the fact. Our post-space-exploration frenzy with its understandable idolatry of facts, figures, and test tubes, created a vacuum in the so-called humanities. With a mighty surge toward intellectual stimulation by the several disciplines, music again felt itself on the outside; so it joined the fray. But, unfortunately, it isn't academic just to blow the clarinet harder and longer, or to place performing groups on a high school credit basis.

The music supervisor has an obligation to encourage music teachers to work closely with the history and English teachers so that the arts can come alive in history and in man's noblest efforts at verbal communication.

The music teacher also needs assistance in using his performing groups[9] as a cultural resource and stimulus to the entire school. And

PLANNING PROJECTS APPROVED BY CATEGORIES[10]

Project Categories	Number	Amount
I. Multiple Purpose Projects	72	$4,687,465
Supplemental and Learning Centers . . .	33	2,361,000
Media and Materials Centers	14	1,385,387
Demonstration Programs.	17	775,675
Cultural Enrichment Programs	8	165,403
Mobile Services.	0	0
II. Special Programs	60	3,940,785
Planning	8	1,129,254
Determine Needs and Resources	24	1,770,231
Curriculum Development.	9	447,984
Guidance, Counseling, Testing	6	235,937
Remedial Instruction.	2	53,110
Special Education	4	81,665
Self-Instruction	4	143,492
Outdoor Education	3	79,112
III. Administration and Personnel.	7	266,104
School Administration	1	76,620
Teacher Inservice Training	5	133,259
Computer Processing	1	56,225
IV. Subject Matter	5	119,441
Language Arts	3	88,465
Arts, Humanities, Social Sciences . . .	1	17,051
Science and Mathematics.	1	13,925
Vocational Education.	0	0
V. Others	3	73,080
Total	147	$9,086,875

he needs assistance in helping his students learn more about music through the performing media. Too often the student is involved only in the technical and skill aspects of music making. The rehearsal period can ideally become a laboratory for deepening knowledge about music.

The Minority Groups in Performance Classes

The poor students, the slow students, and the handicapped students are so frequently by-passed because they could spoil the artistic configuration and pattern set up in a performing organization. They are

OPERATIONAL PROJECTS APPROVED BY CATEGORIES[11]

Project Categories	Number	Amount
I. Multiple Purpose Projects	42	$4,198,154
Media and Materials Centers	6	338,201
Supplemental and Learning Center . . .	17	2,532,329
Cultural Enrichment Programs	9	479,715
Demonstration Programs.	8	773,745
Mobile Services.	2	74,164
II. Special Programs	8	450,673
Curriculum Development.	1	92,800
Guidance, Counseling, Testing	2	122,048
Self Instruction	0	0
Special Education	1	72,808
Outdoor Education.	2	50,414
Remedial Instruction	2	112,603
Pre-School Education	0	0
III. Administration and Personnel.	15	1,006,542
Teacher Inservice Training	3	393,969
Administration	1	138,600
Team Teaching	0	0
Teacher Aides	0	0
Computer Processing	11	473,973
Community Resources	0	0
IV. Subject Matter	3	59,166
Science and Mathematics.	1	13,454
Arts, Humanities, Social Sciences . . .	2	45,712
Language Arts	0	0
Foreign Languages	0	0
V. Others.	2	303,462
Total	70	$6,017,997

RECOMMENDED MATERIALS
FOR CONSIDERATION UNDER TITLE I ESEA PROGRAMS[12]

	RECOMMENDED	INVENTORY		COST	
	Per Teaching Unit and Level	We Have	We Need	Unit Cost	Total Cost
Audiovisual aids and other equipment					
Filmstrip projector	1 per 5 c.r.				
Overhead projector	1 per 5 c.r.				
Radio	1 per 4 c.r.				
Record player	1 per c.r.				
Record player equipped with listening posts and head-phones	1 per 6 c.r.				
Filmstrip and movie screen	1 per 3 c.r.				
Sound motion picture projector	1 per 6 c.r.				
Tape recorder w. microphone	1 per 4 c.r.				
Television set	1 per grade level 1 per 6 c.r.				
INSTRUMENTS FOR USE IN THE CLASSROOM					
Autoharp (12 or 15 bar)	1 per c.r.				
Melody bells (w. case) 1-1/2 octave, chromatic	1 per c.r. K-4				
Melody bells (w. case) 2 octave chromatic, starting below middle C	1 per c.r. 5-8				
Resonator bells (2 octave, chromatic	1 set per 4 rms.				
Piano (spinet or studio) OR	1 per 4 c.r.				
Electric organ (Hohner)	1 per 4 c.r.				
Magnus Electric organ	1 per 4 c.r.				
Melodica (soprano) include	1 per K-4 min.				
Melodic (alto) 4 mouthpieces in each	1 per 5-8 rm.				
Pitch pipe (chromatic	1 per c.r.				
Recorders (Bloc flöte)	1 per c.r. 5-8				
Song flute type instrument	1 per ea. 3d grader, min.				
Rhythm instrument kit	1 per ea. K-3				
Rhythm sticks	8 pr. ea. c.r. K-4				
Sand blocks	3 pr. ea. c.r. K-4				
Sleigh bells	4 per c.r. K-4				
Tambourine	2 in ea. kit				
Triangles (various sizes)	3 in ea. kit				
Cymbals	1 per kit				
Woodblocks	1 set per kit				
Rhythm drum	1 per c.r.				
Tom Tom drum (Indian)	1 per c.r.				
Tom Tom drum (African)	1 per sc.				
Claves	1 per c.r.				
Coconut shells (halved pairs	1 pr. per c.r.				
Hand castas	2 per kit				
Maracas	1 per gr. 5-8				
Cabaca	1 per gr. 5-8				
Temple blocks	1 per school				
Lummi sticks (24 plus record)	1 set per school				
RECORDINGS AND FILMS					
Music included in adopted text for each grade	all recording for each level				
Rhythm records	Graduated for each grade level				
Appreciation records Adventure Series RCA	At least one set of these				

	RECOMMENDED	INVENTORY		COST	
	Per Teaching Unit and Level	We Have	We Need	Unit Cost	Total Cost

Musical Sound Books
Bowmar Listening Library
  with filmstrips
Jam Handy Series of Music
  and Opera Stories, rec. & fs
Special holiday recordings
BluePrints for Musical Under-
  standing (charts & records)
	in each bldg.
	1 set in district
	library or
	co. A-V center
	(same as above)
	3 rec. per grade
	
	1 set per upper gr.				

(multiply by number of schools in district wherever amount for one building is listed)					

STANDARD CLASSROOM SUPPLIES
AND FURNISHINGS
 	
Flannel board, or
Magnetic bulletin board
Large staff-lined chart paper
Staff liner
Staff paper
Music Instrument Charts with
  presentation kit, record, etc.
Transparencies for overhead
  projector overlays
	
	1 per 2 c.r.'s
	
	1 per c.r.
	1# ditto per sq.
	
	1 per school				

BOOKS AND MUSIC Community song books Enrichment reading on composers and music Paper backs on music	 1 per 2 students $5. per yr. per rm. $5. per yr. gr. 6, 7, and 8				

a bother, and we'd rather not be bothered. The English teacher and the mathematics teacher must take them, but we, on our musical island, still afford the luxury of exclusiveness. This day is over. The national thrust demands inclusion.

The Negro, the Mexican-American, the Indian, and many other small national and ethnic groups who have difficulty speaking and providing for themselves—they, too, are to have the same advantages as the majority. Provision must be made. It is the supervisor's responsibility to call attention to this and suggest ways of including those who were inadvertently and deliberately excluded. The issue is one of weighing musical perfection and achievement standards against human rights standards. There is still much room for developing the individual to his fullest capacity.

What the supervisor does about the questions raised will be determined by his orientation to the job and by the objectives he has chosen to follow. The effectiveness of his program will be dependent upon the learned wisdom he applies to problems and situations. ESEA of 1965 has not simplified the life of the music supervisor. In many instances he has taken it upon himself to avail himself of the opportunity of extending his services. In some instances he has been asked to participate in a project with his staff. In many instances his overtures to lead out have been rebuffed. Tables 2 and 3 from *Pacesetter* indicate the kind of planning and operational projects that were approved in the first year of operation of the Title III of ESEA. Nine per cent of funded projects through July 1966 were for the performing arts.

The music supervisor is in a unique position to advise schools how they can spend their Title I and Title II allotments to benefit the students in poverty areas. The accompanying Table of Recommended Materials for the Elementary Classroom Music Program was prepared specifically for schools entitled to Title I funds. The list is a standard minimum. Some districts have gone into large projects involving added personnel and multi-media equipment.

NDEA type of assistance to the humanities, even though small in comparison to the other federal funds, nevertheless holds much for music departments in the form of matching funds. Several school districts through their music consultant pooled available financial resources and requested matching funds with which they purchased equipment needed to establish a fine arts camp.

QUESTIONS FOR DISCUSSION, THOUGHT AND STUDY

1. How would you decide which system of music reading to espouse?
2. How would you help a school set up a sequential system of music reading?
3. How can rote singing predispose children to music reading?
4. Differentiate between music reading and note spelling.
5. Relate studies that give validity to associational crutches.
6. Why do we incorporate emphasis in the several music structural concepts in teaching one song?
7. List singing problems in the classroom you have observed.
8. How does rhythmic sensitivity affect music learning?
9. List preorchestral instruments and indicate appropriate grade levels.
10. Discuss the school's responsibility in teaching social instruments.
11. Justify utilizing the music department in promoting "other than music" life values.
12. Justify student performances for the public.
13. Make a classroom music schedule for an eight-teacher elementary school with time allotments for the entire week.
14. Make a schedule for an elementary instrumental teacher who is assigned to a 30-teacher school two days a week.
15. To what extent should correlation between social studies and humanities take place in the general music program?

16. How can you discover the creative teacher, creative learning, and the critical incident?
17. Outline how to point out the weaknesses of an instrumental program and prevent the teacher from losing face.
18. Present pros and cons about several listed supervisory devices.
19. How would you get music teachers to include students from the several minority groups in the band, chorus, orchestra?

NOTES

[1]Marian Brooks and Harry Brown, *Music Education in the Elementary School,* (New York: American Book Co., 1946).

[2]"Stairs to Musicality" and text adapted from Scope and Sequence Chart, Follett Publishing Co., 1965.

[3]Benjamin Bloom, *Taxonomy of Educational Objectives,* (New York: David McKay, Inc.).

[4]Report on Amateur Instrumental Music in USA, (American Music Conference, 1964).

[5]Calif. Music Guide, *op. cit.,* p. 95.

[6]Russel Morgan, *op. cit.*

[7]Calif. Music Guide, *op. cit.,* p. 2.

[8]Spears, *op. cit.*

[9]NSSE Yearbook, *op. cit.,* Chap. IX, p. 261.

[10]*Pacesetters in Innovation,* Title III, ESEA projects, 1966.

[11]*Ibid.*

[12]Tulare Company, California Department of Education, prepared for Title I, ESEA projects.

Title III Project, Widening Cultural Horizons, Madera Company, Calif.

Chapter 13

Relating Research

Much of the change that has affected music education has been due to research findings. The effects of significant findings are never immediate. They are more like the effects of medication intended to correct a physical deficiency, to cure someone, or to revitalize the body. The desired effect does not happen right away. The medication has to infiltrate into the system, and gradually something may happen, i.e., if the medicine is applied faithfully according to design. Frequently, also just knowing that successful research has been accomplished in an area gives one a sense of well-being and a generalized kind of improvement occurs.

The music supervisor's job is to call attention to significant research and to assist in its implementation. He must be constantly looking for better ways of doing things, or even doing something new. He is on the lookout for new and fresh ideas that carry with them some assurance that the situation will improve. Ideas that have been tested in the crucible of research can carry such guarantees. These ideas must be translated for the teacher so she can use them at the operational level.

Need for New Ideas and New Ways

The day is past when music educators can afford to luxuriate in hastily done research, or even some thesis-centered research of the past. More research pertaining to the classroom setting of various levels of the general music program is needed. Too often scope and sequence have been reconciled with current educational thinking. And in the process the problem has been put into a package that defied inspection. Recall the many years when elementary music education lost itself almost willingly in the enveloping folds of "social studies!"

Research, if it is to be effective, must take into consideration music in the context of the school of our society. The United States Office of Education has indicated four major thrusts in progress now that will shape up all of education. If music is to make significant contributions to the educational growth of children it too must be part of this thrust, or risk insulating itself into insignificance. These are (1) individuality of instruction, (2) quality of instruction, (3) equality of instruction, and (4) community action.

All education, to be effective, must finally cross the threshold separating the school and its total effective component parts into the community. There is no purpose for the school unless this happens. The music program loses validity if it remains insular, if it does not involve itself in the four major points above. And, it cannot exist unless it produces an end product that is musically effective in the affairs of the community. Do our choral students sing in church choirs? Do our band and orchestra students play in community groups or assist in bringing music into depressed areas? Do our musical consumers influence community taste in music?

Analysis, evaluation and revision of objectives in terms of procedures must be a continuing process throughout the entire structure called education. This includes management on through supervision, planning, analysis to obtain raw material, the learning process, the influence of the instructional program, the implementor (teacher), the predicted end behavior, and the transfer into society to ideal community involvement. Every step along the way is a significant rung on the ladder or link in the chain. Each is so dependent upon the other that chance operation will not suffice; only a critical program of related research can hold the process through to a meaningful goal.

In music education, the supervisor in his role as catalyst and assurer of instructional quality must depend on the foundation stone of the system, i.e., the administration, before he can proceed up the steps (see below) to a significant and valid outcome.

There are supervisory tasks to be performed just to "keep the ship afloat." These none of us in music supervision can escape. A function that supercedes all of these is that of assuring quality of instruction.

The NSSE Yearbook *Basic Concepts in Music Education*[1] opens the question for the need for further search. Thurber Madison describes several kinds of concepts thus: (*a*) as abstractions and generalizations, (*b*) as communication vehicles, (*c*) as the line that leads from concrete to abstract, (*d*) as means and ends (aims and objectives), (*e*) as symbolic pattern (wedding music, holiday music), (*f*) as common-sense data and as theory, and (*g*) as intuition and postulation.

There is a relatedness in all of these. Currently there is a revitalized (or belated) concern for teaching concepts, rather teaching for concepts in the hope that transfer will be facilitated. There seems to be a growing body of research that deals with aspects of validation of concepts (see recent issues of JRME). Following are some of the things that need to be done to get tested ideas into the music teaching act:

1. Make a listing of the teacher-encountered problems at all levels and in all areas of the music program
2. Develop a concrete program through which teachers and supervisors work at these problems in real teaching situations
3. Establish a research center to which the results of these workers can be brought for further study, refinement and fact dissemination

If teacher and supervisor are to work together on searching for answers, these are some important considerations:[2]

1. What conditions need the music supervisor arrange that will give the teacher freedom to state problems in music teaching as she sees them, and to give the reasons for the importance of such problems?
2. After the problem has been recognized, what is the peculiar context in which this problem is typically found? Can the solution be found in this context?
3. In setting up a problem, are there considerations of time limitations? How fast or slow should one go in finding a solution?
4. Should the teacher be turned loose on it alone . . . or should consultant, supervisors, and teachers work together on it?

Identifying Problems for Research

Significant problems can often be pinpointed by hearing the complaints, difficulties, and frustrating experiences of teachers. We recall one teacher who was so emotionally involved that it was difficult for her to express herself logically and coherently. After she had expressed her complaints it was discovered, even though she talked around the problem, that she had outlined a real and live one, just waiting for someone to do something about it. She had expressed herself in the symbolic language of peeves.

The supervisor should be alert to unanswered questions. By working closely with teachers in search for answers on the scene, he is assisting them in a practical form of research called *action research*.

The workshop type of in-service programs described in Chapter 9 are examples of the kind of research accomplished in the teacher-learning setting of the school. The Tulare County study dealt chiefly with the teacher in her own setting. The nine teachers observed were so-called run-of-the-mill. Their music background, their music teaching ability, their orientation to teaching, and their demonstrated teaching ability ranged from very poor to excellent. There was no positive correlation between musical ability and music teaching competency. There seemed to be a high correlation between good teaching and good music teaching, though. The poor teacher improved somewhat but reached a plateau, whereas the good teachers kept on improving, and even twelve years after the study they remain the "improving" kind.

Action research is here to stay in spite of the mandate for exact research in all areas of music education. Action research must be the genuine "problem finder" so that the pure researchers have something of significance to work at. Action research can expose the problem and point to directions for solutions. It can thus be a *prerequisite* for laboratory research. It also ought to be the *postevaluation* or tryout for pure research, if for no other reason than to point out how findings work out in ordinary situations. The two following résumés involved elementary school teachers. They are in part action research because of the involvement.

The strength of action research is that it tends to do something positive to the teacher, the students, and the local situation. The values inherent in such involvement tend to provide motivation and incentive for change and improvement.

Research on Classroom Music Teaching

A study by Linton[3] indicates "The tendency has been to emphasize three areas of content organization in pre-service training of teachers: (a) a theoretical approach to the so-called rudiments of music, (b) a verbal approach, with certain practical emphases, to the techniques of teaching music to children, and (c) a formal approach to music appreciation. For the most part, there has been little effort to establish relationships between these areas with the teacher education program as a whole, or with the musical experiences of the children." He summarizes trends of opinion held by many educators throughout the United States, as follows:

1. "All children need music of a kind that will be intimately related to the living they do in and out of school.

2. The classroom teacher must be prepared to accept more responsibility in bringing worthwhile musical experiences to children.
3. Predominating programs of musical experiences in teacher training institutions reflect the assumption that the problem involves a more rigorous conservatory approach to training the specialist and loses sight of the fact that we are, first of all, educating classroom teachers.
4. A promising solution exists within the limitation of six semester hours by developing a preservice program with (*a*) experiences with music that are direct, rich, varied, and immediately adaptable for use with children, (*b*) a continuity of experiences . . . something that parallels the musical development of the child, (*c*) a functioning relationship with the whole teacher education program."

He identifies certain classroom teacher needs:

1. "To understand the place of music in the lives of children and the nature of their music development
2. To acquire an attitude of responsibility for bringing children into worthwhile contact with music
3. To develop musically in such a way that he may receive personal values from music and organize worthwhile musical experiences for children."

To accomplish this, he suggests (*a*) class participation, (*b*) professional laboratory experiences, (*c*) individual projects, and (*d*) development of fundamental concepts. All these methods can be part of one another, not necessarily separate and compartmentalized.

Fleming[4] completed a research project in 1951 under the auspices of New York University to determine the necessary musical experiences needed by elementary teachers in Maryland to develop musical competencies in keeping with school music expectations. She selected eighty-three school music activities as representative of a total elementary music education program. These activities were divided into seven categories: singing, listening, creative, instrumental, music reading and reading readiness, rhythmic, and interpretative. Her study revealed a resulting list of eighty-eight college level musical experiences for the potential teacher.

Examples of Basic Research Affecting Music Education

Some studies deal with small but significant aspects of the music program. Some of these were not done by people involved in the educative process. This does not detract from their validity. It adds to their objectivity.

Bean[5] discovered that the pattern reader was a more effective and a more rapid reader.

Blethen[6] stated: "No music skill can be studied as an individual item. Our aims and methods must focus around experiences that promote musical growth through responsiveness." It hints at the complexities involved in musical learning. Because one can read notes, this does not say that one has become musical. There are many other interrelated factors involved in music reading.

Creitz[7], in experimenting with the piano as a space frame for learning note reading, found that children learned faster when they learned with a keyboard.

Earhart and *Gatto*[8] found that students who played instruments could sight read with greater ease.

Egbert[9] advocates learning note reading by visualizing the musical score in connection with the keyboard. Other research workers bear this out also. Ernst and Dykema each have written articles to call attention to the advantage of keyboard music reading.

Gaston,[10] in his studies put considerable doubt on the efficacy of the movable *do*. He said it is not the only way, neither is it the best nor the most economical way to learn music reading.

Jersild and *Bienstock*[11] discovered that youth has nothing to do with a child's ability to sing difficult songs.

King,[12] in trying to find a relationship between aural and visual ability, discovered that memory, movement, pitch, and time are greater factors in music-reading ability than aural sense.

King[13] discovered a definite relationship between intelligence and the ability to read music.

Reimer[14] found that students learned more effectively when they used the "known-melody" method than by formal drill.

Smith and Vitto[15] each worked on the idea of developing musicalness through symbolizing melodies. *Leonhard*[16] worked out a methodology of teaching by the song approach.

Both *Weaver*[17] and *Ortmann*[18] did research in visual span and eye fixations. They discovered that word reading and music reading are related; and that music reading difficulties can be attributed to the child's inability to see notes in larger perceptual units. These ideas are being utilized in more recent textbook productions. There are more attempts at printing the entire phrases of a song on one line instead of breaking it up. This method of writing notation ought to promote musical thought reading.

Wheelwright[19] discovered that spacing note symbols so they were consistent with time symbols would be conducive to better reading. Also sharp print aids in note reading.

These studies deal with segmented aspects affecting the total music education program. Their implications affect learning situations, however. On examining the studies and checking recent classroom music materials, one can see that many resulting ideas have been incorporated into the learning programs. There is need for much collateral research which focuses attention on these findings to determine whether the conclusions hold up under many kinds of situations.

Research, no matter how free and informal or how sharp, cruel, counting, and unrelenting, is a way of evaluation based on a very definite foundation. The act of research connotes a prior dissatisfaction, or an evaluation.

Relating Research from Other Areas to Music Education

Brooks and *Brown*[20] tried to analyze music learning in terms of linguistic learning: ". . . it may be stated that the four significant facts about the child's learning to understand oral language and to express himself in speech are: (a) the child's social need to express himself and to understand what is said to him is the impelling force of learning; (b) imitation is the chief basis for linguistic learning; (c) learning is accomplished through an enormous amount of repetition; (d) great interest attends all of the child's efforts in this respect. These same principals apply to expression of thought and feeling through the medium of song, to playing a musical instrument, and to reading music from the score." "Reading is a muscular and interpretative process which has three aspects, namely: (a) the muscular movements of the eye connected with its movements and fixation pauses; (b) the retinal work of the eye in sentence perception; and (c) the mental process involved in apprehending the meaning of the printed words . . . it is believed that the best reasons for mastery of the musical score in the elementary school are (a) to open to the child the vast storehouse of music literature which otherwise would be closed to him and (b) to put him in possession of a means of musical expression."

This is an example of drawing upon the research literature and making recommendations for classroom teachers. This, however, is but an infinitesimal aspect of the music learning program.

Of recent years a number of studies affecting music education have come to light. They yield food for thought and provide incentive for directional planning:

Kyme[21] made a comparative study of several systems of teaching sight-singing. Using 183 students in his study, he found that the evidence showed that the group instructed by means of "shaped notes" tested superior to groups instructed in one of several other systems.

Blyler[22] made a study of song choices of children in elementary grades. The following table represents grade by grade and sex breakdown:

Baumann[23] reported on teen-age music preferences.

Kelly[24] also made a study of the musical preferences of adolescents.

THE CHOICES OF BOYS AND GIRLS

Grade	Prefer	Dislike
II Boys	Songs about our country, animals, nature, fanciful situations, cowboys	Songs about everyday experiences and objects
Girls	Songs about our country, animals, nature, flowers, people	Songs about everyday experiences and objects, nursery rhymes
III Boys	Songs about our country, pioneers, the West, humor, lullabies	Songs about everyday experiences and objects, animals, slogans, and moralizing
Girls	Songs about our country, God, birds, love, humor, lullabies	Songs about everyday experiences and objects, animals, slogans, and moralizing
IV Boys	Songs about our country, the armed services, nonsense (birds and animals), cowboys	Songs of love and lullabies
Girls	Songs of our country, nonsense (birds and animals), God, and lullabies	Songs about animals
V Boys	Songs of our country, the armed services, humor of a more subtle type, heroes	Ballads about birds and animals
Girls	Songs of our country, humor of a more subtle type, love, God	Ballads about birds and animals, cowboy songs
VI Boys	Songs of our country, love and romance, heroes, God	Songs of nature, pioneers, nonsense
Girls	Songs of love and romance, our country, God, nature	Ballads, birds and animals, humor and nonsense

THE FIFTY SELECTIONS
OF THE MUSIC PREFERENCE INVENTORY
RANKED IN ORDER OF POPULARITY
WITH 1600 TEEN-AGERS

Rank	Title, Description, and/or Artist	Number like most	like least
1	*In the Mood*, Glenn Miller Orchestra	1263	50
2	*Rock Around the Clock*, Bill Haley and Comets	1216	144
3	*Boogie-Woogie*, Tommy Dorsey Orchestra	1091	122
4	*San Antonio Rose*, Western guitar, Chet Atkins	962	181
5	*In the Jailhouse Now*, Webb Pierce	909	329
6	*It Is No Secret*, popular sacred, Foley and Andrews Sisters	877	149
7	*Akaka Falls*, Hawaiian guitar, Benny Kalama	863	121
8	*Hesitating Blues*, trumpet, Mugsy Spanier	848	211
9	*The Waltz You Saved for Me*, Wayne King Orchestra	835	85
10	"You'll Never Walk Alone" from *Carousel*, movie sound track	832	192
11	*Wiener Blut, Walzer*, Op. 354 by Strauss, Boston "Pops"	805	195
12	*The Hot Canary*, popular violin, Florian ZaBach	804	159
13	*Away in the Manger*, Fred Waring Chorus	754	109
14	*Who?* Benny Goodman Trio	753	242
15	"Heigh-Ho" from *Snow White*, London Symphonic Band	730	120
16	*Those Foolish Things*, Dave Brubeck Quartet	721	188
17	*Washington Post*, American Legion Band of Hollywood	705	160
18	*Buffalo Gals*, hoedown, Old Timers	693	344
19	*Llegaste Tarde, mambo*, Chuy Reyes Orchestra	672	335
20	*Jersey Bounce*, popular organ, Lenny Dee	650	247
21	*Canadian Capers*, ragtime, Joe "Fingers" Carr	641	232
22	*Mexican Hat Dance*, Mexican band	633	230
23	*23° N — 82° W*, Stan Kenton Orchestra	585	398
24	*Oh! Susanna*, Fred Waring Chorus and Orchestra	578	200
25	*Deep River*, Tuskegee Institute Choir	565	314
26	*Love Letters*, The Strings of Stordahl	559	384
27	*River, River*, Peggy Lee and Gordon Jenkins Orchestra	555	259
28	"Hallelujah Chorus" from the *Messiah* by Handel	481	343
29	*Israel*, cool jazz, Miles Davis, *et al.*	479	414
30	*Goodbye, Old Dixie, Goodbye*, Barbershop Quartet	451	311
31	*Symphony No. 5 in C Minor* by Beethoven (opening phrases)	434	585
32	"Procession of the Nobles" from *Mlada* by Rimsky-Korsakov, American Symphonic Band of the Air	360	541
33	*Symphony No. 1 in C Minor* by Brahms, fourth movement	381	517
34	*Revolutionary Etude* by Chopin, Goldsand	394	719
35	*Serenade for Strings in C Major* by Tschaikowsky	339	455
36	*Anecdote No. 2* by Segovia, classical guitar, Almeida	294	472
37	*Concerto for Violin in E Minor* by Mendelssohn, last movement	274	648
38	"Menuetto" from *Clarinet Quintet in A Major* by Mozart	272	764
39	*Appalachian Spring*, by Copland	269	648
40	*The Afternoon of a Faun*, by Debussy	255	648
41	"Liebestod" from *Tristan and Isolde*, Kirsten Flagstad	241	726
42	"I Am the Monarch of the Sea" from *H. M. S. Pinafore*	229	692
43	*Toccata and Fugue in D Minor*, by Bach (fugue section), organ	222	690
44	*Matona, Lovely Maiden*, madrigal by de Lassus	161	802
45	*Petrouchka*, by Stravinsky (piano theme)	150	922
46	*The Frog Went Courting*, sung by John Jacob Niles	144	937
47	*Die Fledermaus* by Strauss (soprano and tenor duet)	142	1063
48	*Die Forelle*, Op. 32 by Schubert, Bjoerling	134	997
49	"The Burning Tapers" from *Lucia*, Lily Pons	88	1234
50	*Quartet No. 5* by Bartok, Finale	64	1188

It indicated that preferences were related to grade level, parents' musical training, and membership in certain musical camp organizations. More than half of the subjects preferred listening to live performances.

Yingling[25] reported on reaction patterns in listening to music. Educational implications suggested that (*a*) the intellectual response to music appreciation is too narrow a base of instruction; (*b*) a physical sensing of music is important to its apprehension; (*c*) taste can be developed by calling attention to emotional element of music; and (*d*) programmatic connotations are valid in certain types of music.

Petzold[26] reported that auditory perception of musical sounds is influenced by the cumulative influence of the music program upon the child; that heterogenous grouping of children in classes is a mandate for developing teaching procedures that take differences into account; that music programs of the school must include a variety of activities designed to stimulate and challenge children so that they can develop an aural understanding of musical sounds. Routine rote instruction is not enough since it is, too often, the result of mechanical imitation and not the result of intellectual thought.

Smith[27] tested the idea of group vocal training of nursery school children and discovered that this approach was successful with three and four year olds. Improvement in the lower range was more pronounced. The report suggests that group vocal training is appropriate for young children and that the focus of such training should be in the range from c^1 to a^1.

Ordway[28] reported on music activities of high school graduates in two communities. There was an implication that the more high school music participation occurred, the more students became involved in community music after graduation. There was a further indication that students graduating more than ten years ago participated more readily now. This was explained because of the possible burdens of young people in getting started on a job and in a family.

Barnes[29] completed a study on the effectiveness of programmed instruction in music fundamentals for prospective elementary teachers which indicated that learning was significantly greater in the experimental group. The implications were that a prospective teacher can save countless hours by the use of such material outside of the regular course time—and that class time can then be used for building on competencies learned.

Flederer's[30] study on the responses of children to musical tasks embodying Piaget's Principle of conservation carried the following implications: The principle of conservation as used by Piaget means the invariance of a given empirical factor throughout observed changes of stage. Only as the given material element remains permanent and independent of changes in its form can the mind use it in building a conceptual framework of the physical world . . . Piaget views concept development in terms of conservation, marked by an increasing stability of a particular concept in the face of changes in the stimulus field.

1. Stages of conservation were apparent in the children's solutions to rhythmic tasks. Solutions often were arrived at by the intervention of physical activity (clapping, etc.). Overt interaction of the child with the musical problem would seem important.

2. Children need models to imitate which serve as feedback mechanisms. Teacher-supplied models (clapping, etc.) should be properly matched with the child's existing mental schemata.

3. There is a necessity for supplying a variety of musical experiences. Musical problems must be commensurate with the child's musical understanding. The musical experiences designed to clarify incipient concepts must precede intellectualization of the specific concept in question.

4. Experience with a large repertoire of desired patterns in many and varied guises is necessary to sharpen the child's ability to discriminate between patterns and to follow thematic development of patterns.

5. Learning situations based on the child's use of his original rhythm patterns in varied tonal contexts and original tonal patterns in varied meters and rhythmic contexts would aid . . . the child with the kind of experience to build a conceptual musical framework.

Rainbow's[31] study to investigate the constructs of Music Aptitude suggests that educators may be able to improve their accuracy of prediction by giving due consideration to relevant extramusical variables, such as interest in music, home enrichment, and socioeconomic background, which may be important factors.

Luce's[32] study on the ability of instrumental music students discovered that a significant relationship between sightreading and earplaying was found for all instrumental students tested. Implication suggested that methods for teaching earplaying should be devised, and as much instruction time spent on it as on sightplaying.

Choate's[33] résumé of recent research appears in *Music Education* *JRME Vol. XIII, No. 2.*

Colwell and *Rundell*[34] discovered no significant differences between groups in auditory-visual achievement in a one-semester experiment comparing keyboard study and ukulele study with regular vocal music experiences. There was a significant gain of the ukulele group over the keyboard group. A follow-up study showed that the keyboard group showed more retention than the other two.

Osborne's[35] study on the validity of making notation metric and representational points up the need for a simple or more easily comprehensible notation that spells out not only highs and lows with accuracy but also presents the rhythmic units in visually measurable terms.

Joseph's[36] *Vocal Growth in the Human Adolescent and the Total Growth Process*, is a study that finds that the ability to produce tones of certain ranges, height or lowness, is closely related to sex, and general body build. Skeletal development, height, shoulder breadth, weight, and attitudes toward singing are considerations in classifying voices. Choate says boys ordinarily do not exhibit adult sonorities before the age of 15 years.

Movsesian[37] discovered that teaching specific music-reading skills has a positive effect on the development of primary reading skills.

The foregoing is a mere sampling, indicating the significance of research to the effective working of a music supervisor. If the music supervisor doesn't relate research finding to the teaching-learning situation, then who will? Research can answer why we do certain things or why we ought to be doing other things. Until better and more conclusive research appears, some of the findings we now have serve as beacon lights guiding the music educative process. There is still a notable lag between significant music education research and real practice. We are still influenced by tradition and greatness. Note how we willingly abandon the best we know about learning for simple stimulus-response drill, Pavlov and faculty psychology just because certain renowned European masters espouse a mechanistic program of music education.

Teacher Aids Embodying Research Results

New ideas tested by research can be distilled by the local music supervisor in a practical form for teachers. This involves artistic ability and the ability to project. The form that becomes the vehicle for ideas may be a brief bulletin. The following criteria were established by a group of teachers and supervisors who were aware of getting useful material into the hands of the teachers:

1. It must be short, no more than three to six pages
2. It must be attractive, so that teachers will pick it up
3. It must be most specific; its objectives must be clear
4. It must be outlined to the extent that teachers can determine with a glance whether it contains what they want
5. There must be only one idea per bulletin, such as
    (a) Learning to listen in the primary grades
    (b) Making Latin-American instruments in upper grades
    (c) Beginning concepts of music reading for primary grades
    (d) Aids for the beginning part-singing teacher
    (e) Steps in helping poor singers

This type of functional bulletin is produced by hundreds of music supervisors in all parts of the country, and there may be duplication of effort. It seems reasonable that many of the ideas can be pooled and produced in quantity, then distributed to teachers. This would be economical, but it overlooks the factor of a supervisor having the specific problems of one or several teachers in mind. Mass-produced items can lose their savor because they risk losing the personalized frame of reference of teacher versus supervisor.

The worth of an idea is determined whether it is used by anyone at all. It is inadvisable to distribute materials to teachers indiscriminately. Use is usually assured when the teacher receives such materials at the close of a workshop or clinic session, or, as on-the-spot aid at a time and place where it is most needed. It is also a way of letting the teacher know that you thought of her concerns. The writer knows of colleagues who use prepared bulletins as a wedge to get at the teacher, or a way to get into her room.

Music Guides, a Distillation of Pertinent Research

Most states, large cities, and music supervision departments publish courses of study in music, often called music guides. Their value is that they present the total program for consideration. The existence of a guide is representational and also serves as a conscience to the school and the teacher. Its presence is a spur to action. If it contains a program of worth it deserves to be implemented. Here, of course, the supervisor who noted a need and wrote the document, must also bear the responsibility that something happens.

The accompanying form makes provision for succinctness, readability, and attractive layout. It is a planned way of presenting written materials:

STANDARD FORM FOR CURRICULUM GUIDE PROJECTS
(as used by one city school system)

I. Standard First Page (See sample attached)

    A. Curriculum guide for (subject and grade)

    B. Prepared by: (chairman and committee members)

    C. Names of Director, Deputy and Superintendent

    D. Project Number

    E. District and address

    F. Date of publication

II. Table of Contents
(optional with committee)

III. All pages of the guide are to be numbered within the project or within major sections such as social studies units.

IV. Brief foreword, statement, point of view, etc.
(optional with committee — less than a full page)

V. List of Instructional Materials

    A. At top — (subject, grade), instructional materials

    B. Basic materials (other headings may be substituted for "B" and "C")

        Author   Title   Distribution   Source of Supply

    C. Supplementary materials

        Author   Title   Distribution   Source of Supply

      1. Do not use codes. Write out distribution and source of supply.
      2. If audiovisual materials are listed, do not use catalogue numbers.
      3. Use of a grade level column is optional.
      4. "Tear-out" sheets for ordering may follow materials pages.

VI. General Outline (if desired)

    A. General objectives

    B. Brief overview of years' work — not more than two pages

    C. Suggested approaches

VII. Main Guide Headings

The three divisions below should constitute the main body of the guide and be setup in column form as shown. Use exact spacing as shown.

What to Teach (Specific Objectives)	How to Teach (Suggested Experiences)	Where to Find Help (Aids & References)

The General Course of Study
(a codification of pertinent research)

Most large school systems have developed their own courses of study. They usually contain a music section where a minimum program is laid out grade by grade, and often in correlation with other learning areas. The course of study is frequently in the form of an outline making provision for (*a*) objectives, (*b*) suggested experiences, (*c*) pertinent content, and (*d*) resources for such grade level. The sequential sections are listed either by grade level or by age level.

The course of study ordinarily is preceded by several pages of scope and sequence charts in which age levels are treated in keeping with known developmental considerations.

The music section of several courses of study starts out at each grade level by introducing as the major consideration of music education a developmental concept for all grades: "music should be part of the cultural, social and emotional experiences of each child, so that he may grow in musical awareness, initiative, insight, discrimination, and skill. Music should help children in grade————through such experiences as——"

Research a National Concern[38]

More than $7,000,000 of Title IV, ESEA, money has been invested in twelve regional laboratories and twelve clearinghouses for educational research. President Johnson announced: "These laboratories should be large and significant enterprises, equal in size and scope to the major tasks they seek to accomplish. They ought to be conceived as comparable in their way to the large-scale laboratories of the defense or atomic energy establishments. Nothing less will do. Their missions are equally important."

The projects planned by these laboratories will be the development of packages of instructional material for all areas of all grade levels. Special features will be the development of model schools for the demonstration of new ideas and providing a richer education for the underprivileged. Evaluation units will provide for change of programs in progress. Special innovation centers will also be established. These are the federally financed laboratory locations, to date:

1. Albuquerque—Southwest Cooperative Educational Laboratory
2. Philadelphia—Research for Better Schools, Inc.
3. Berkeley—Far West Laboratory for Education Research and Development
4. St. Louis—Central Midwestern Regional Educational Laboratory

5. Kansas City—Mid-Continent Regional Educational Laboratory
6. Portland—Northwest Regional Educational Laboratory
7. Greeley—Rocky Mountain Educational Laboratory, Inc.
8. Charleston, W. Va.—Appalachia Educational Laboratory
9. Tallahassee—Southeastern Educational Corporation
10. St. Paul—Upper Mid-West Regional Educational Laboratory
11. New York City—Center for Urban Education
12. Santa Monica—Southwest Regional Laboratory for Educational Research and Development

It is entirely predictable that by the time this book is in print major problems related to music education will be underway in one or the other of these laboratories. The fact that the national government has entered into the picture is quite understandable. As one writer stated aptly, "Educators have a propensity for arguing most astutely about the most irrelevant things, and coming up with solutions which are never implemented." This may be an overstatement, but it points up a need and unfulfilled commitments. Somewhere we have promised all the American people some mighty wonderful things in the arts, and we know they have not been happening even in half measure. The federal government has a justifiable concern. Its promotion of research will force the issue of finding better ways to make the arts effective to more children.

Ole Sand, in his article, "Schools for the Seventies"[39] emphasizes the accelerated accumulation of knowledge: (a) 1750 marked the first doubling of knowledge since A.D. 4; (b) 1900 marked the second doubling of knowledge; (c) 1950 marked the third doubling of knowledge; and (d) 1960 marked the fourth doubling of knowledge.

This reality forces music educators to ask for research. For these reasons certain favored programs may have to make room for programs that carry out the national policy. The formidable gap between the intent of curriculum projects and what really happens must close. Music educators also stand guilty of Feldman's scathing condemnation, "scorn for the wooly teacher with a chalkboard, the little phony world we have in school, and one lousy road to learning . . . vocational education has to pick up our casualties." He asks that we help students "escape from the constant drone of instruction so they can really learn something."

The research laboratories have already produced plans of the new school. Some of these schools have been built. One fine day your school will have the new features. Will you be ready to change your view on what is the music curriculum? With knowledge doubling less than every ten years, has music education changed to meet the challenge?

In a plea for more significant research, Hazel Morgan points out that "research done with little effort is likely to yield results of little importance. Let us be fully aware that much valuable research had been done by music education scholars. Let us accept the challenge to find the marble in the mountains of our graduate music students and encourage capable ones to make beautiful statues that will endure. Let us hope that future research by music educators will yield an ever increasing body of knowledge which can be universally helpful and universally available."[40]

Robert Petzold[41] says, "basic research is characterized by: (1) careful delineation of a fundamental problem leading to the formulation of hypotheses to be tested; (2) development of definitive and objective procedures for collecting valid and reliable data; (3) systematic treatment and analysis of these data; and (4) testing of the hypotheses and formulation of statements regarding conclusions and implications that are based on the finding of the study." He warns against "the inherent unreliability of common sense" and questions "the validity of much that we perceive through our senses." Basic research is most importantly concerned in not only the *what* is happening, but also the *why* and the *how*.

Paul Lehman has compiled a list on behalf of the Music Education Research Council of MENC as a service to music educators seeking support for research activities. It can be found in its entirety in the February-March 1966 issue of the *Music Educators Journal,* pp. 82 and 85.

QUESTIONS FOR DISCUSSION, THOUGHT AND STUDY

1. What has research to do with the learning process?
2. Where is the nearest federally supported research center? Who is the director?
3. Name five music educators whose work establishes them as researchers.
4. If you have done research, how has it changed you?
5. How can the supervisor relate research finding for the teacher?
6. Outline a research design whereby you can find answers to problems in your district.
7. What are favorable conditions for carrying out research?
8. What are the dispositional qualifications of a researcher?
9. How do your teachers identify problems?
10. Differentiate between basic and action research.
11. List pros and cons for action research.

12. Go through your district's course of study or music guide and outline how research influenced the content.
13. How can you solicit the interest of teachers and administrators in carrying out local research on pertinent music education problems?
14. Classify the research studies listed topically and according to pertinence.

NOTES

[1]Thurber Madison, *Basic Concepts in Music Education,* NSSE Yearbook LVII, (Chicago: University of Chicago Press, 1948), Chapter I.

[2]Harold Spears, *Improving the Supervision of Instruction,* (New York: Prentice-Hall, Inc., 1953), p. 268.

[3]Chas. Leonhard, *A Song Approach to Music Reading,* (New York: Silver-Burdett Co., 1953), pp. 6-10.

[4]Jessie Fleming, "The Determination of Musical Experiences Designed to Develop Competencies Required of Elementary School Teachers in Maryland," *Journal of Research in Music Education,* I, No. 1, (Spring, 1953), pp. 59-97.

[5-19]SEE Research Section in Bibliography for references.

[20]Marian Brooks and Harry Brown, *Music Education in the Elementary School,* (New York: American Book Company, 1946).

[21-37]SEE Research Section in Bibliography for references.

[38]Berlie Fallon, *Educational Innovation in the U. S.,* (Bloomington: Phi Delta Kappa, 1966), pp. 95 & 162.

[39]Ole Sand, "Schools for the Seventies," *MENC Journal,* Vol. 52, No. VI, (J–J 1966), p. 40.

[40]Hazel Morgan, "First Steps in Research for Graduate Students," *MENC Journal,* Vol. 52, No. I, (S-O 1965), p. 76.

[41]Robert Petzold, "Direction for Research in Music Education," *MENC Journal,* Vol. 50, No. 3, (Jan. 1964), p. 39.

Idyllwild Arts Foundation, Idyllwild, Calif.

Chapter 14

Growing Professionally

The schools of this and the next decade will need leadership in the arts of a caliber and commitment never before apparent. The need exists because education is changing. There is coming into being a new kind of school and a new kind of curriculum. These new molds will require modes of operation never envisioned ten years ago. All of this is not because of a passing fancy. For years educators have promised the good life and all of the skills and attitudes and attributes that are needed to keep afloat in this luxuriant age. The message has finally reached the lowliest, and they are wanting what we have said is their right and their heritage. We, as music educators, had better be prepared to give it from here on in. Yes, we will still have our excellent bands, choruses, and orchestras. They may be even bigger and better. More importantly, we will have done something about providing valid learnings in the arts to those heretofore untouched.

The Headstart programs, nursery schools and other preschool programs will be the starting points from which will procede sequential learning programs in keeping with growth and development. The musical tastes, proclivities and reactions of the total student population will be the future concern. All students will enjoy a guaranteed significant minimum. Many can move ahead to heights unknown.

The music supervisor of today and tomorrow must be a person of vision and one who is part of the vast exciting change taking place in education. He must, as it were, lead his flock of music teachers to the new vantage point in such a way that they can function comfortably and with the same dedication as within the old molds.

To be a working partner in this renaissance in education, he, the music supervisor, must become more than a traveling classroom teacher, a budget maker, an order filler, and an evaluator. New insights, new views, and new skills will be required. These require the services of a person ever growing professionally. And, unless the leader grows, the music curriculum will recede more and more into insular obsolescence.

The great question is, "Just how does the leader grow?"

There are traditional ways by which professional leaders in education have grown. Many of these have been haphazard, and the result has been that the individual really grew only in the area in which he was performing already quite acceptably. The choral director is said to have grown when he can produce a more beautiful tone. The band director, when he can produce a better band sound, or play more difficult music. The music supervisor is known to have grown when he achieved a larger budget, a bigger festival, was elected to a position of respect, etc. One prominent educator recently said, "Music educators are doing an ever increasing good job of the things they are doing . . . but are they the right things?" The kind of growth needed today is what takes place when one adopts a new mold and does something entirely different. The patterns of reaction cannot follow the old convenient paths.

Familiar Growth Agents[1]

Local Professional Staff Meetings

The local scene is where things happen. What ought to occur in staff meetings is a growth in understanding of the total educational commitment of the district and its special concerns. The music supervisor cannot afford to be absent. His presence gives him awareness of the framework through which he works. Here he also learns the rules of the local educational game. He learns by hearing others, from the top administrator down to his peers in other learning areas. Many ideas can be reworked and become useful to his own work. He also grows whenever he contributes to the thinking of the group. He may be asked to react. He ought to volunteer reaction. The resulting interaction is a growth factor. He may make a presentation of his program. He may have to answer searching questions; he may have to defend and justify what he espouses. A curriculum staff can be relentlessly critical of the special supervisor, and especially the music supervisor's program because it takes a large financial slice out of the budget and a large time slice out of the school day.

Community Involvements

Most music supervisors at some time or other find themselves actively engaged in working with lay groups, either assisting them in worth-while projects or soliciting their aid to further the cause of music. One cannot help growing in perspective, in sensitivity to others, and in the appreciation of the task other groups espouse.

The Parent-Teacher Association is a most excellent group through which one can establish good public relations for the music program. Mothers want the best in culture for their children. They react to the school music person as did the mothers in *Music Man*. The writer had an opportunity to bring an opera company to town to present special performances to school children. Neither the school, the boards, nor other legitimate groups were able to shoulder the financial responsibility. The P. T. A. mothers took over and the money flowed in; ushers and chaperones were provided.

Contacts with the several service clubs provide wholesome opportunities. Learn to understand their goals. Work with them. They will help finance students to music camps, or even buy instruments.

The press and communications media are not to be ignored. One grows mightily preparing material that is acceptable. It takes much learning to have material accepted. Just because you are a college graduate and an excellently trained musician and educator, this doesn't make you a writer. You grow in communicative ability by writing.

Community Music Associations and Local Symphony Associations

These are growth affiliations for the music supervisor. They provide consumer and performer outlets for your musical products. In our small town, leaders of these groups are doctors, lawyers, business people, and undertakers. Also included on the roster of local leaders are several nonteaching graduates of Julliard and Eastman schools of music, several who sang in European opera companies and others who played in major symphony orchestras before moving here.

Professional Affiliations

It is a professional responsibility to join several complementary organizations. You support them by contributing annual dues. They help you grow by meetings, associations, projects, books and periodicals. These are some:

local teachers' club
area teachers' association
state teachers' association
N. E. A.
local supervisors' association
regional supervisors' association
state supervisors' association

Association for Supervision and
Curriculum Development
local music teachers
county music teachers
regional music teachers
state music teachers
Music Educators National Conference

The periodicals of the state and national supervisors and music teachers associations provide a wealth of growth materials. One cannot exist as a music supervisor without a fair knowledge of things reported in the journals. The *Music Educators Journal* and the *Journal of Research in Music Education,* laid out sequentially over the years, form a pretty accurate time line of the history of conceptual growth and progress in music education. The yearbooks published by both music educators and the ASCD are stopping places, saying, as it were: "We are here today, and we are headed that direction."

Meetings, Conventions, Conferences and Clinics

Both the Association for Supervision and Curriculum Development and the Music Educators National Conference hold periodic meetings and stage conventions and clinics at the several levels, national, divisional, state, regional, county or large district.

Local Music Educator Clubs

Present-day complex interrelationships push into the background much of what we know is good about face-to-face relationships. To counteract the effects of this trend, several county music coordinators have encouraged the development of an organization where music teachers could meet face to face, express themselves on problems and issues, and plan and work together toward solutions. The coordinator serves *ex officio* as observer, advisor, and catalyst. Over the years many of the music teachers were able to receive personalized attention and counseling; and the entire group could move forward together toward mutually acceptable goals. Yes, the supervisor grew by remaining somewhat in the background and rearranging circumstances so that many kinds of growth could happen. He grew most in human relations and in techniques of motivating others to action.

Regional Music Educators Clinics

Whatever has been traditionally said about the music supervisor, he is still looked up to by his colleagues as a leader. He is assigned leadership roles and is expected to carry them out. In one area of a large western state there is an organization of five hundred school music teachers. Its fifteen-member board of directors has always been made up of at least four supervisors, three college professors, and eight teachers (the teachers usually were department heads, and in essence, supervisors). The steering committee and the program committee were usually directed by supervisors.

The professional growth of the supervisor results from his leadership involvement for others' benefit. The writer served on the regional music educators board of directors representing one community for twelve years in various capacities; and out of thirty clinics held, he was host at six and assisted in setting up the program for at least ten others.

This kind of involvement forces one to grow. Such a leader must acquire the skill to sense area-wide needs and to set up growth situations so music teachers can help themselves.

State, Division and National Music Educators Conventions

The musical tastemakers and the appetite whetters are present in varying degrees and color shadings at the conventions. The music teachers and supervisors from every kind of community are also present, eager for a circus of ideas, the residual of which can carry them to the end of a wearisome school year and provide inspiration and courage to change some things for the better. A sad commentary is that probably no more than one-fourth of the school music teachers attend each year. Of these, a large percentage never get beyond the display tables. They miss the thought that ties the profession together toward a forward-moving goal.

Prominent in leadership roles are the music supervisors. Also prominent at planning conferences preceding conventions are the music supervisors. I am sure they have not made themselves prominent. Most of them are too busy for that kind of status-seeking sport. They have been sought out by a profession that respects its leadership.

It is quite redundant to discuss the areas in which growth takes place in this connotation. Suffice it to add, "The leader grows by his contacts while preparing for leadership at conferences, and in his personal preparation. The listener or consumer grows only to the extent that he 'tunes in' . . . and statistically, that can be as little as twenty per cent of the time."

The wares and the ideas that bombard the consciousness of the supervisor at a convention, force him to evaluate in terms of home; and to assimilate what is immediately apropos.

Association for Supervision and Curriculum Development[2]

The ASCD and its state and regional subdivisions are in all probability the real curriculum policy makers. Their members, drawn from the ranks of all areas of supervisors, are constantly studying new ways of implementing learning programs. The mother organization is recognized by administrators as the oracle in in-service matters. Supervisory personnel gladly rely on the authoritative studies made by the various groups in this organization.

The studies have found their way into the organization's many books, periodicals, and yearbooks. It is interesting to note that the national educational concern for the year is usually reflected in the title of the yearbook of the year.

At the state level ASCD is divided into working committees representing each area of curricular concern:

1. Early childhood committee
2. Educational television commission
3. The music committee
4. The committee for non-English-speaking children
5. The committee on drop-outs
6. The social studies committee

Each of these meet during regional and state meetings, also in the intervals between meetings, and work at projects that promote the improvement of learning situations in their respective areas. The music committee may meet to work at ideas such as these:

1. Preparing guidelines for including music expansion under ESEA Title I, II and III requests for Federal Funds
2. Establishing a clearing house for exchange of in-service ideas
3. Developing a framework for music education to affect programs throughout an area or state
4. Formulating criteria for selecting music texts

Music Educators National Conference

Two periodicals, three yearbooks, and a host of publications representing every branch of the school music teaching arena are the credits of MENC. The periodicals and publications present a distillation of the ideas, workings and research of the more verbal leaders. The avenues of growth to the supervisor, merely by reading the literature, are unbelievably many. Here also the supervisor grows by contributing of his knowledge. He grows when he is forced to refine and distill his ideas into a form readable and understandable to the vast host and variety of music teachers.

N.E.A., the mother organization of both MENC and ASCD, is also a source of growth to all who come in contact with its writings.

Books, Guides, and Courses of Study[3]

A rich source for professional growth are the many guides and courses of study produced by state departments of education and large school administrative units. The value in seeing what others have written lies in that we recognize there exists a community of music education concerns. Writers on music education tend to reflect the best of what we know. There is value also in placing the host of guides and courses under the spotlight of critical evaluation. In this way can the realists and the idealists come to terms on important issues. The music supervisor's growth lies in his critically reading much and then translating it for others. This process alone activates the professional growth potential.

There is no single satisfactory list of books that is a *must* for the supervisor. This is certain—his reading ought to be broad, covering the total cultural spectrum. He ought to see the relationship between music and poetry or art, between large forms and drama. He ought to become aware of new movements in education, i.e., new philosophical thought. He ought to have a verbal acquaintanceship with new approaches to learning, concept development, educational objectives, and evaluations. These areas are undergoing dramatic changes in perspective. He ought to be aware of and knowledgeable in recommended ways of scheduling school programs. The future of music programs will be dependent on the supervisor's flexibility in adapting to flexible programs. His reading program must be so intense that his verbalization on issues is reflected in succinctness and crystal clarity.

The Music Supervisor as Teacher[4]

Growth takes place when one translates theory into action. Many music supervisors are master teachers; otherwise they could not have been selected for the job. The supervisor needs to go back to the classroom at times to present a crystallization of his ideas. He ought to do this either before children and/or before adult teachers. This kind of interaction will force him into a succinctness of expression that will give credibility to theory.

Every music supervisor ought to teach a course in music education, if for no other reasons than (1) to bolster his program, (2) to give him an opportunity to clarify and update his thinking, and (3) to give him a measure of desirable status.

Study, Research, Pilot Programs

Equally important ways to grow professionally are through (1) study groups; (2) action research with teachers; (3) setting up pilot programs in schools; (4) attending seminars and graduate courses in advanced problems of music education and supervision; (5) travel, even busmen's holidays of visiting other departments in districts far from home.

Studying real field problems with peers in music supervision can provide tremendous insights. Each person in the group challenges the thinking of the others. Such groups can become the testing ground for mutual problems and untried ideas (the leavening for otherwise ponderous thought and new ideas).

Action research needs reemphasis here, since it also is a testing ground for theories and ideas. It implies trying out ideas in the home teaching situation and relaying findings back to the group for further refinement and evaluation. This is on-the-job research. To the music supervisor it is like owning the test tube and doing the experiments instead of merely reading about them. Action research and pilot programs, if carried out with scholarly exactitude, are quite synonymous.

Travel and study are among the obvious professional growth factors. Travel's effect is similar to that when the artist stands back and looks with the perspective that distance offers on his handiwork. New life, new ideas, and new vigor come from travel. One is forced out of the societal and self-imposed track for a while, and is given the experience of going a new way and being open to different things. Problems and projects may be approached in a new light. Old, obsolete ways of functioning make room for the new. Travel can give that magic touch or impetus to revitalized activities.

The discipline of sitting in a graduate seminar with classroom teachers, peers from other areas of instruction, administrators, and college teachers can be as effective in changing the music supervisor as being involved in a program of sensitivity training. Here the chips fall as they may, and the abrasive effect of rubbing elbows with other disciplines cause one to examine his own stance with utmost care. Recently the federal government sponsored seminars on the arts and humanities in different parts of the country. These seminars provided not only a meeting of minds, but a hammering out of common goals, leaving again, crystal clear the significant differences between these similar disciplines.

Preferably this kind of intensive study ought not take place after four o'clock once a week. Very few educators can profit from the four o'clock in-service "quickie." By that time they have been drained and need a change. It takes both time and place away from job deadlines.

Meeting Teachers as People

One of our teacher friends has a husband who is supervisor for a utility company; another's is vice-president of a bank. Another teacher operates a large range on the side. We also know a number of teachers whose spouses are superintendents of large school districts. One teacher's husband runs a travel agency. The family has traveled by air to all parts of the world. These people have grown by right of what they are and the families they have. Don't get too excited if they tune you out in a meeting. It might just be that they have been there before and have heard all too often what you are talking about. Supervisors tend to "talk down" to teachers.

It may be of great value to make a chart of many of the classroom teachers you are expected to work with, listing their family occupation, hobbies, interests, and special experiences. It might just be that the little third grade teacher who sort of smiles inwardly when you come around has been what you are, a music consultant, but in another district. Many of these remain hidden in a school system.

Music supervisors grow by meeting teachers as special people. We grow when we have the good sense and tact to utilize their great abilities and experiences to build a good music program.

Some Do's to Help in Growth of Understanding Others

1. The music supervisor ought to find ways of reaching into his past for clues in understanding the problems of the present. He must ask himself, How did I act, really, when I was a beginning teacher?

Did I seek help? Did I accept help with ease? How did I look at my supervisor?

2. The music supervisor ought to put his ears to the railroad track and be able to pick up the signals from a freight train and from a streamlined jet-propelled train. Is he so accustomed to the old familiar sound of the slow-moving freight that the whirr of the fast-moving Twentieth Century Limited is on him before he can step aside, not even to speak of climbing on board?

3. Do you recognize that most educators (this includes teachers and administrators) come from a lower class? How is it possible that we have lost the common touch so soon? Do you remember the days when you attended a more primitive school than the worst one in your district? You made it, somehow? What was the critical incident? Who helped you?

4. Music supervisors ought to remain tuned in on children—how they grow and how they respond to music. They ought to remain tuned in on teachers. They may know more than you can see. It is for you to find a common ground from which teacher and supervisor can proceed.

5. The music supervisor must open herself up. Drop the pretense. Let the status wall crumble. Be willing to admit deficiencies. Give trade secrets. Empathize with teachers. By opening yourself up you make yourself vulnerable. You expose yourself to critical evaluation by peers. You reveal the great goodness within you, and in this revelation you expose yourself to hurt. The rewards are greater than any hurt experienced.

6. It has been said that people can sympathize and cry at the grief and sorrows of others; but only angels can rejoice in others' joys and successes. Sympathy is easy. You feel sorry for something; in fact, you place a value judgment on a deficiency. But can you empathize? Can you feel with someone in his failure and in his success? And from this empathy can you move forward with him?

7. The music supervisor also grows by knowing himself, his personal, educational, and musical strengths and weaknesses. The Socratean dictum Know Thyself holds the same validity now as when it was uttered almost 2400 years old. Psychotherapists work at putting their patients in a position where they must look at themselves for what they are, before real therapy can take place. Growth happens when supervisors recognize their limitations and see themselves as they are.

8. The music supervisor must give himself to his cause before he can anticipate success. Before he can grow he must involve himself

thoroughly in the things he is espousing. Great people in all fields respect no time limitations.

9. The music supervisor's growth is also dependent on his ability to see through the differences that separate him from those with whom he works. He must seek out the likenesses, and possibly even probe through the differences to the area of feelings.

10. Each of the above is tied together with a small observation, i.e., our tragic uninvolvement in people, problems, issues, research, music, and everything that affects the job of the supervisor is the limiting agent that inhibits growth and progress.

Growth is not to be confused with *change*. "CHANGE is the substitution of one thing for another; but GROWTH, or improvement, assumes a fundamental reorganization of thinking."[5] "All growth is change, but all change is not growth." "The typical (supervisor) behaves in ways that are partly a result of notions gained during his training and partly because of his in-service experience. He begins to grow when he is dissatisfied with his performance and seeks a greater understanding and control of the events under his jurisdiction. Growth, in effect extends his accumulated knowledge. It goads him into a mastery of more sophisticated skill and techniques and a more perceptive grasp of the subtleties which exist in the interplay between himself and those who he hopes to affect."

Rubin envisions the professional growth of the teacher (and/or supervisor) as something that satisfactorily deals with these phenomena:

1. The nature of growth
2. The conditions for growth
3. A strategy for growth
4. The growth facilitator
5. The supporting growth promoting agency

Growth occurs when the music supervisor is confronted by a situation which cries for change or improvement. Once he is aware of it he experiences a certain amount of unrest until he looks into the problem more fully to comprehend its cause and effect relationships, and then uses the resulting evidence to reorganize his understanding.

The Music Supervisor Improves by Demanding a Continual Search for New Evidence to Rearrange His Way of Thinking

Select a number of leaders in music education. By examining their actions and reactions you will be able to discover the key to their success. Is it not the one who has a zeal for performing his mission extremely well? Look at Miss D. She's at the state convention chairing several section meetings. Someone said the committee asked her because she has such a live-wire program going in her district. Most of the teachers teach their own classroom music. The performing groups are the best. They say she has a revolutionary system all her own and everyone is excited about it.

Obviously she is the artist type supervisor. She functions above and beyond preconceived ways of doing things. She is the master of her environment and as such dances to the nuances of the learning situation and as such continually plots her own betterment. She is on the alert to grasp ideas as thoroughly as if she really dreamed them up herself. She has the facility to integrate an idea with everything she knows about the art of supervision.

Miss D did not grow as a matter of course. Certain conditions were present. Many school systems are inhibiting factors. They just will not permit music supervisors to function beyond the minimal level needed for survival. This is probably why so many "supervisors" race from room to room teaching the youngsters. At least the system is content that they are busy . . . and anyhow, "the classroom teacher doesn't do a good job."

Miss D grew because of a personal desire. Not many years ago she came to a new position where she was relegated to a minimal function level, i.e., doing the musical chores for classroom teachers; picking up the tab in preparing P. T. A. programs; and performing such antics that tended not to rock the proverbial educational boat. She became aware of a higher level of functioning; she desired it for herself, and she worked with all diligence toward achieving it. She just did not want to remain the organ grinder's monkey who occupied her time by doing crazy antics and collecting money.

How did Miss D ever get out of her dilemma? Yes, she was aware of better ways. She was dissatisfied in living out her life racing about in little musical circles. Someone or something prodded her into action. An external force, either in the form of a person, a situation or an idea gave her the impetus. And she was aware of rewards—yes, probably even monetary rewards. Today a glowing feeling of satisfaction alone can tend to wear thin.

The external force that caused the initial restlessness and zeal to change and grow could have been a person, an organization, or a situation. Remember, a kind word from a person a step higher on the educational ladder can do much. Especially if this kind word is coupled with a plan to assist or facilitate new ideas. The professional growth of a music supervisor is affected by how others deal with him. One is reminded here of a statement offered by Goethe:

> If you treat an individual as he is, he will stay as he is, but if you treat him as if he were what he ought to be and could be, he will become what he ought to be and could be.

Rubin[6] calls the person who does the treating *the facilitator*. Ideally this person could easily be the music coordinator working, not out of the district office, but from a service center which is, in some areas, the county school office, in others, the intermediate unit. Newer terminology calls it the *consortium*. He feels strongly that such a *facilitator* has the task of serving as a support person assisting teachers and consultants to exploit their own potential in self-determined and self-directed programs of growth. His role encompasses three major dimensions: creator, sustainer and mediator:

1. must draw attention to the problem
2. must create and sustain the conditions necessary for growth
3. must assist the teacher to put improvements into practice and to measure their consequences

The facilitator working out of an educational consortium can be the external prod to supervisors, consultants, and teachers in his area toward growth. Just recently such a coordinator addressed an audience of eight music consultants and forty-five special music teachers. In his talk he outlined unmet challenges on topics such as planning for integration within performing groups, changing contest festival format, developing new approaches to teaching general music, and looking at objective and evaluation techniques.

The ideas were presented as if he were the spokesman for the unspoken desires of the many music people present. Even though no mandates were given, the effect was as follows:

1. Several music consultants asked to work on a program to improve their ability to work with teachers
2. A number of music instructors presented plans which could revolutionize festival structure
3. There was more talk about "we are paid to teach music better to more students"
4. Two consultants wanted to form a study group to explore grade level objectives in school music, and to work at evaluation criteria

These consultants and music teachers are growing with the external assistance of the facilitator. The facilitator or "catalyst" will not shape the teachers and consultants into a preconceived mold. Hopefully he will catalyze some reaction, but he cannot predict what the reaction will be. It is assumed that one of his major responsibilities will be to generate mutation. The word *mutation* is apt because it is a change that cannot be predicted. Whatever mutation occurs, however, is likely to serve as a start to the chain reaction of cumulative professional growth.

In summing up the innumerable factors and the specific theories by which music supervisors grow professionally, it is apropos to outline the affective domain of the taxonomy of educational objectives because these contain the growth pattern steps:[7]

1. The music supervisor should place himself in the position of being a receptor. He must be open to ideas and change. This means,
   (a) he must be AWARE of new ideas and problems in his field
   (b) he must be WILLING to receive the ideas
   (c) he must be DISCRIMINATE in selecting the stimuli most likely to offer complementary results
2. The music supervisor having heard the "call," and placed a priority on the ideas that presented themselves must respond by indicating a desire:
   (a) he must comply with, and/or acquiesce (as it were "this is *my mission*—I will")
   (b) he must indicate a willingness to respond to the "call"
   (c) he will experience a feeling of satisfaction once the "die is cast," and he finds gratification, joy and pleasure in his decision
3. The music supervisor, in his commitment, will place a value or worth on what he has selected. His attitude will reflect the acceptance of a value.
   (a) he accepts and believes in what he wants to do
   (b) he becomes committed to the value he espouses; it becomes an all-encompassing *commitment*
   (c) he becomes devoted to the carrying out of the idea.
4. The music supervisor organizes what he wants to accomplish into a systematic value configuration. It again systematizes and places priorities of values on concomitant ideas that present themselves in the pursuit of the project.
   (a) he conceptualizes whatever value is part of his growth program; he compares it with what is known to him and extracts generalizations from the known
   (b) he weighs alternatives and decides in favor of the values most consistent with what he is seeking.

5. In the process of professional growth the music supervisor decides on a priority of values that have to do with the specific growth he is working at. His consistent reaction to selecting priorities reflect how he has *internalized* or made "into his own" the learning
   (*a*) he becomes known for his view (really a generalization of his reaction pattern).
   (*b*) finally, his new growth behavior assumes a CHARACTER; he is then known to have such and such a philosophy; he exemplifies a philosophy which determines his reaction

Thus the music supervisor *receives* impulses; he makes them his *mission;* he becomes *committed* to the accomplishing of the task; he places *priorities* on the task or values he encounters; these he organizes into a *value system;* finally he *internalizes* what he is after so it becomes part of his being.

QUESTIONS FOR DISCUSSION, THOUGHT AND STUDY

1. What has research to do with the learning process?
2. How did your own research affect your thinking?
3. Trace your own growth through the steps presented immediately above.
4. Classify research studies you found in the *Music Educators Journal* over the past three years. What per cent deal with learning? What per cent deal with in-service education?
5. Suggest a research design to find the answers to pressing supervisory problems.
6. What are favorable conditions for carrying out research?
7. What values are in action research?
8. How would you relate research to improved classroom functioning?
9. Look in your Music Course of Study or Guide and pinpoint the places where research was utilized. What per cent is opinion? and what per cent research?
10. How would you interest your school in carrying action research? How can you make it something *they* want?

NOTES

[1]Thelen, *Dynamics of Groups at Work,* (Chicago: Univ. of Chicago Press, 1963).
[2]ASCD Yearbooks (see Bibliography).
[3]Louis Rubin, *The Nurture of Teacher Growth,* (Center for Coordinated Education, Santa Barbara, 1966).
[4]Louis Rubin, *The Professional Growth of the Educator,* (Center for Coordinated Education, Santa Barbara, 1966).
[5]Louis Rubin, *The Nature of Teacher Growth.*
[6]Louis Rubin, *The Professional Growth of the Educator.*
[7]Benj. Bloom, *Taxonomy of Education Objectives,* (New York: David McKay, Inc., 1964).

Idyllwild Arts Foundation, Idyllwild, Calif.

Chapter 15

Evaluating Programs, Processes and People

Evaluation in music education is more than making value judgments on the basis of cursory observation. It is more than applying a device to test the effectiveness of certain procedures in teaching music. Most testing devices shed but a glimmer of light on a small segment of musical learning. Tests of musical achievement tell very little about progress toward objectives and about learner change in relationship to objectives.

To the music supervisor, evaluation ought to involve looking critically at the process of gathering and weighing evidence that will reveal changes in terms of a desirable music educational product. This ought not be limited to the use of usual tests but ought to extend into multitudinous devices and instrumentalities that will provide answers to such questions as these:[1]

1. Are the objectives of music education realistic? (Can what is predicted really happen?) Are they musically oriented, or do they espouse "other than" musical values?
2. Are the methods employed to reach the objectives effective (methods refer to the means used)? Is the personality of the teacher part of the means; and what does the degree of teacher knowledge about music have to do with method?
3. If we declare the objective to be realistic and the methods to be effective, what progress is being made, and what is the rate of progress toward the objectives? Is movement toward objectives good enough?
4. Is the student any different because of being taught with certain objectives in mind? Has his progress toward the goals been satisfactory to himself, to the teacher, to the school, and to society? What kind of behavior ought a musically taught student manifest? What

do we really have after going through this tremendous fuss and bother about "music for all and all for music" in our schools?

The role of the evaluator (in this case the music supervisor) is not simple. The role implies examining many procedures for the teaching of music in order to determine whether they fulfill the hoped for ideals. It means placing values on programs, on people and on means, however in terms of objectives.

The Music Supervisor as a Diagnostician

No matter how you look at it the music supervisor's first task is to look over the territory and decide for himself what needs to be done to make it a comfortable place to live in and a comfortable situation to live with. He *evaluates*. He determines as well as is possible through observational means:

1. The lay of the land (the music educational climate)
2. The kind of neighbors (the educational peers)
3. The physical facilities (office, or whatever space is allowed)
4. The tools (what you offer teachers that help them teach)
5. The principals (what they care about music)
6. The teacher corps, both special and classroom (their expertise)
7. The community (the general cultural interests and the pockets of no culture)
8. The district's financial structure (salary, budget to provide mobility of action)
9. The philosophy of the district (something by which one can bet on futures)

While the music supervisor is evaluating the district, this same district is evaluating him. They are looking at a file containing such items as (*a*) personal history record; (*b*) high school and college records including grades, majors, and minors; (*c*) recommendation from college teachers; (*d*) recommendation from other employers, both education and other; (*e*) activity and interest record; (*f*) family.

The district has evaluated its own circumstances and has determined what kind of person it wants to hire to do the job they envision. Also the applicant music supervisor has already evaluated himself in terms of strengths and weaknesses, interests and ambitions; and he is looking at the district to see whether the potential for the kind of future he seeks can be ascertained from the available evidence. Employer and applicant are handing each other a report card. It is more like the contract subscribed to by the colonial indentured servant and his master. The two parts of the contract have to mesh.

The likelihood exists that in the future the music supervisor's past, plus his ideas, character analysis, and all other items under consideration, will be placed in a computer along with the district's specifications. The result could save much time, money, and energy.

After the supervisor is on the job, there isn't an act that he engages in that does not include evaluation. *That's what it's all about!* Each chapter in this book talks about a different phase of the process of evaluation in which the music supervisor engages:

1. Looking over the field
2. Looking at the music supervisor and his job
3. Looking at the situation—the people, the problems
4. Looking at typical problems
5. Looking at job expectancies and interrelationships
6. Looking at interrelationship and involvements
7. Looking at administrative responsibilities
8. Looking at curriculum, personnel, budget, material and space
9. Looking at in-service programs
10. Looking at facilitating aids
11. Looking at big issues
12. Looking at practises
13. Looking at research
14. Looking at self-improvement

The music supervisor's life is one of placing value on something and then doing something about it. He is constantly diagnosing anything that pertains to his responsibility in order to see (*a*) whether it is working, (*b*) whether it is relevant, and (*c*) what he needs to do to improve the situation.

Knowledge of Objectives Makes Evaluation Meaningful

What do music supervisors really want from their job associations? What do we really want for a music program? What does the district and community want in music for its children? First of all, the music supervisor must clear in his mind once and for all time the reason for his existence. *Basically, his* raison d'etre *is to bring about the improvement of the teaching of music in the schools at whatever level he is assigned, or what specialty is his responsibility.*

The problem is how to decide correctly and wisely. Educators have struggled with this kind of decision making and have shackled themselves with evaluation procedures that have very little validity but have become so ingrained by usage that they are part of the culture of our society. We evaluate, we grade youngsters, we tag them for life with a mark of approval or disapproval. Our educational tags are lifetime blemishes or beauty marks. They are not, even though we argue to the contrary, diagnostic tools.

The doctor diagnoses a broken leg and then does something about it. After a while the leg is no longer broken. It doesn't bother the victim or those around him. A doctor diagnoses a cancerous condition; if it has not progressed too far, he cures or removes it. The patient goes back into society as a useful accepted citizen.

Of course, the reason for this inability to use evaluation as a valuable tool in the learning process is that we don't know enough about it. More light is being shed on this phenomenon in recent years. CSEIP, the Center for the Study of Evaluation of Instructional Programs, at the University of California in Los Angeles, is engaged in research that will yield new ideas and new tools of analyzing and evaluating instruction. Staff members are creating new ways to evaluate content of curricula, methods of teaching, and the multiple effects of both on students. Their investigations will also involve cost-effectiveness of instructional programs. The Center is under the direction of Dr. Merlin Wittrock and is staffed by a group of nationally renowned scholars. Still in embryonic stage, its contributions to clarity in educational evaluation should prove to become monumental.

The Skill of Stating Educational Objectives

Were educational objectives stated clearly, the job of evaluation would be considerably simplified. One would know what is to be evaluated. Clarity in stating objectives is dependent upon the following:

1. Objectives in music instruction must be stated in performance terms.
2. The particular music instructional objective must contain a statement or statements defining minimum acceptable performance.
3. The performance items must be appropriate to the evaluation of the objectives.

Three terms will cover and explain the above more succinctly: (*a*) behavior, or visible activity of the learner; (*b*) terminal behavior, the kind of observable musical behavior your student should exhibit by the time you are finished with the instructional unit and are ready to eval-

uate; and (c) criterion, the measure against which the observable terminal musical behavior is evaluated.

There are also three considerations in setting up objectives. They
are (a) prerequisites, or what the student ought to be able to do to
qualify for the particular musical instruction you have in mind; (b)
a thorough description of the program of learning in which your student will be involved; and (c) an exact description of what the successful music student is able to do when he has completed your course and
has followed all of the rules. The course description we referred to
earlier is *process*. The objective is the *product*. The music educator
must choose between a general objective and one that has specific
meaning to the learner. Here some words of caution are in order:

SUGGESTED PREFERENCE CHART

I prefer listening to	Daily	Twice Weekly	Once a Week	Once a Month	Never
Preclassical music					
Classical music					
Romantic music					
Modern music					
Composers					
National music					
Rhythmic music					
Songs					
Instrumental music					
Mood music					
Programmatic music					
Musical drama					
Semiclassical music					
Popular music					
Progressive jazz					
Folk songs					
Folk dance					

1. What you want to have happen at the end of the course or at a testing station—give it an action name so the learner knows that he has achieved the goal.
2. Define the behavior, listing the conditions under which it will be expected to function.
3. What is the minimum acceptable behavior, the criteria of acceptable performance that will describe how well the learner must be able to perform at the time when evaluation takes place.

If your objective is that each child in Grade 6 should love music by the end of the year, it will behoove you to spell out quite succinctly what you mean with *love*. What actions on the part of the learner spell out love? This the learner is entitled to know, if you want his progress to be evaluated. First of all, it will be necessary to delimit the scope of music to be loved because it takes a life time of working at this idea of loving. It may be relevant to list many kinds of music and ask the student to check his preferences as indicated in the two research studies listed in Chapter 13.

Each category of this chart must also be subdivided into titles of at least thirty of forty selections in each section:

NAME OF SELECTION My preference rating	I Very Much	II Much	III Some	IV Little	V None
1.					
2.					
3.					

This kind of evaluation can easily involve 500 or more items that need to be checked. The question then is this: Are these items part of the original objectives? Are they contained in the course of study? Does the student know he will be rated on these? If he is to be rated on "loving" music, then it holds that he must have been taught or exposed to music in a fairly orderly fashion. His exposure must have been of such a nature that there remained a residual effect predisposing him to make choices.

What are some of the activities that a music appreciator goes through? Does he sigh in ecstacy when listening to Bach? Does he buy a stereo system and $500 worth of records? Can he answer correctly 100 questions on music history? Does he know (is he able to discuss) the plots of fifty operas? Does he go into a trance when hearing the latest beat?

Mager[2] says:

1. An instructional objective describes an intended outcome rather than a description or summary of content.
2. The outcome should be stated in behavioral, or performance, terms that describe what the learner will be doing when demonstrating his achievement of the objective.
3. The statement of objective for an entire program of instruction will consist of several specific statements.
4. The objective which is most usefully stated is one which best communicates the instructional intent of the person selecting the objective.

Teacher Evaluates Supervisor

The following checklist is a teacher's rating of her supervisor. This list presupposes a succinct understanding of the terms: *services, help, competent, expanded, democratic procedures, more competent, failed, resources, teaching practises, familiar.*[3]

	Often	Seldom	Never
Has the instructional supervisor offered his services to you?			
Have the services given been of help to you?			
Do you feel the supervisor is competent in offering help?			
Would you wish for more expanded services of the supervisor?			
Does the supervisor employ democratic procedures while giving service?			
After requesting the supervisor's help or service, have you felt that as a result of this service you became more competent as a teacher? (In a particular instance)			
Has the supervisor failed to give you the service you requested?			
Have the resources which the supervisor has identified or accumulated been of help to you?			
Would you like to invite the supervisor into your classroom to observe your teaching practices?			
Are you familiar with the services that the supervisor can offer to classroom teachers?			

__ A supervisory checklist (self-evaluation)[4]

__ Do I

__ Set up a schedule of activities for each week?

__ Make changes easily?

__ Use criticism to improve my procedures?

__ Get more teachers to experiment?

__ Stimulate action research?

__ Get parents involved in the work of the school?

__ Secure an increase in the reading of professional books and participation in professional organizations?

__ Succeed in increasing the amount of cooperative planning?

__ Get teachers to be more self-directing?

__ Increase the use of a wider variety of instructional materials?

__ Promote increased pupil achievements?

__ Obtain a full description of the school's program on a given date
to serve as a base line in determining the amount of progress that is
being made in program development?

__ Bring teachers, pupils, parents, and community members into the
judgments concerning the progress that has been made?

__ Encourage revision of goals or procedures in areas in which the
group decides progress is unsatisfactory?

__ Judge my success by the progress of the school program toward goals
accepted by the group?

Supervisor Evaluates Materials

One of the music supervisor's functions is selecting instructional
materials. The following critera have been set up by a group of prominent music textbook authors and educators as a guide to evaluators:[5]

Criteria for Evaluating Music Materials
Kindergarten Through Grade Eight*

The guiding principles in the recommendation of a series of music
textbooks should be the excellence of their musical content and the
potentialities of that content for contributing systematically to a total
program of music education. The necessity for *quality* is paramount.

    I. Quality of Material

        A. Music

            1. *Melody*: Each musical selection should have a melody of
expressive quality. It is desirable that each book contain
numerous examples of each of several characteristic melodic

*By permission of California State Department of Education.

Criteria for Evaluating Music Materials
Kindergarten Through Grade Eight (Con't.)

structures, i.e., patterns that move by scale, by chord, by repeated tones, or in sequence, or that include such devices as inversion, augmentation, and diminution.

2. *Harmony*: The accompaniment to each song should be appropriate to the style of its melody and to the period from which it comes. All accompaniments should conform to generally accepted principles of harmony, both traditional and contemporary. In part songs, the voice parts should be singable and move according to accepted harmonic procedures.

3. *Rhythm*: The rhythm of each melody and the verbal pattern of the text should conform to each other artistically. Accented beats of the measure and accented words or syllables normally should coincide. In pupils' books, rhythmic structures so difficult as to require rote learning entirely should be held to a minimum. In general, the rhythmic notation of songs should be comprehensible to children who will use the books.

4. *Structure*: Each book should contain many songs in which the musical relationships among phrases are so precisely defined that children can readily recognize them and thereby discover the form.

5. *Musical Content*: Instrumental compositions and songs included in the books should be of excellent quality and of varied types. Folk songs should be balanced by songs composed by significant composers of the past and present and should be appropriate to the age-grade level. Folk songs should be representative not only of various countries but also of various regions of the United States.

6. *Voice Range*: The music for each part in each song should be within the voice range of the majority of pupils for whom it is intended.

B. Texts

1. The text of each song should possess intrinsic merit and be suitable to the age level for which it is intended.

2. Each book should include some songs in the foreign languages in which they were originally written. It is desirable that phonetic indications of correct pronunciations be included. Translations of these songs should be included in poetic or prose form in books for pupils or teachers. Translations may also be included as texts of songs if they possess poetic quality, are appropriate in content for the age level involved, and conform to the music.

Criteria for Evaluating Music Materials
Kindergarten Through Grade Eight (Con't.)

3. Translated texts of art songs, oratorios, and operas should convey the same general ideas they did in the original foreign language.

II. Music Listening

A. Each book for pupils should contain some material that will encourage them to listen for specific features of songs and instrumental compositions recorded for listening. Similarly, materials for teachers should include an adequate number of suggestions designed to aid in developing the ability of children to listen to music intelligently, to enjoy it, to understand it, and to appreciate its value.

B. Compositions recommended in the textbooks for listening should include varied media of performance and, to promote a sense of the historical development of music, contrasting styles and periods.

C. Books for pupils in grades two through eight should include some themes of musical compositions recommended for listening and authentic verbal material related to the music itself. Materials for teachers should include additional information designed to assist in the promotion of an understanding and appreciation of music by the children.

III. Organization of Material

The selections within each book and within a complete series should be organized to promote a sequential program of musical growth. To accomplish this, the books for pupils and for teachers should be organized so as clearly to set forth this sequence.

IV. Type of Content

A. In each book the following types of material should be represented in reasonable balance with the others: folk songs, art songs, seasonal songs, songs expressive of moral and spiritual values, and patriotic songs. For middle and upper grades, selections from operas and oratorios appropriate to the grade level are desirable.

B. Materials for pupils and for teachers should include information which will promote understanding of the cultural significance and expressive meaning of songs.

C. Books for pupils should contain some material organized systematically to promote an increasing understanding of the meaning of symbols of musical notation and increasing skill in using them. Books for teachers should include clearly stated directions for implementing this program.

Criteria for Evaluating Music Materials
Kindergarten Through Grade Eight (Con't.)

D. In books for grade four, very simple two-part songs are acceptable. In addition to unison songs, books for grade five should contain a considerable number of songs in two parts and may contain some simple three-part songs. Books for grade six should include some unison songs and a considerable number of songs in two and three parts.

E. The books for seventh and eighth grades should contain songs to be sung in unison and songs to be sung in two, three, and four parts (SA, SSA, SAT, SAB, and SATB). Not more than half the songs should be for unison singing.

F. In books for grades seven and eight, some part songs should contain the melody in parts other than that for the soprano voice. It is particularly important that some songs have the melody written in the bass clef in a range which will be comfortable for boys with changing or changed voices.

G. The notation of numerous songs in books for both pupils and teachers should include authentic indications for tempos and dynamics.

H. Beginning with grade two, songs and suggested listening activities in books for pupils should promote an ever-deepening appreciation of music as a part of our cultural heritage.

V. Instrumental Activities

A. Materials for each grade should include some songs that suggest the use of either simple classroom instruments or orchestral instruments. In books for pupils, the notation of instrumental parts to be played by children should be included in some instances.

B. All books should contain indications of the correct chords for songs that may appropriately be accompanied by the autoharp or similar chordal instruments. In books for both pupils and teachers of grades four through eight, the notations of appropriate rhythm patterns for some accompaniments should be included.

C. For grades four through eight, materials for pupils should contain some songs scored for orchestral instruments to be played by the children.

D. Books and other materials for grades two through eight should stress visualization of the relationship between the piano keyboard and the music staff.

E. At appropriate points where the books contain material directly related to groups of instruments or to one instrument or another, pictures of these instruments and brief factual informa-

Criteria for Evaluating Music Materials
Kindergarten Through Grade Eight (Con't.)

tion about them should be included. These illustrations should
be authentic and also accurate in showing the relative sizes of
instruments within a given family.

F. In books for grades five through eight, it is desirable to have
at least one page in each book that shows a reproduction of a
page of full orchestral score related to music children are studying. A brief explanation of the score's most important features
should be included.

VI. Helps for Teachers

A. Technically superior recordings of the majority of songs in
each text should be available. These recordings should include
a variety of voice types, but all should be appropriate for children to imitate. The songs should be sung at an appropriate
tempo. The words should be understandable. Instrumental accompaniments should be tasteful and should not overpower the
vocal character of the songs. Melodic and rhythmic content in
each recording should correspond to the score printed in the
books used by pupils and teachers.

B. The catalog numbers of the records and the page numbers of
the recorded songs should be cross-referenced in the books for
pupils and teachers.

C. Materials for teachers should include piano accompaniments
that are harmonically correct, appropriate to the style of the
melody, and playable by some pupils or teachers.

D. A teachers edition to assist in the effective use of materials
used by pupils should be available. Its relationship to the cor-
responding book for pupils should make its use convenient for
the teacher. Pagination should be the same in both books.

E. Material for teachers should be organized to help them carry
on a program of instruction dealing systematically with the
constituent elements of music and their relationships.

F. Material for teachers should indicate ways in which they can
help children learn how to explore music creatively and how
to investigate and discover for themselves the nature, meaning,
and structure of music.

G. It is desirable that books for teachers include suggestions for
original and exploratory activities—including movement to music—through which musical concepts can be developed.

H. Suggestions for teachers at all grade levels should provide for
musical activities which will lead to learning in the cognitive,
effective, and psychomotor domains, e.g., understanding, appreciation, and skill.

Criteria for Evaluating Music Materials
Kindergarten Through Grade Eight (Con't.)

VII. Physical Features

The format and other physical features of the books should conform to acceptable standards in the following ways:

A. General appearance should appeal to children.

B. Printing

1. Both texts and musical notation should be clear and easy to read.

2. In part songs included in books for grades four through eight, the notation of the individual parts should be clearly defined and easy to read. Many of the part songs should be notated, with each part on a separate staff.

C. Bindings should be strong and durable and should permit the book to lie flat. Bindings must not obscure inner margins.

D. An attractive cover design is desirable.

E. Whenever possible, the songs should be set up on the page so that the phrase structure is easily apparent, with no phrase broken between two lines.

F. Illustrations

1. Each book should be attractively illustrated to stimulate interest in the music and to enhance its mood and spirit. These illustrations should not interfere with musical notation.

2. Illustrations picturing children participating in activities related to the music should include a variety of ethnic groups.

G. Index

1. The materials in each book for pupils should be indexed alphabetically and classified as to topics and types of music. In the books for teachers, materials should be additionally classified in terms of concepts to be developed.

These are specific objectives describing the end product of how a music book should look and what it should contain. Does it answer these questions: What will the learner be provided? What will he be denied? The terminal behavior is what the book(s) look(s) like to the trained observer (the music supervisor). Does the book resemble the descriptions listed and the restrictions listed?

How well do the books come up to the description of the ideal books? The descriptions list the minimum acceptable book *behavior,* also called the criteria (less than this, the books are unacceptable.)

The *rating sheet for preliminary evaluation of books* provides an opportunity to place a value on music books, the criteria of which are

California State Curriculum Commission

RATING SHEET FOR PRELIMINARY EVALUATION OF MUSIC BOOKS [6]

Publisher_____ Series title, if any_____

Title_____ Grade(s)_____

Author(s)

You may, if you wish, use a single rating sheet for a series of textbooks. If you do, please indicate in your comments below whether your rating applies to the series as a whole or whether you wish to differentiate among the titles in the series. Because a variety of material may be selected for Kindergarten and Grade 1, books for these grades should be evaluated separately. Teachers manuals only will be provided for Kindergarten and Grade 1. Books for Grades 2 through 6 should be evaluated as a series. Books for Grades 7 and 8 should be evaluated separately.

RATING

	Excellent	Superior	Satis-factory	Unsatis-factory
1. Musical quality of songs and listening materials				
2. Systematic organization of content for developing purely musical concepts				
3. Accuracy and authenticity of musical and verbal content (including texts)				
4. Musical quality of the recordings* (including tone quality, accuracy, appropriateness of style and instrumentation)				
5. Overall rating (not necessarily an average of ratings on separate items)				

DISPOSITION

Check One

Retain for final evaluation			
Eliminate			

Directions: Please indicate any particularly noteworthy features, such as related art work, other illustrations, layout, legibility, suitability for slow, average, or advanced pupils. Also, if the book has been submitted for more than one grade, indicate the particular grade or grades to which your rating applies, or indicate separate ratings for each grade.

COMMENTS

*Note that recordings at the present time cannot legally be supplied by the State.

CALIFORNIA STATE DEPARTMENT OF EDUCATION
Bureau of Textbooks and Publications Distribution
September 15, 1966   _____
                                                      Signature of evaluator

well in mind as are the standards against which the evaluator is making his judgment. All series of books were written by known authorities in the field. Most of these and their publishers had educational criteria in mind. Many authors and prominent educators collaborated in making criteria based on the desirable, and based on how the intended musical product (the student) should act upon instruction. Scores of responsible music educators studied the books submitted carefully and with the help of the criteria graded the books.[7]

In order to be able to evaluate wisely one needs objectives. These objectives must be spelled out operationally and they must include a set of minimum acceptable standards or *criteria*. These are the rules by which people, situations, events, or things are judged.

Evaluating ESEA Title III Projects

The Elementary and Secondary Education Act of 1965 provides rules or guidelines (criteria) for its various titles. Title III's guidelines are contained in PACE, a booklet containing the rules. After the various requests are completed and submitted they are given to a committee of educators who also know the rules. It evaluates the requests, using the standards and translating its judgement onto the following evaluation form (p. 310).

Evaluating Operational Objectives

The following SKILL chart represents an operational breakdown of music educational objectives grade by grade and by concepts. (See pp. 312-313.)

Criteria for Objectives

Setting up evaluative procedures must be logical and must observe criteria controlling the sphere of the classification of educational objectives[8] (these are merely a reiteration of logical steps indispensible to determining operational objectives, the success of which can be measured):

I. Knowledge or remembering methods, specifics, and concepts about the subject at hand
   1. Specifics—information—pertinent elements
      a. Terminology—the verbal and non-verbal set of symbols (notes, etc.) that can be used that refer to the subject at hand
      b. Facts—dates, places, events, persons—(composers, keys, modes, style, etc.)—things that put certain constraints on the subject at hand that make it more identifiable

DEPARTMENT OF HEALTH, EDUCATION AND WELFARE
OFFICE OF EDUCATION
WASHINGTON D.C. 20202

REVIEW AND RECOMMENDATION BY STATE EDUCATIONAL AGENCY OF PROPOSED PROJECT
Title III. P.L. 81-874. As amended by P.L. 89-10

INSTRUCTIONS: Please review and make the applicable recommendations for each project, as specified in this questionnaire. Attach a brief summary statement, to support your recommendations.

Type of Project
"X"

_____ PLANNING

_____ OPERATIONAL

PART I — GENERAL INFORMATION

NAME OF STATE AGENCY	PERSON OE MAY CONTACT (Name, address, title)	TELEPHONE (Area code, local no.)
NAME OF LOCAL EDUCATIONAL AGENCY	TITLE OF PROJECT	DATE SUBMITTED TO STATE AGENCY

PART II — REVIEW

(The letters O for operational, P for planning, and OP for both operational and planning, indicate the type of project to which each item applies)

	ITEM	"X" APPLICABLE RATING No. 1 = Highest No. 5 = Lowest				
		1	2	3	4	5
1	O Extent to which this project meets the educational and cultural needs of the highest priority in the area served					
2	P Adequacy of the plans to identify and document the need for a proposed center or service					
3	P Quality of the pilot projects to test the proposed service					
4	O Adequacy of description and documentation of the need for the proposed center or service					
5	O P Extent to which the project is innovative					
6	O P Extent to which the project is exemplary					
7	O Evidence of supplementation of the regular school program by the Proposed Project					
8	O P Representation of other educational and cultural agencies in the planning and operation of the project					
9	O Degree of awareness of similar programs, research findings, or the knowledge of recognized experts					
10	O P Adequacy of the size and qualifications of the staff					
11	O P Adequacy of the facilities, both existing and proposed, for the conduct of the project					
12	O P Economic efficiency of the proposed project					
13	O Provision for participation of those to benefit from the project					
14	O P Provision for evaluation of the project					
15	O Provision for communication of results of the project, through demonstrations, publications, and other methods					

PART III — RECOMMENDED ACTION ("X" 1, 2, or 3)

1. RECOMMENDED FOR FUNDING ("X" 1, 2, or 3)

   a._____ Preferred   b._____ Medium   c. _____ Low

2. _____ Negotiable Changes (Attach a brief statement emphasizing recommendations for changes

3. _____ Not Recommended

NAME AND TITLE OF CHIEF STATE SCHOOL OFFICER (Type) SIGNATURE   DATE

2. Methods of dealing with the subject at hand—organizing, judging, critically examining the nature of the subject at hand. Being aware of
   a. Conventional ways of dealing with the subject at hand, practices, styles, forms, techniques
   b. Direction, trend and sequence of how the subject at hand operates in time (melodic, phrase, form)
   c. Categories in which the subject at hand can be found or placed (programmatic, impressionistic)
   d. Basic rules or criteria by which the subject at hand is evaluated (interpretation, exactness, sound, etc.)
   e. Appropriate method of investigating the validity of the subject at hand (aesthetic values)
3. Knowledge of the organizational schema (form) in which the subject at hand is organized
   a. Abstraction and principles that contribute toward accurate evaluation of the subject at hand
   b. The theories and structures—the body of principles and generalizations and their interrelations which contribute toward a clear view of the subject at hand

II. Skills and abilities, or modi operandi and techniques appropriate to the subject at hand—most suited to deal with it
   1. A general understanding of the subject at hand indicating the individual knows what is being communicated
      a. Translating the message from one symbolic language to another—(translating notes into symbolic hand placements on a musical instrument, and translating this into sounds, finally translating the sounds into music)
      b. Putting meaning in the communication (note above: adding musical significance by use of phrasing and dynamics; also the application of varied tempi, rhythms and timbre)
      c. Ability to extract a corollary skill that can be applied to similar situations (can the scalewise and choral motives in "Dixie" be applied to "My Pony" or to other songs that contain similar kinds of motives?)
   2. The actual use of ideas presented in the immediate subject in other situations; the ability to predict that this kind of application can be successful
   3. Analyzing the subject at hand into elements that present in its sequence of contributing factors (analysis of the melodic motive factors in "Dixie" to see what makes "Dixie" tick and classify these in order of learning importance)
      a. Identifying the element (the motives)
      b. Seeing the connection between the elements (motives) and the subject at hand ("Dixie")
      c. Organizing the elements (motives into phrase, phrase into parts of AB, or ABA, etc.)

GRADE BY GRADE MUSICAL SKILL CHART[9]

	MELODIC	RHYTHMIC	HARMONIC
KINDERGARTEN	Learning to use the singing voice Singing accurately melodies of short lengths	Interpretation of rhythm through imitative and creative movement Ability to move, clap, and play rhythm instruments in time Ability to imitate rhythmic patterns by moving, by clapping, and by playing instruments	Singing and listening to melodies with an accompaniment Listening to an accompaniment played independently of the melody Listening to and experimenting with the grouping of musical tones into chords Listening experience with modern as well as traditional harmonies
GRADE I	Singing melodies accurately Playing, on the piano or bells, simple melodic patterns or those based upon the pentatonic scale Utilizing chalkboard and hand motions to indicate melodic direction and contour Identifying melody and mood relationship	Interpretation of rhythm through imitative and creative movement Singing, moving, playing, and responding with bodily movement "in time" Illustrating rhythm of the melody by body movement or by drawing on chalkboard or paper	Beginning experience with autoharp Some opportunity to play the autoharp individually for one-chord songs Learning some of the chord letter-name designations Participation with resonator bells and piano if available
GRADE II	Learning to read repeated tones, skips, and steps Indicating melodic direction Reading, singing, and playing simple melodies Creating melodies to fit poems	Distinguishing between the rhythm of the melody, of the meter, and of the accent, especially in $\frac{2}{4}$ and $\frac{3}{4}$ meter Clapping, moving, or playing rhythm instruments in time with music Recognizing and performing rhythmic patterns Dramatizing songs rhythmically	Singing simple rounds Playing chants, ostinatos, and other tonal patterns on resonator bells or piano if available Playing simple chord accompaniments on autoharp, bells, or piano Listening for chord change
GRADE III	Distinguishing between the sound of whole and half steps Ability to sing a melody accurately Recognizing the sound of the major scale Ability to recognize sequences Creating original melodies	Ability to hear and respond accurately to: ♪ ♩ ♩ ♩. ♩ ♩ ♩ ♪ ⁊ ▬ ▬ Sensitivity to syncopated rhythms sung and heard Ability to create rhythm accompaniments to songs Ability to conduct simple meters	Ability to sing harmonized endings to songs Ability to sing two-part rounds Ability to sing and play simple descants Using chord accompaniments on the autoharp and resonator bells
GRADE IV	Recognizing sequences aurally and visually Finding and singing melodies by phrases Associating pitch with syllable, number, and letter names Using familiar tonal and rhythmic characteristics when sightsinging Using the flute as a music-reading device Recognizing minor tonalities aurally and visually	Sightreading rhythmic patterns in $\frac{2}{4}$, $\frac{3}{4}$ and $\frac{4}{4}$ meters Using percussion instruments to play rhythmic song accompaniments Identifying and responding aptly to the symbols for dotted rhythm patterns Identifying and responding aptly to the symbols for syncopated rhythms Recognizing the relation of the tempo to the meter signature	Playing song accompaniments from chordal notation on the autoharp, using the three primary chords Using the autoharp to develop song accompaniments by ear Singing rounds and canons effectively Sustaining a harmony part against a melody line Distinguishing aurally between consonance and dissonance
GRADE V	Recognition, identification, and response to tonal patterns in a melodic line Identification and naming of intervals Recognition of melodies based on major, minor, pentatonic, and chromatic scales Creation of original melodies in various modes Increased ability in melody reading Use of the flute in melody reading	Recognition and response to simple rhythm patterns in $\frac{2}{4}$, $\frac{3}{4}$, $\frac{4}{4}$, $\frac{6}{8}$, and $\frac{2}{2}$ meters Ability to use percussion instruments to play notated and improvised song accompaniments Identification and accurate response to symbols for dotted rhythms, the tie, syncopation, and the triplet	Ability to play chordal accompaniments from chord symbols with autoharp, ukulele, bell or piano Ability to form chords with voices, to harmonize melodies by ear, to sing rounds descants, and chants effectively Use of accompaniments in the pentatonic mode Ability to sustain a harmony part against a melody line
GRADE VI	Determining the phrase structure of melodies and singing melodies by phrases Recognizing major and minor melodies by sight and sound Singing and playing accidental and chromatic tones as well as diatonic patterns Sight-reading complex melodies	Ability to read music in various simple and compound meters Reading diverse subdivided beat, triplet, and syncopated rhythm patterns	Singing a harmony part in a round, descant companion song, or two- or three-part so Playing an autoharp accompaniment from chord symbols, and improvising simple autoharp accompaniments Writing major and minor chords and distinguishing aurally between them Hearing and seeing the differences among triads, seventh chords, and fourth chord

NOTATIONAL	FORM AND STRUCTURE	INTERPRETATION
g phrase-by-phrase 'ying the musical phrase by listening through movement recognition of like, different, or similar 'ases: like movement for the phrases; 'erent movement for different phrases	Illustrating with the hand, with the body, or on the chalkboard the direction of melody Showing with the hand, with the body, at the chalkboard, and with pitch-producing instruments various levels of pitch Illustrating with the hand, with the body or on the chalkboard the meter, accent, and rhythms of simple melodies Indication of phrase repetition, variations, or change	Singing, playing, moving, and listening to music utilizing dynamic contrast and contrasting tempos Experimenting with different dynamic levels and tempos Singing and identifying phrases as complete musical and literary ideas Singing texts with understanding, enunciation, meaning, articulation, and feeling for phrasing Recognizing certain instruments, types of voices, and ensembles
g phrase-by-phrase 'ying the musical phrase by listening through movement recognition of like, similar, and trasting phrases response to phrasing: (1) like vement for like phrases; different vement for different phrases; (2) like truments for like phrases; different truments for different phrases	Illustrating with the hand, with the body, or at the chalkboard, the direction of the melodic line Showing with the hand, with the body, at the chalkboard, and with pitch-producing instruments the various levels of pitch Illustrating with the hand, with the body, or at the chalkboard, the meter, accent, and rhythms of simple melodies Indication of phrase repetition, variation, or change	Singing, playing, moving, and listening to music utilizing more extensive dynamic contrast and more extensively contrasting tempos Experimentation with several different dynamic levels and tempos Singing and identifying phrases as complete musical and literary ideas Singing texts with understanding, enunciation, meaning, and feeling for phrasing Recognition of certain instruments, types of voices, and ensembles
nizing repetition, similarity, and trast in music through singing, playing, tening, and visual association nizing structure in music, both visually aurally	Learning to use syllables or numbers for music reading Reading notational symbols to produce melodic and rhythmic patterns, harmony, suitable interpretation Developing a feeling for the home tone or key center	Identifying and responding to dynamic and tempo markings Interpreting a song according to the text Singing with good phrasing, enunciation, and feeling Dramatizing songs while they are being sung Suggesting and performing suitable accompaniments
nizing like, similar and contrasting 'ases standing the meaning and use of nbols indicating form structure g. A–B–A–C) edge of rondo and suite forms	Finding the key signature of a song and locating the home tone Singing tonal patterns found in songs in the book Finding the starting tone of a song Understanding of "measure," "bar line," "meter" Ability to count rhythmic note values Learning to use syllables, numbers, or letters for music reading	Ability to read and use symbols of interpretation (p, mf, etc.) Ability to express the mood of a song by interpreting the meaning of the words Ability to change tone quality as well as dynamics to suit each song (e.g., chantey vs. lullaby) Ability to phrase properly
fying the musical phrase aurally and ually 'ying repetition, contrast, and the forms ·B, A–B–A, and through-composed) these eate, in songs nizing aurally repetition, contrast, and hniques of variation	Learning to find the home tone, key, and starting tone in an unfamiliar song Recognizing and identifying minor tonality by sound and sight Applying letter names accurately to bells and piano keyboard Responding accurately to melodic, rhythmic, tempo, and dynamic symbols while sightreading appropriate songs	Identifying an appropriate mood in music heard Being able to decide how to interpret a song from the textual implications Identifying and responding accurately to basic tempo and dynamic markings Identifying instruments aurally Learning to determine and to sing musical phrases accurately
and visual identification of phrases and visual identification of two- and ee-part forms in song repertoire y to determine form in music heard y to discuss with some understanding i to listen intelligently to larger sical forms	Ability to identify key signature, key, home tone, and starting tone in an unfamiliar song Accurate use of syllable and number names to recall pitch relationships in independent music reading Use of bells, piano, and flute to read melodic and rhythmic notation Ability to read rhythmic patterns in basic meters with chanting, clapping, and percussion instruments	Ability to determine appropriate interpretation for songs Ability to recognize suitable interpretation in music listened to Accurate identification and response to basic tempo and dynamic markings and symbols Recognition of instrumental tone colors Determination of musical phrases and ability to sing melodies by phrases
y to identify phrases gnizing two- and three-part song form, nata-allegro form, and rondo form iving sectional elements of larger forms ing two-, three-, and four-phrase melodies monstrating such forms as A–B; A–B–A; A–B–A; A–B–A–C	Notating original melodies Writing and playing major and minor scales Singing and playing chromatic melodies	Ability to determine appropriate mood, style, tempo, dynamics, and phrasing by analysis of the song Using symbols and terms of interpretation as guides in determining one's personal interpretation

4. Reconstruction of the elements into more meaningful whole
   a. Using the elements in reconstructed form to convey an idea (using the rearranged elements—scale-wise and chordal in making up a new tune . . . creative application)
   b. Producing a plan or a set of activities that will guarantee success to a new task at hand
   c. Generalize on the basis of success with (a) and (b) and to develop ability to use generalizations to further continue the creative process
5. Make value judgments about materials and methods. Make quantitative and qualitative judgments about how the materials and methods satisfy the criteria
   a. Evaluate for accuracy—logicalness, consistency of the hypothetical criteria . . . the internal—untested
   b. Judge in relation to what is remembered or successfully applied

Accordingly any talk about evaluation must include objectives. It must take into account knowledge of setting up valid objectives, realistic objectives, and measurable objectives. They must be stated in such a way that they can be seen, understood, and counted. The old adage "the proof is in the pudding" is apropos. It must be visible, touchable, tasteable, manipulatable. And, "the proof is in the eating." It must be clean, healthful, attractive, and palatable.

The music supervisor is the catalyst in the educational milieu. As change-agent and growth-cultivator he must evaluate everything he surveys. Among the most difficult matters to evaluate are the learnings the children are to accomplish after a stipulated course of instruction or a period of time with music. The chart on the next page attempts to indicate the complexity of the problem. It is an evaluation instrument whereby administrators can evaluate their own music programs at the primary level. It can also be used by individual teachers as a self-evaluation profile for what goes on in the classroom. The supervisor can look at it diagnostically, and from it form opinions and suggestions to change or improve the program.

According to Leonhard,[10] evaluation involves three steps: (1) identification, formulation, and validation of objectives; (2) collection of data relevant to status in relation to those objectives; and (3) the interpretation of the data. His rationale for evaluation is (1) appraisal of progress, (2) guidance, (3) motivation, (4) improvement of instruction, (5) program improvement, (6) selection for leadership or special help, (7) maintenance of standards, and (8) stimulation toward research. He suggests evaluating all aspects of musical learning. The thirty-one criteria

EVALUATING A CLASSROOM MUSIC PROGRAM IN OPERATIONAL TERMS (Teacher Self-Evaluation) FOR PRIMARY GRADES[11]

	Daily	3-times weekly	Twice weekly	Weekly	Seldom	Never

I. DOES YOUR SINGING PROGRAM —

a. <u>Give pleasure</u>. Do the children:
Sing for the joy of singing, alone and with others.

b. <u>Develop skill</u>. Do the children:
Learn to sing with others.
Learn to sing alone.
Learn to sing with a tone expressive to the song.
Learn to sing smoothly.
Learn to sing words clearly.
Learn to sing a melody accurately.
Learn to sing in tune.

c. <u>Develop creative capacities</u>. Do the children:
Take part in singing conversations, stories, calls.
Make up songs and chants.
Make up extra verses and new words to known songs.
Create introductions, interludes and codas.
Add simple descants and chants to songs.

d. <u>Develop knowledge of music literature</u>. Do the children:
Learn many songs of child interest, of permanent interest.
Learn songs representative of the world and its people.

e. <u>Develop understanding of music symbols</u>. Do the children:
Follow a song in a song book while singing.
Recognize tonal pattern aurally and visually.
Read familiar patterns in new songs.
Help to write down a song composed by the class.
Use musical terms to express musical ideas.

f. <u>Develop understanding of human feelings and their expression</u>. Do the children:
Recognize and express basic childhood emotions through songs.
Express and recognize these emotions by others, through songs.
Develop ability to work with a group, as a group.

II. DOES PLAYING ON INSTRUMENTS —

a. <u>Give pleasure</u>. Do your children:
Freely explore rhythm and melody instruments.
Discover effects which are musically pleasing.
Play an instrument alone and with a group.

b. Develop skill. Do your children:
Learn ways of using rhythm and melody instruments
to keep time and to enrich the melody.
Become sensitive to pitch, tone, color and rhythm
through instruments.

c. Develop creative capacities. Do your children:
Add sound effects to stories, poetry and songs.
Discover effects which are musically pleasing.
Make up tune with instruments.
Create introductions, interludes, descants, codas
and ostinato with instruments.

d. Develop knowledge of music literature. Do your
children:
Play many songs with rhythm and melody instruments.
Play these instruments with piano and recorded music.
Create various moods through playing instruments.

e. Develop understanding of music symbols. Do your
children:
Associate aurally and visually the musical contrasts
(up and down) with instruments.
Learn that lines and spaces of the staff symbolize
pitches.
Follow symbols while playing rhythm instruments.
Learn to express crescendo, diminuendo, acceler-
ando, etc., from symbols.

f. Develop understanding of the structure of music.
Do your children:
Recognize phrases while playing.
Play introductions, interludes, and codas for
songs.
Play the various parts of music — i.e., the accom-
paniment, the melody, the harmonies, etc.

g. Develop understanding of human feelings and their
expression. Do your children:
Recognize and express basic childhood emotions
with instruments.
Recognize and portray instrumentally the basic
emotions of self and others.
Understand the music of various cultures — i.e.,
the Latin excitement vs. the oriental restraint in
music.

III. DOES YOUR LISTENING PROGRAM —
a. Give pleasure. Do the children:
Listen to music prior to singing, playing or movement.
Listen to music for enjoyment and relaxation such
as:

Teacher making music for the children.
Individual children making music for other
children.
Guests making music for the children.
Radio, recordings, and other reproductions of
music.

b. Develop skill. Does it help your children to:
Learn to recognize pitch, instrument, tempo and mood changes.
Learn to match pitch.
Learn to sing rote songs.
Learn to improve tone quality.
Learn to recognize tunes.
Learn to pronounce words accurately.
Learn to respond to music by movement, and with instrument.
Learn to recognize mood in music.
Learn to recognize sounds of instruments.
Learn concert-audience manners.

c. Develop creative capacities. Do your children:
Plan individual responses to music through art and bodily movement.
Make up of stories and the plan of dramatization music.
Discover music for sound effects with stories, poetry, and songs.

d. Develop knowledge of music literature. Do your children:
Listen to recordings of familiar songs.
Listen to selected instrumental recordings.
Listen to recordings which children bring from home.
Listen to school and classroom concerts.
Listen to radio and television music.

e. Develop understanding for music symbols. Do your children:
Hear the "up and down" of notes.
Hear long and short notes.
Hear scale and chord patterns.
Hear characteristics such as holds, slurs, repeats, and accents.
Hear patterns in rhythm and melody.

f. Develop understanding of the structure of music. Do your children:
Become aware of phrases, and repetitions.
Become aware of group and individual interpretations of moods.
Reach out toward other peoples so far as readiness and maturity of children permit.

IV. DOES MOVING TO MUSIC —
a. Give pleasure. Do your children:
Interpret songs, instrumental and recorded music through free rhythmic motion.

b. Develop skill. Do your children:
Keep time (accent and beat) with large muscles while walking, running, skipping, swinging, galloping, clapping, etc.
Respond to fast and slow tempos.
Interpret moods, rhythms, changes through body movement.

c. Develop creative capacities. Do your children:
Respond through art, bodily movement, and
dramatization.

d. Develop knowledge of music literature. Do your
children:
Take part in rhythmic songs and folk dances.
Rhythmic dramatization and instrumental
music.
Discover types of orchestral music.

e. Develop understanding of music symbols. Do
your children:
Respond to long and short notes as they appear
in songs.
Respond to accent and observing accent in
songs.
Respond to the swing of music and discover the
meaning of the top number of the meter sign.

f. Develop understanding of the structure of music.
Do your children:
Demonstrate phrase lines by movement.
Demonstrate basic forms (AB, ABA, etc.)
through movement.

g. Develop understanding of human feelings and
their expression. Do your children:
Express basic childhood emotions in movements.
Appreciate the feelings of self and others through
the playing of singing games, and simple folk
dances.
Interpret words of songs through movement.

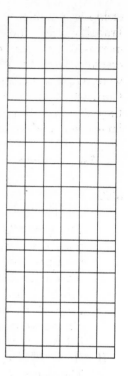

he lists give the entire evaluative process direction and meaning (NSSE Yearbook, 57th Basic Concepts, Chapter 13).

All federally aided projects must be evaluated. All programs funded by federal or foundation funds must be evaluated. Educators are frantically searching for evaluation instruments that carry a guarantee of validity. They are also searching for evaluators who are trained to look at objectives in order to determine whether they are stated in a manner that they lend themselves to operation. If they can be carried out, then it should be possible to evaluate them also. Federal and foundation funds also insist on built-in evaluation as part and parcel of the entire project process. We don't test only at the end. We also look over the situation before we start in order to determine direction, materials, personnel, etc. We also test along the way to determine whether we are headed toward the objectives.

The high cost of education makes evaluation of programs, methods, materials and personnel mandatory. No school system can longer afford the luxury of harboring ineffective materials, ideas, methods or persons.

In conclusion: Much has happened in supervision during the past five years. Music supervision has improved. More real educational leadership is in evidence. The reasons for this improvement are conjectural. Probably the national thrust toward education for all, probably the increased criticisms of education, have had something to do with increase in quality. In one state not more than seven years ago there were no more than six music supervisors holding the doctorate degree. Currently, there are fifteen. Although degrees do not assure quality, they are an indication of increased standards, expectancies, dedication, knowledge, and vision.

The Outcomes of the Music Program Are the Objectives of Effective Music Supervision[12]

Skills

I. He will have skill in listening to music

The generally educated person listens with a purpose. He recognizes the broad melodic and rhythmic contours of musical compositions. He is familiar with the sounds of the instruments of the orchestra and the types of human voices. He can hear and identify more than one melody at a time. He can recognize patterns of melody and rhythm when repeated in identical or in altered form. He can concentrate on sounds and the relationships between sounds.

II. He will be able to sing

The generally educated person is articulate. He uses his voice confidently in speech and song. He sings in a way that is satisfying to himself. He can carry a part in group singing. His singing is expressive.

III. He will be able to express himself on a musical instrument

A generally educated person is curious. He is interested in how instrumental music is produced and willing to try his hand at making music, if only at an elementary level with a percussion instrument, a recorder, or a "social-type" instrument. He experiments with providing accompaniments for singing and rhythmic activities. He is familiar with the piano keyboard.

IV. He will be able to interpret musical notation

The generally educated person is literate. He understands arithmetical and musical symbols. He is able to respond to the musical notation of unison and simple part songs. He can follow the scores of instrumental compositions.

Understandings

V. He will understand the importance of design in music

The generally educated person understands the structure of the various disciplines. He knows the component parts of music and the interrelationships that exist between melody, rhythm, harmony, and form. He is able to recognize design elements aurally, and he uses musical notation to confirm and reinforce this recognition. He realizes that the active listener can, in a sense, share in the composer's act of creation. By understanding how music communicates, he has come to gain insight into what it communicates.

VI. He will relate music to man's historical development

The generally educated person has historical perspective. He recognizes that music has long been an important part of man's life. He understands that its development in Western civilization is one of the unique elements of his own heritage. He is familiar with the major historical periods in that development and the styles of music which they produced. He has acquaintance with some of the musical masterpieces of the past and with the men who composed them. He relates this knowledge to his understanding of man's social and political development.

VII. He will understand the relationships existing between music and other areas of human endeavor

The generally educated person integrates his knowledge. He has been helped to see that the arts have in common such concepts as design resulting from repetition and variation. Sociology and politics are recognized as pertinent to the development of art as well as to economics. He understands how literature and music enhance one another and together illuminate history. The mathematical and physical aspects of music are known to him through aural experiences as well as through intellectual inquiry.

VIII. He will understand the place of music in contemporary society

The generally educated person is aware of his environment. He understands the function of music in the life of his community and he accepts some responsibility for exercising his critical judgment in order to improve the quality of music heard in church and on radio and television. He is aware of the position of the musician in today's social structure and understands the opportunities open to him to engage in musical endeavor both as a vocation and as an avocation.

Attitudes

IX. He will value music as a means of self-expression

A generally educated person has developed outlets for his emotions. He recognizes music not only as a source of satisfaction because of its filling his desire for beauty, but also because of the unique way in which it expresses man's feelings. If he is not prepared to gain release by actually performing music, he has learned to experience this vicariously. He looks to music as a course of renewal of mind and body, as an evidence of benefi- cence in his life. He recognizes the importance of performers and composers and is grateful for the pleasure and inspiration which they give him.

X.   He will desire to continue his musical experiences

The generally educated person continues to grow. He seeks addi- tional experiences in areas in which he has found satisfaction. He looks for community musical activities in which he can participate. He attends concerts and listens to music on radio, television, and recordings. He keeps informed concerning happenings in the world of music by reading newspapers and magazines.

XI.   He will discriminate with respect to music

The generally educated person has good taste. He has learned to make sensitive choices based upon musical knowledge and skill in listening. He evaluates performances and exercises mature judgments in this area. He is not naive with respect to the functional use of music for commercial purposes nor to the commercial pressures which will be exerted to obtain what money he can spend for music.

QUESTIONS FOR DISCUSSION, THOUGHT AND STUDY

1. Using Mager's ideas on setting up objectives, develop a set of criteria for student public performances at the high school level.
2. Devise an evaluation instrument to determine what kind of elementary school program your school has currently.
3. What are the essential objectives in a high school general music program?
4. List the dangers of evaluation.
5. Discuss how music supervision is a process of evaluation.
6. How can music supervision itself be evaluated?
7. Make a self-evaluation instrument for the supervisor.
8. Make an instrument whereby the teacher evaluates the music supervisor.
9. Devise an instrument whereby the administrator evaluates the music supervisor.

NOTES

[1]Robert Mager, *Planning Instructional Objectives,* (Palo Alto: Fearon Publishing Co., 1966).
[2]Mager, *Ibid.*
[3]Reba Burnham and Martha King, *Supervision in Action,* ASCD, 1961.
[4]Wiles, *Supervision for Better Schools, op. cit.,* adapted.
[5]Calif. State Dept. of Education, *Criteria for Evaluating Materials,* (Sacramento, 1966).

[6]Calif. State Dept. of Education, *Rating Sheet for Preliminary Evaluation of Music Books,* (Sacramento, 1966).

[7]Dept. Health, Education and Welfare, *Evaluation of Title III ESEA Projects,* (Washington, D.C., 1966).

[8]Benjamin Bloom, *Taxonomy of Educational Objectives,* (New York: David
[9]Adapted from Scope and Sequence Chart, American Book Co., 1966.
McKay, Inc., 1964).

[10]Madison Thurber et.al., *Basic Concepts in Music Education,* 57th Yearbook, National Society for the Study if Education, (Chicago: University of Chicago Press, 1958), Chapter VIII.

[11]Kurt Miller, adapted from Evaluation Instrument devised for USADEG Schools, 1960.

[12]From *Music in General Education,* edited by Karl D. Ernst and Charles L. Gary. Washington: Music Educators National Conference, 1965, pp. 4-8. Used by permission.

Bibliography

A. Administration

Commission on School Administration in Newly Reorganized Districts. Washington, D.C.: American Association of School Administration, 1965, 1-82.

Imperatives in Education. Washington, D.C.: American Association of School Administration, 1966, i-80.

KYTE, GEORGE C., *The Principal at Work* (revised ed.). Boston: Ginn and Company, 1952, 111-531.

OTTO, HENRY, *Elementary School Organization and Administration*. New York: Appleton-Century-Crofts, 1964, xi-409.

REEDER, WARD K., *School Boards and Superintendents*. New York: The Macmillan Company, 1954, v-234.

Music Administration

ERWIN, MAX T., *The Function of the Administrator*. Kenosha: Leblanc Corporation, pp. 2–11.

FLAGG, MARION, "The Elementary School Principal and His Music Program," *The Elementary School Principal*, XXX, No. 4, (February, 1951), 12-22.

MENC, *Music Buildings, Rooms and Equipment*. Washington: MENC rev. 1965.

B. Curriculum

BUSH, ROBT. N. and ALLEN, D., *A New Design for High School Education*. New York: McGraw-Hill Book Company, 1964, v-197.

FALLON, BERLIE J., *Educational Innovations in the U.S.* Bloomington, Ind.: Phi Delta Kappa, 1966, iii-248.

KRUG, EDWARD, *Curriculum Planning*. New York: Harper and Brothers, 1950, 14-306.

MIEL, ALICE, *Changing the Curriculum*. New York: Appleton-Century-Crofts, 1946, v-241.

OTTO, HENRY J., *Principles of Elementary Education.* New York: Rinehart & Company, Inc., 1948, v-430.

SMITH, B. OTHANIEL, STANLEY, WILLIAM O. and SHORES, J. HARLAN, *Fundamentals of Curriculum Development.* Yonkers-on-Hudson: World Book Company, 1950. 9-159.

SPEARS, HAROLD, *The Teacher and Curriculum Planning.* New York: Prentice-Hall, Inc., 1951. 1-163.

U.S. Office of Educ., *PACE—Projects to Advance Creativity in Education.* Washington, D.C.: USOE, 1965. 1-73.

U.S.O.E., *PACESETTER, Funded Title III ESEA Project Reports.* Washington, D.C.: H.E.W.

Music Curriculum

AMC, *Report of Amateur Instrumental Music in USA—1964.* Chicago: Am. Music Conf., 1965.

ANDREWS, GLADYS, *Creative Rhythmic Movement for Children.* Englewood Cliffs: Prentice-Hall, Inc., 1954. v-198.

BURROWS, ROBERT M., "What Is Keyboard Experience," *School Musician,* XXII, (April, 1951). 6–.

CECELIA,—SISTER, S.D., "Music Reading in the Elementary School," *Catholic Journal,* LIII, (September, 1953). 206-207.

CMEA and CASCD Committee, *Teachers Guide to Music in the Elementary School.* Sacramento: California State Department of Education, 1963. 11-149.

DODGE, VINCENT (Editor), *Music Education for Elementary School Children.* Washington: NEA, Department of Elementary School Principals, 1960. 1-40.

DYKEMA, PETER, "Some Fundamental Questions about Music Reading," *Music Educators Journal,* XXV, (1948). 24-26.

EARHART, WILL and GATTO, FRANK, "Value of Instrumental Teaching in Public School Music," 1935.

ERNST, KARL D., "Place of Reading in the Elementary Music Program," *Music Educators Journal,* XXIX, (January, 1953). 26-28.

FARWELL, GAYLORD H., *Curriculum Planning in Music Education,* Vol. VII, Fall, 1964, No. 3. p. 231.

GINGELAND, DAVID, *Music Activities for Retarded Children.* New York: Abingdon Press, 1965. 1-140.

HARTSHORN, WM. C., *Music for Academically Talented.* Washington: NEA and MENC, 1960. 1-127.

HEFFERNAN, HELEN, and others, *Music Education in the Elementary School.* Sacramento: California State Department of Education, 1939. vii-152.

HOFER, CHARLES, *Teaching Music in Secondary Schools.* Belmont, Calif.: Wadsworth Publishing Co., 1966.

KENDALL, J. C., "Music Education for Today," *Journal of Education* 133: (May, 1951). 146-148.

LAWLER, VANETT and GARY, CHARLES, *Student Music Activities.* Washington: National Association of Secondary School Principals, Vol. 48, No. 294, 1964.

McLAUGHLIN, ROBERTA, *Music in Everyday Living.* Washington: MENC and NEA, 1960. ix-63.

MENC, NEA, *Contemporary Music for School*. Washington: NEA, 1966.
MENC, *The Music Curriculum in Secondary Schools*. Washington: NASSP, 1959. 2-15.
MENC, *Music in Senior High School*. Washington: MENC, 1959. 4-112.
MENC, *The Study of Music in the Elementary School*: MENC, 1967.
MYERS, N., "Music an Essential Part of the Curriculum," *Peabody, Journal of Education*, XXX, (May, 1953). 3, 6-7.
NYE, R. D., "If You Don't Use Syllables What Do You Use," *Music Educators Journal*, XXVII, (February, 1951). 31-33.
REA, RALPH C., "Music Reading Films," *Journal of Research in Music Education*, II, No. 2, (Fall, 1954). 147-155.
WEYLAND, RUDOLPH H., *Establishing a Creative Arts Service Center for Young People*. Visalia: Tulare County Department of Education, ESEA Title III Proposal. i-87.
———, *Guide for Teaching General Music in the High School*. Visalia: Tulare County Department of Education, rev. 1964. 1-81.

C. Methods

BAIR, M. and WOODWARD, R., *Team Teaching in Action*. Boston: Houghton-Mifflin Co., 1964. v-229.
CORSINI, R. J. and HOWARD, D. D., *Critical Incidents in Teaching*. Englewood Cliffs: Prentice-Hall, Inc., 1964.

Music Teaching Methods

AUSTINE, V. D., "Put Music in Every Classroom," *Music Educators Journal*, XL, (January, 1954). 40—.
BERGETHON, B. and BOARDMAN, E., *Musical Growth in the Elementary School*. New York: Holt, Rinehart and Winston, 1963. v-276.
BROOKS, MARIAN B., and BROWN, HARRY A., *Music Education in the Elementary School*. New York: American Book Company, 1946.
BRYAN, JANICE W., "Musical Growth of the Classroom Teacher," *Music Educators Journal*, XXXVII, (June, 1951). 28—.
CARABO-CONE, MADELEINE, and ROYT, BEATRICE, *How to Help Children Learn Music*. New York: Harper and Brothers, 1955. v-138.
CHOATE, ROBERT M., "Music Instruction in the Self-Contained Classroom," *National Elementary Principal*, XXX, (February, 1951). 9-11.
DYKEMA, PETER, and CUNDIFF, HANNAH M., *School Music Handbook, New Edition*. Boston: C. C. Birchard & Company, 1955. v-669.
EGBERT, MARION S., *Seeing What We Sing*. Boston: C. C. Birchard Company, 1954.
ERNST, KARL D., "What Should Be Expected from the Elementary Teacher," *National Elementary Principal*, XXX, (February, 1951). 26-31.
HARTSELL, O. M., *Teaching Music in the Elementary School*. Washington: MENC and ASCD, 1964.
HUMPHREYS, A. W., "Orienting the Classroom Teacher in Music," *Music Educators Journal*, XXIX, (September, 1952). 28-30.
LEONHARD, CHARLES, *A Song Approach to Music Reading*. New York: Silver Burdett Company, 1953. vii-149.
LOVELESS, M., "Music for the Classroom Teacher," *Education*, LXXII, (September, 1951). 39-41.

MARTIN, L. B., "Basic Musical Needs of the Elementary Teacher," *Music Educators Journal,* XXXVIII, (January, 1952). 52–.

MATHEWS, PAUL WENTWORTH, *You Can Teach Music.* New York: E. P. Dutton and Company, Inc., 1953. xx-178.

MATTERN, D., "Essentials in the Training of Classroom Teacher," *Music Educators Journal,* XL, (February, 1954). 66–.

MOHN, N. C., "Critical Look at Teacher Training in Public School Music," *School Musician,* XXII, (September, 1950). 14.

MORGAN, HAZEL N., "Music and the Elementary School Teacher," *Education,* LXXII, (September, 1951). 28-32.

MURSELL, JAMES L., *Education for Musical Growth.* Boston: Ginn and Company, 1948. v-343.

——, *Music and the Classroom Teacher.* New York: Silver Burdett Company, 1951. v-304.

——, *Music in the American Schools.* New York: Silver Burdett Company (Revised), 1953. iii-312.

MYERS, LOUISE KIFER, *Teaching Children Music in the Elementary School.* New York: Prentice-Hall, Inc., 1955, (2nd Ed.). iii-374.

NEWTON, M., "Music for the Elementary Teacher," *Music Educators Journal,* XL, (September, 1953). 67–.

NYE, ROBERT E. and NYE, VERNICE, *Music in the Elementary School.* Englewood Cliffs, New Jersey: Prentice-Hall, Inc., 1957. vii-289.

PITTS, LILLA BELLE, "The General Music Program in the Elementary School," *The National Elementary Principal,* XX, No. 4 (February, 1951). 5-8.

QUILTY, M. E., "Attention Classroom Music Teacher," *Educational Music Magazine,* XXXI, (September, 1951). 13–.

SHEEHY, EMMA DICKSON, "Music and the Classroom Teacher," *The National Elementary School Principal,* XXX, No. 4, (February, 1951). 31-40.

SWANSON, BESSIE, *Music in the Education of Children.* Belmont, Calif.: Wadsworth Publishing Company, 1964. vii-306.

WEIL, L., "Can the Elementary School Teacher Teach Music," *Kentucky School Journal,* XXX, (February, 1952). 18-20.

WERSEN, L. G., "You Can Teach Music," *National Education Association Journal,* XLII, (March, 1953). 157-158.

WEYLAND, RUDOLPH H., *Learning to Read Music.* Dubuque: Wm. C. Brown Company Publishers, 1961. xi-231.

WHITTAKER, H. H., "Classroom Music Program," *Music Educators Journal,* XXIX, (June, 1950). 50-51.

WILSON, HARRY R., *Music in the High School.* New York: Silver Burdett Company, 1941. iii-440.

WINSLOW, ROBERT W. and DALLIN, LEON, *Music Skills for Classroom Teachers.* Dubuque, Iowa: Wm. C. Brown Company Publishers, 1958. iii-141.

D. Philosophy

DEWEY, JOHN, *Experience and Education.* New York: The Macmillan Company, 1939.

DEWEY, JOHN, *Reconstruction in Philosophy.* Boston: The Beacon Press, 1949. XLVII, 224 pp.

LANGER, SUSANNE, *Philosophy in a New Key*. New York: The New American Library, 1942. 1-239.

SMITH, T. V., and LINDEMAN, *The Democratic Way of Life* (reprinted). New York: The New American Library of Word Literature, Inc., 1953.

Philosophy of Music Education

BURROWS, R. M., *Present Day Trends in Music Education*. New York: Columbia University, Teachers College Record, LII, (January, 1951). 213-225.

CLARK, F. E., "Music, a Vital Force in Education," *Music Educators Journal*, XL, (April-May, 1954). 21.

DYKEMA, PETER, and GLENN, MABELLE, "The Child's Bill of Rights in Music," prepared for the Music Educator's National Conference. *The National Elementary School Principal*, XXX, No. 4, (February, 1951). 47.

GIAUDRON, ANGELO et al, *Music in the School Curriculum*. Washington: Joint MENC and AASA, 1965.

HUNT, HEROLD, "Music the Common Ground of Mankind," *Music Educators Journal*, XXXV, (January, 1948). 19, 20, 56–.

MADISON, THURBER, *Basic Concepts in Music Education*. Chicago: Univ. of Chicago Press, National Society for Study of Education, 1958. v-364.

MORGAN, RUSSEL V., "A Forward Looking Program for Music Education," from *Music, A Living Power*, Silver Burdett Company.

MURSELL, JAMES L., *Music Education Principles and Programs*. Morristown, New York: Silver Burdett, 1956. vii-385.

REED, RAY, "Some Basic Educational Concepts," *Music Educators Journal*, XL, (November and December, 1953). 52–.

SOMMERS, H. H., "Music in the Modern School Program." *School Executive*, LXX, (May, 1951). 46-47.

SQUIRE, RUSSEL N., *Introduction to Music Education*. New York: The Ronald Press Company, 1952. v-185.

SUNDERMAN, LLOYD F., "Great Issues in Music Education," *Education*, LXXIV, (September, 1953). 3-10.

WILLIS, BENJAMIN, "Stake of Music in Education," *Music Educators Journal*, XLI, (June, 1954).

E. Psychology of Teaching and Learning

BLOOM, BENJAMIN S., *Taxonomy of Educational Objectives, Handbook II*. New York: David McKay Company, Inc., 1964. v-196.

BRUNER, JEROME S. *The Process of Education*. New York: Random House, 1960. vi-97.

———, *Toward a Theory of Instruction*. Cambridge: Harvard University Press, 1966. 1-176.

CORRIGAN, ROBERT E., *Practical Application of System Technology to Education and Training*. Anaheim: Litton Instructional Materials, Inc., 1965.

COREY, STEPHEN M., *Action Research to Improve School Practices*. New York: Bureau of Publications, Teachers College, Columbia University, 1953. v-161.

DEHUSZAR, GEORGE B., *Practical Applications of Democracy*. New York: Harpers, 1945. 14-140.

KELLEY, EARL C., *The Workshop Way of Learning*. New York: Harper and Brothers, 1951. 14-169.

LEWIN, KURT, "The Dynamics of Group Action," *Educational Leadership*, I, (January, 1944). 194–.

MAGER, ROBERT F., *Preparing Instructional Objectives*. Palo Alto: Fearon Publishers, 1962. vii-62.

RUBIN, LOUIS, *The Nurture of Teacher Growth*. Santa Barbara: Center for Coordinated Education, 1966. 1-20.

SNYGG, DONOLD and COMBS, ARTHUR W., *Individual Behaviour*. New York: Harper and Brothers, 1949. vii-386.

THELEN, HERBERT, *Education and the Human Quest*. New York: Harper and Brothers, 1960. 1-224.

Psychology of Music Teaching and Learning

BISHOP, M., "Psychology of Music Participation," *Music Educators Journal*, XL, (November, 1953). 46–.

LUNDIN, ROBERT W., *An Objective Psychology of Music*. New York: The Ronald Press Company, 1953. v-303.

MURSELL, JAMES L. and GLENN, MABELLE, *The Psychology of School Music Teaching*. New York: Silver Burdett and Company, 1931. v-343.

REVESZ, G., *Introduction to the Psychology of Music*. Norman: University of Oklahoma Press, 1954. (Translated from the German by G. I. C. de-Courcy). vii-261.

F. Research In Education

GOOD, CARTER V., BARR, A. S., and SCATES, DOUGLAS E., *The Methodology of Educational Research*. New York: D. Appleton-Century, 1941. v-890.

Research in Music Education

BARNES, ROBERT A., "Programmed Instruction in Music Fundamentals for Future Elementary Teachers," *Journal of Research in Music Education*, XII, No. 3, (Fall, 1964). 187.

BAUMANN, VICTOR H., "Teen-Age Preferences," Washington: MENC, *Journal of Research in Music Education*, VIII, No. 2, (Fall, 1960). 75.

BLETHEN, E., "Music Education versus Solfeggio," *Music Educators Journal*, XXXIX, (February, 1953). 62-64.

BLYLER, DOROTHY, "The Song Choices of Children in the Elementary Grades," *Journal of Research in Music Education*, VIII, No. 1, (Spring, 1960). 9.

BLYTHE, J. B., "Elementary Teachers Should Use Keyboard Experience," *School Musician*, XXV, (March, 1954). 24-25.

BRITTON, ALLEN P., "Research in Music Education," *Education*, LXXIV, (September, 1953). 40-44.

BRODY, VIOLA A., "The Role of Body-Awareness in the Emergence of Musical Ability: Its Application to Music Education, the College Basic Music Course, and Critic Teaching," *Journal of Research in Music Education*, I, No. 1, (Spring, 1953). 21-29.

CHOATE, ROBERT A., "Research in Music Education," *Journal of Research in Music Education*, XIII, No. 2, (Summer, 1965). p. 67.

COLWELL, RICHARD and RUNDELL, GLENNA, "An Evaluation of Achievement in Auditory Visual Discrimination Resulting from Specific Types of Musical

Experiences among Junior High Students," *Journal of Research in Music Education*, XIII, No. 4, (Winter, 1965). 239.

COLWELL, RICHARD, "An Investigation of Music Achievement among Vocal Students, Vocal-Instrumental Students, Instrumental Students," *Journal of Research in Music Education*, XI, No. 2, (Fall, 1963). p. 123.

CREITZ, DALE P., "A Study of the Use of the Piano as a Space Frame in Teaching Vocal Music to Children." Unpublished Master of Arts Thesis, University of Kansas, 1943.

FLEDERER, MARILYN, "The Responses of Children to Musical Tasks Embodying Plaget's Principles of Conservation," *Journal of Research in Music Education*, XII, No. 4, (Winter, 1964). p. 251.

FLEMING, JESSIE L., "The Determination of Musical Experiences Designed to Develop Competencies Required of Elementary School Teachers in Maryland," *Journal of Research in Music Education*, I, No. 1, (Spring, 1953). 59-67.

FOWLER, CHARLES, "Discovery Method, Its Relevance to Music Education," *Journal of Research in Music Education*, XIV, No. 2, (Summer, 1966). p. 126.

GASTON, E. THAYER, *A Study of the Trends of Attitude Toward Music in School Children*, University of Kansas Studies in Education, Vol. 2, No. 6.

GORDON, RODERICK D., "Doctoral Dissertations in Music and Music Education," *Journal of Research in Music Education*, VII, No. 1 (Spring, 1964), p. 119, and Vol. II, No. 1, (Spring, 1965), p. 45. Vol. XIV, No. 1, (Spring, 1966), p. 45.

HUTTON, DORIS, "A Comparative Study of Teaching Two Methods of Sight Singing in the Fourth Grade," *Journal of Research in Music Education*, I, No. 2, (Fall, 1953). 119-126.

JERSILD, ARTHUR, and BIENSTOCK, SYLVIA, "A Study of Developing Children's Ability to Sing," *Journal of Educational Psychology*, XXV, No. 6.

JOSEPH, WARREN, "A Summation of the Research Pertaining to Vocal Growth," *Journal of Research in Music Education*, XIII, No. 2, (Summer, 1965). p. 93.

———, "Vocal Growth in the Human Adolescent," *Journal of Research in Music Education*, XIV, No. 2, (Summer, 1966). p. 135.

KELLEY, DAVID, "A Study of the Musical Preferences of a Select Group of Adolescents," *Journal of Research in Music Education*, IX, No. 2, (Fall, 1961). p. 118.

KING, HARRY, *Auditory and Visual Characteristics of Poor Music Readers*. Music Educators, National Conference Yearbook, Vol. 50.

KING, HARRY L., "A Study of the Relationship of Music Reading and I. Q. Scores," *Journal of Research in Music Education*, II, No. 1, (Spring, 1954). 35-37.

KYME, GEORGE H., "An Experiment in Teaching Children to Read Music with Shaped Notes," *Journal of Research in Music Education*, VIII, No. 1, (Spring, 1960). p. 3.

LEHMANN, C. F., "Investigation of Musical Achievement and Relationship to Intelligence and Musical Talent," *Journal of Educational Research*, XLV, (April, 1952). 623-629.

LARSON, WM. C., "Bibliography in Research Studies in Music Education, 1949-1956," *Journal of Research in Music Education*, V, No. 2, (Fall, 1957). p. 225.

LINTON, STANLEY, "Music for the Pre-Service Classroom Teacher," *Journal of Research in Music Education*, II, No. 1, (Spring, 1954). 3-10.

LUCE, JOHN R., "Sight-Singing and Ear Playing Abilities as Related to Instrumental Music Students," *Journal of Research in Music Education*, XIII, No. 2, (Summer, 1965). p. 101.

ORDWAY, CLAIRE, "Music Activities of High School Graduates in Two Communities," *Journal of Research in Music Education*, XII, No. 2, (Summer, 1964). p. 172.

ORTMANN, OTTO, *Span of Vision in Note Reading*, Music Educators National Yearbook, (1937).

OSBORN, LESLIE, "Notation Should be Metric and Representational," *Journal of Research in Music Education*, XIV, No. 2, (Summer, 1966). p. 67.

PETZOLD, ROBERT G., "The Development of Auditory Perception of Musical Sounds by Children in the First Six Grades," *Journal of Research in Music Education*, XI, No. 1, (Spring, 1963). p. 21.

RAINBOW, JOHN R., "A Pilot Study to Investigate the Constructs of Musical Aptitudes," *Journal of Research in Music Education*, XIII, No. 1, (Spring, 1965). p. 3.

REIMER, A. J., "A Comparison of Two Methods of Teaching Instrumental Music to Beginners," Master of Arts unpublished study, University of Kansas, 1944.

SMITH, EDGAR F., "The Value of Notated Examples in Learning to Recognize Musical Themes Aurally," *Journal of Research in Music Education*, I, No. 2, (Fall, 1953), 97-104.

SMITH, ROBERT B., "The Effect of Group Vocal Training on the Singing Ability of Nursery School Children," *Journal of Research in Music Education*, XI, No. 2, (Fall, 1963). p. 137.

VITTO, B., "Ear Training Through Symbolizing Melodies A New Approach," *School Musician*, XXII, (January, 1951). 8-10.

WATKINS, J. GOODRICH, "Objective Measurement of Instrument Performance," *Contribution to Education*, Teachers College, Columbia University, No. 684, 1942.

WEAVER, H. E., *Studies of Ocular Behavior in Music Reading*, Psychological Monograph, Volume 55, No. 1.

WEYLAND, RUDOLPH H., "The Effects of a Workshop on Certain Fourth-Grade Teachers' Skills in Teaching Music Reading," Unpublished doctoral dissertation, University of California, Berkeley, 1958. iii-252.

WHEELWRIGHT, LOUIS F., *An Experimental Study of Perceptibility and Spacing of Musical Symbols*. New York: Contributions to Education, No. 775, Teachers College, Columbia University.

WHYBREW, WM. E., *Measurement and Evaluation in Music*. Dubuque: Wm. C. Brown Co. Publishers, 1962. v-184.

YINGLING, ROBERT W., "Classification of Reaction Patterns in Listening to Music," *Journal of Research in Music Education*, X, No. 2, (Fall, 1962). p. 105.

G. Supervision

ANTELL, HENRY, "Teachers Appraise Supervision," *Journal of Educational Research*, XXXVIII, (April, 1945). 606-11.

BARTKY, JOHN A., *Supervision as Human Relations.* Boston: D. C. Heath & Co., 1953. 3-308.

BURNHAM, REBA and KING, MARTHA, *Supervision in Action.* Washington: ASCD (NEA), v-66.

BURTON, WILLIAM and BRUECKNER, LEO, *Supervision a Social Process.* New York: Appleton-Century-Crofts, Inc., third ed., 1955. v-715.

GLENN, NEAL E., "Human Relations and the Supervisor," *Education,* LXXIV, (September, 1953). 27-30.

HARRIS, BENJAMIN, *Supervising Behavior in Education.* Englewood Cliffs: Prentice-Hall, Inc., 1963. 1-557.

KYTE, GEORGE C., *How to Supervise.* Boston: Houghton Mifflin Company, The Riverside Press, 1930. v-468.

MACKENZIE, GORDON N., and COREY, STEPHEN M., *Instructional Leadership.* New York: Bureau of Publications, Teachers College, Columbia University, 1954. v-209.

McKEAN, ROBERT C., *The Supervisor.* Washington: Center for Applied Research in Education, 1964. x-117.

MELCHIOR, WILLIAM TOBIAS, *Instructional Supervision.* Boston: D. C. Heath & Co., 1950. 3-485.

NEAGLEY, ROSS L., and DAVIS, N. D., *Handbook for Effective Supervision of Instruction.* Englewood Cliffs: Prentice-Hall, Inc. v-275.

RUBIN, LOUIS, *The Professional Growth of the Educator.* Santa Barbara: Center for Coordinated Education, 1966. 1-16.

SPEARS, HAROLD, *Improving the Supervision of Instruction.* New York: Prentice-Hall, Inc., 1953. vii-478.

WILES, KIMBALL, *Supervision for Better Schools.* New York: Prentice-Hall, Inc., 1950. v-330.

Supervision of Music

BLAKELY, LLOYD G., "The State Supervisor of Music," *Journal of Research in Music Education,* VIII, No. 2, (Fall, 1960). p. 99.

CHOATE, ROBERT A., "Supervisor and the Curriculum," *Educational Music Magazine,* XX, (November, 1950). 8-9.

FRISCH, F. T., "What Happened at the Workshop," *Music Educators Journal,* XXXVII, (November, 1950). 24-25.

GIDDINGS, THADDEUS P., "On Supervision," *Music Educators Journal,* XXXVII, (April, 1951), 46–.

HERMANN, EDWARD J., *Supervising Music in the Elementary School.* Englewood Cliffs: Prentice-Hall, Inc., 1965. vii-210.

MENC, *Music Supervision and Administration in the Schools,* Music Education Research Council, Bulletin No. 18. MENC, Chicago, (Now Washington, D.C.) 1949. 4-30.

National Council of State Supervisors of Music, *State Supervision of Music.* Washington: MENC and NEA. 1-58.

NYE, R. C., "On Call Elementary Music Supervision," *Education Digest,* XVI, (March, 1951), 30-31.

SNYDER, KEITH O., *School Music Administration and Supervision.* Boston: Allyn and Bacon, Inc., 1959. p. 365.

WATSON, JACK M., "The New Role of the Music Specialist," *Music Journal,* (March, 1954).

WEYLAND, RUDOLPH, H., "Band Teacher Becomes Music Supervisor," *The Instrumentalist*, February 1965. p. 46–51.

H. Yearbooks

ASCD, *Action for Curriculum Development*. Washington: NEA, 1951. v-246.
——, *Fostering Mental Health in Our Schools*. Washington: NEA, 1950. iii-320.
ASCD, *Leadership for Improving Instruction*. Washington: NEA. 1960, iii-198.
——, *Leadership Through Supervision*. Washington: NEA, 1946. 1-163.
——, *Organizing the Elementary Schools for Living and Learning*. Washington: NEA, 1947. 4-211.
——, *Research for Curriculum Improvement*. Washington: NEA, 1957. v-350.
——, *Role of the Supervisor and Curriculum Direction in a Climate of Change*. Washington: NEA. 1965, iii-170.
——, *Toward Better Teaching*. Washington: NEA, 1949. iii-282.
PARKER, J *Group Process in Supervision*. Washington: NEA, 1948. 3-130.

Music Education Yearbooks

MENC, *Music in American Education*. Washington: MENC Source Book No. II, 1955. iii-365.
MENC, *Perspectives in Music Education*. Washington: MENC Source Book No. III, 1966. 3-579.
MORGAN, HAZEL, *Music Education Source Book No. I*. Chicago: MENC, 1947. iii-250.

Index